Early Literacy S
@ your library®

Partnering
with Caregivers
for Success

Saroj Nadkarni Ghoting and
Pamela Martin-Díaz

AMERICAN LIBRARY ASSOCIATION
Chicago   2006

While extensive effort has gone into ensuring the reliability of information appearing in this book, the publisher makes no warranty, express or implied, on the accuracy or reliability of the information, and does not assume and hereby disclaims any liability to any person for any loss or damage caused by errors or omissions in this publication.

Composition by ALA Editions in Tekton and Berkeley using QuarkXPress 5.0 on a PC platform

Printed on 50-pound white offset, a pH-neutral stock, and bound in 10-point coated cover stock by Data Reproductions

The paper used in this publication meets the minimum requirements of American National Standard for Information Sciences—Permanence of Paper for Printed Library Materials, ANSI Z39.48-1992. ∞

"Clap Your Hands" and "Horsey, Horsey," by Carol Rose Duane, from *Lively Songs and Lullabies: Songs for Baby*, vol. 1 (audiotape). Courtesy of Carol Rose Duane.
"Roll Your Hands," by Carol Hammett and Elaine Bueffel, from *Toddlers on Parade* (compact disc). Courtesy of Kimbo Educational.
"Little Flea," by Pamela Beall, from *Wee Sing for Baby* (audiotape).
"Rainbow Kittens" from *Kidstuff* 4 (7), 12.

Library of Congress Cataloging-in-Publication Data

Ghoting, Saroj Nadkarni.
    Early literacy storytimes @ your library : partnering with caregivers for success / Saroj Nadkarni Ghoting, Pamela Martin-Díaz.
        p.   cm.
    Includes bibliographical references and index.
    ISBN 0-8389-0899-3
    1. Children's libraries—Activity programs—United States. 2. Storytelling—United States. 3. Libraries and preschool children—United States. 4. Libraries and caregivers—United States. 5. Preschool children—Books and reading—United States. 6. Reading—Parent participation—United States. I. Title: Early literacy storytimes at your library II. Martin-Díaz, Pamela. III. Title.

Z718.3G56 2005
027.62'51—dc22   2005016437

Printed in the United States of America

10   09   08   07   06   5   4   3   2   1

For my parents, who read to me and told me stories.

For library staff, who continually seek ways to reach and serve children, their families, and their caregivers.

—*Saroj*

For my parents, in endless gratitude, and for Zoë, Lucía, and, most especially, Elisiana, who teach me about learning every day.

—*Pamela*

Contents

Appendixes

Index
261

Preface

The library's role in preschool and early childhood education has long been established. Historically, we have offered strong picture book collections, readers' advisory assistance to parents and teachers using books and other materials with young children, and, of course, storytimes. Storytimes, with our use of puppets, finger plays, songs, and rhymes, have played a key role in bringing books and children together and in developing language. For many young children, the public library is where the first contact with the world of books and reading takes place. For library staff and the adults who bring young children to the library, storytime has been seen as a way to help children on the path to reading.

Research has validated much of what we intuitively inferred. Studies on brain development and the skills required for young children to become readers emphasize the importance of the child's interaction *with* an adult around books. The importance of early literacy and the key role of the parent/caregiver in its development in children newborn through age five can propel the library, with all of our resources, into a prominent role in the development of the reading child.

In 2000 a partnership between the Public Library Association and the Association for Library Service to Children, both divisions of the American Library Association, and the National Institute of Child Health and Human Development (NICHD) of the National Institutes of Health developed a project to strengthen the bond among groups crucial to a child's development. In this way, the work and activities of researchers, library staff, and parents/caregivers join to support young children in becoming successful readers.

According to NICHD research, the development of early literacy skills in a child's life can better prepare that child for success in reading when he or she enters school. The thinking behind the project, called "Every Child Ready to Read® @ your library®," is that library staff are ideally suited to inform parents and caregivers about early literacy research. Through workshops for parents and caregivers we provide them with crucial research about early literacy and teach them behaviors to help children become readers. Because of our intermittent contact with each child, we have limited direct impact. However, by teaching parents and caregivers about early literacy skills and ways to incorporate them in their daily lives, we make a difference in the child's development by supporting the parent/caregiver. (For more on the program, go to http://www.pla.org/earlyliteracy.htm.)

What can this mean—what does this mean—for library services to young children and their parents and caregivers? Based on the premises and conclusions of the "Every Child Ready to Read @ your library" project, library staff can support children's early literacy development by emphasizing the importance of the parent/caregiver role in the development of early literacy in their children,

explaining to parents and caregivers the components that make up early literacy, and

providing parents and caregivers with a variety of activities that support each of these components while helping them understand the relationship between the early literacy skill and the activity.

To inform parents and caregivers about the research behind early literacy, a series of workshops was developed for libraries. Fourteen demonstration sites were chosen to evaluate the effect of these workshops on the early literacy behaviors of participants. These sites presented the workshops both in and out of the library and to parents and to childcare providers. The full evaluation and a list of the demonstration sites are available at http://www.pla.org/earlyliteracy.htm. In addition to workshops, these sites have applied this early literacy information to other aspects of library service by

enhancing storytimes with the inclusion of early literacy information for adults,

incorporating early literacy skills into reading programs,

doing more outreach programs,

changing the library environment to be more language rich,

incorporating early literacy information into the one-on-one interaction (via reference and readers' advisory interviews), and

expanding collections.

In *Early Literacy Storytimes*, we focus on one of those aspects—enhancing storytimes with early literacy information. Our experience with the project has taught us a great deal about how to integrate early literacy skills into the fabric of our work. Traditional storytimes already incorporate many, if not all, of the components of early literacy. For example, we express the fun of sharing books, include songs and rhymes, explain words that may not be familiar to children, and have children chime in with repeated phrases and sometimes point to the text as they repeat the words. We can strengthen our storytimes by becoming more knowledgeable about early literacy and by sharing this information with parents and caregivers, who are with the children every day. As we learn more about early literacy and develop early literacy enhanced storytimes based on our traditional models, we strengthen our services in at least four ways:

1. We become more aware of how storytime components support early literacy.
2. We can better articulate early literacy information to other staff and to administrators.
3. We become better child advocates in the community.
4. We not only model but also explain early literacy information to parents/caregivers during storytimes, giving them information and skills they can use when sharing books and promoting language development with their children.

We can use storytimes to explain to parents/caregivers the key role they play in their children's early literacy development and ways they can support them. Some storytime presenters question why library staff should take on this task, which seems so close to teaching. We offer two responses to this question:

1. *The public library is a key provider of services to young children and their families.* We need to reexamine how we implement this role in light of what we have learned from research. Because of the critical role of parents and caregivers and the importance of the child's first five years, we must share information with them to support early literacy development in their children.

2. *Societal circumstances and changes in academic expectations require that we reassess the library's role in early childhood education.* More families need information about what is expected for "school readiness." Information on early literacy is an important part of this information.

As long as storytimes continue to be enjoyable, engage the child in story and the fun of language, and encourage parents and caregivers to share books and language, then the traditional storytime can only be enhanced with this approach.

Book Organization

This book is divided into three sections. The first section covers the theory and research on early literacy as well as tips on how this information can be integrated into storytime. It summarizes the research (brain development and early literacy), articulates how the components of storytimes support early literacy development, and offers practical examples for library staff and parents/caregivers.

The second section offers storytime planning suggestions and presents sample storytimes for three groups: early talkers, who range in age from newborns to two-year-olds; talkers, who typically fall in the two- and three-year-old range; and prereaders, or four- and five-year-olds. The sample storytimes show how library staff are able to integrate early literacy information into traditional storytimes. You can either try these sample storytimes or just browse them for some ideas for your own storytimes. The second part of this section provides tips, tools, and how-tos for developing your own early literacy storytimes.

Finally, the third section provides tools for assessing your storytime and information on how to promote early literacy in your community.

Supporting documents can be found in the appendixes.

We look forward to the time when the information in this book will be second nature to us, when this book will be unnecessary because we will have internalized its content and its intent, its approach, and its goals. For new library staff, the content and approach here will be integrated into storytime training tools and texts.

As you use this book, we hope you will not feel constrained by the information but rather that you will take this as a seed, help it grow, use your own creativity to make it your own, and share it with those you serve.

Join us on the journey!

Acknowledgments

We owe a huge debt of gratitude to those far-thinking librarians who are behind the "Every Child Ready to Read @ your library" program, sponsored by two divisions of the American Library Association, the Public Library Association, and the Association of Library Service to Children. They include Harriet Henderson, director of Montgomery County (MD) Public Libraries; Elaine Meyers, head of Children's and Young Adult Services, Central Library, Phoenix (AZ) Public Library; Clara Bohrer, director of West Bloomfield Township (MI) Public Library; Gretchen Wronka, youth services coordinator of Hennepin County (MN) Library System; Greta Southard, executive director, and Barb Macikas, deputy director, of the Public Library Association; Malore Brown, executive director, and Linda Mays, program officer, of the Association for Library Service to Children; Dr. Virginia Walter, associate professor of Information Studies at University of California–Los Angeles Library School; Kathleen Reif, currently director of St. Mary's County (MD) Library; and Sara Laughlin, of Sara Laughlin Associates. We thank the members of the boards of the Public Library Association and of the Association for Library Service to Children, the Joint Task Force for the Program, and staff representatives from the fourteen demonstration sites. Without their foresight, planning, and advocacy, this book would not exist.

We appreciate the work and time taken in the development of "Every Child Ready to Read @ your library" workshops by Dr. G. Reid Lyon, chief of the National Institute for Child Health and Human Development of the National Institutes of Health, and the research conducted by Dr. Grover (Russ) Whitehurst, Dr. Colleen Huebner, and Dr. Christopher Lonigan.

Laura Pelehach and the ALA Editions staff have been extremely patient and forgiving.

—Saroj and Pamela

Allen County Public Library staff have been generous with their support, talent, and time as they energetically embraced the "Every Child Ready to Read @ your library" program and ran with it. Thanks to senior management for their praise and support of our work. Children's library staff Mary Voors, Teresa Walls, Karol Caparaso, Condra Ridley, and Deb Noggle have been steadfast not only in their support of early literacy but in developing new program pieces. With Nancy Magi keeping everything, all the time, on course, we have been able to keep moving ahead. Thanks to my coworkers at Shawnee Branch for their encouragement, especially Heather Grady, who is able to happily remind me that it really isn't just work, that what we do is more than just a job.

To my friends and colleagues in Head Start centers and schools, especially Temple Head Start, in Fort Wayne, Indiana—here's to you! My Chicago connections keep me thinking and working toward the common good. Barbara Becker, your influence has been enormous; I am grateful.

My husband, Rosendo, supports me in all endeavors. Thank you so much for encouraging me, for happily giving me the time and opportunity to work on this book, and for being with me.

—Pamela

Because this book is the culmination of so many interactions and experiences, it is impossible to thank everyone. By the same token, there are some I need to specifically thank related to the development and completion of this book: so many colleagues and friends in Montgomery County (MD) Public Libraries, including Amy Alapati, Michelle Schuster, Judy Furash, Kate McCarthy Bond, Nancy Knauer (who got me over the hump to be able to do storytimes for babies), and Bonita Glatstein; to our partners, including Maribel de la Cruz and Teresa Wright, of Montgomery County Public Schools, who helped me reach and work with the Latino communities; Dale McGee Fry, currently of Early Head Start; Beth Molesworth, of Early Childhood Services of Health and Human Services; and so many from Head Start, from Early Childhood Services of the Public Schools, home-visiting programs, the Maryland Infant and Toddler Program, and numerous child-care providers.

My thanks also to Elaine Czarnecki and Gilda Martinez, of Resources in Reading; Deirdre Murphy, of San Antonio (TX) Public Library's Little Read Wagon; Brianne Williams and Jane Corry, of Multnomah County (OR) Library; Sue Tracy, Linnea Christensen, Dana Bjerke, and Jenna Miller, of Hennepin County (MN) Library System; Cindy Christin, of Bozeman (MT) Public Library; Dianna Burt, of Allen County (IN) Public Libraries; and to the children's and Read to Me staff of Santa Cruz (CA) Public Libraries.

Thank you to Betsy Bybell and Cathy Ensley, of Latah County Library District (Moscow, ID), and Kathleen Ahern, of Neill Public Library (Pullman, WA), who gave constructive comments on the drafts. Special thanks to Renea Arnold, early childhood resources coordinator of Multnomah County Public Library System, for her knowledge, questioning mind, and strong support; and to Judy Malamud, of Montgomery County Public Libraries, who always comes through when I need to know or find something, and who is, more importantly, able to evaluate and incorporate new ideas in ways that always reflect her commitment and dedication to children.

Last but not least, warm thanks to my husband, Vinod, who supports me in whatever I do.

—Saroj

PART

I

Learning It!

1

Early Literacy
Research—Explained

In 2000 the National Reading Panel, headed by then assistant secretary for elementary and secondary education of the U.S. Department of Education Susan B. Neuman, published a document, available on the Web, called *Teaching Children to Read*.[1] This clear, well-reasoned report describes the lessons learned from years of research about what it takes for *school-age* children to become fluent readers. The researchers concluded that three areas of reading instruction are paramount:

1. Alphabetics
   Phonemic awareness
   Phonics
2. Fluency
3. Comprehension
   Vocabulary
   Text

(For further information on this report, go to http://www.nationalreadingpanel.org/Publications/summary.htm.)

This report raised some interesting questions: If we know the areas that are crucial to reading success in school-age children, what does this mean for younger children? Is there a way to lay the foundation in earlier years? What skills do younger children need in preparation for formal reading instruction, and what can be done in early childhood to pave the way for instruction in the areas listed above?

To find answers to those questions, we look to the research conducted by the National Institute of Child Health and Human Development (NICHD) of the National Institutes of Health. Based on research, NICHD set forth six early literacy skills, which are precursors to the reading skills themselves:

Print motivation—a child's interest in and enjoyment of books

Phonological awareness—the ability to hear and play with the smaller sounds in words

Vocabulary—knowing the names of things

Narrative skills—the ability to describe things and events and to tell stories

Print awareness—noticing print, knowing how to handle a book, and understanding how to follow the written words on a page

Letter knowledge—knowing that letters are different from each other, that the same letter can look different, and that each letter has a name and is related to sounds.

Phonemic awareness is often confused with phonological awareness. Phonemic awareness is being able to hear the *smallest* sounds in words, for example, being able to hear the individual sounds in *tiger*: /t/ /i/ /g/ /e/ /r/. Phonological awareness also includes the ability to hear parts of words, not necessarily the smallest parts, for example, the ability to hear the two parts of the word *tiger*: ti-ger; being able to hear when two words rhyme; or being able to say the sound a word starts with.

As table 1-1 shows, there is a significant overlap of content between the three key areas of reading instruction, as described in the National Reading Panel's report, and the components of early literacy, as defined by NICHD. There is a direct connection from early literacy skills to the acquisition of later reading skills, all of which culminate in the development of a reading child. (Note: It is *not* appropriate for parents/caregivers to expect young children to read. The school-age skills are noted here to show how the components of early literacy, offered in ways that are fun and child centered, lead the way to future reading.)

TABLE 1-1
Comparison of Early Literacy Components and Reading

EARLY LITERACY COMPONENT	READING
Phonological awareness Letter knowledge	Alphabetics
Vocabulary Phonological awareness Letter knowledge Narrative skills	Fluency
Vocabulary Narrative skills	Comprehension

To have strong reading skills, children must have a strong foundation—strong early literacy skills. But the question remains: how do we build this foundation? How do we ensure that young children, in the absence of a formal school environment, will develop the skills that portend success when they begin to read?

Empowering the key adults in children's lives to develop these skills is the mission of the "Every Child Ready to Read @ your library" program. Library staff, knowledgeable about early literacy, are ideally suited to convey this information to parents and caregivers, who can then develop these skills in their children. As noted earlier, this information can be provided in a variety of ways, through workshops and other outreach efforts. In *Early Literacy Storytimes*, we consider how to enrich one of the most common services we offer—the storytime—to provide information on early literacy.

By providing parents and caregivers with crucial early literacy information, modeling behavior, and offering ideas on ways to build these skills in children, we help parents provide a strong foundation for reading success. Many other skills children learn in storytime, such as fine and gross motor development, are important for the full development of the child and, as such, do support early literacy. This book, however, deals with the skills that are most directly related to early literacy.

Before getting into the storytimes themselves, let's define early literacy and summarize the research surrounding it.

What Is Early Literacy?

According to NICHD, early literacy is what children know about reading and writing before they actually learn to read and write. To clarify, early literacy is *not* the teaching of reading. It is building a foundation for reading so that when children are taught to read, they are ready. We often hear the terms *emergent literacy* or *reading readiness*. But neither of these quite captures the essence of early literacy. Emergent literacy has the connotation that these skills "emerge" without help from adults, that they naturally evolve. Each of these skills develops as a child grows; however, the skills *do* need interaction and assistance to develop.

Reading readiness, on the other hand, is a maturational point of view of early literacy, the concept that children have to reach a basic, specific maturity or age to be ready to learn to read. According to the *Position Statement* of the International Reading Association and the National Association for the Education of Young Children, reading readiness

> assumes that physical and neurological maturation alone prepare the child to take advantage of instruction in reading and writing [and] implies that until children reach a certain stage of maturity all exposure to reading and writing, except perhaps being read stories, is a waste of time or even potentially harmful.[2]

The early literacy perspective asserts that reading readiness starts at birth, when the parent or caregiver begins talking with the baby. Adherents now believe that "experiences throughout the early years affect the development of literacy. . . . Failing to give children literacy experiences until they are school age can severely limit the reading and writing levels they ultimately attain."[3]

Early literacy encompasses *language readiness* (knowing how oral language "works"); *background knowledge* (as children develop word knowledge, they also develop world knowledge based on their experiences), which supports comprehension; and *print components* (understanding that print has meaning and that print relates to what is spoken).

> Early literacy is what children know about reading and writing before they actually learn to read and write.

Early Literacy Research

Research that sheds light on early literacy falls into several areas:

> biological research—the brain research that shows the physiological components involved in learning to read;
>
> environmental aspects—research on young children in their homes, how they interact with the adults in their lives, and the effects of their families' income and education;
>
> how children acquire the skills that they need to learn how to read; and
>
> early literacy skills themselves.

What follows is a brief description of some of the key findings. Additional resources are cited in appendix E.

Brain Research and Early Literacy

We have heard the phrase "The first years last forever," and the I Am Your Child Foundation has even published a book with that title.[4] Now scientific evidence confirms that early experiences and interactions directly affect the nature and extent of adult capacities.

Much of the information about how the brain works in young children is the result of new technologies. For example, magnetic resonance imaging (MRI) and positron-emission tomography (PET) scans, which are noninvasive and can be performed on children while they are awake, allow studies to be conducted on healthy children.

BACKGROUND

Babies are born with one hundred billion neurons, or brain cells, but these neurons are not connected. Sensory experiences—seeing, smelling, hearing, touching, and especially tasting—stimulate connections, or electrical impulses, among the brain cells. The development of these electrical impulses across a synapse, or gap between the cells, is the basis for children's learning. Chemicals such as serotonin enable and enhance the transmission of this electrical signal. Figure 1-1 shows the connections across the synapses of an infant,

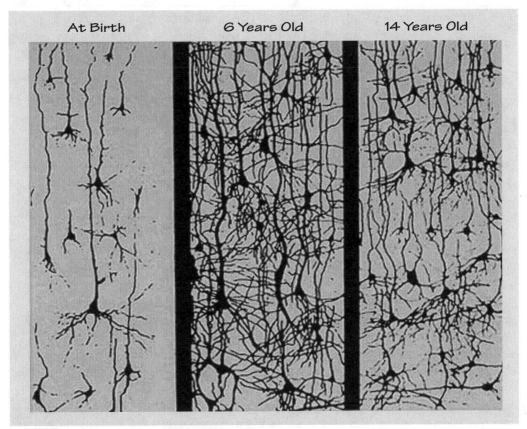

FIGURE 1-1 Synaptic Density

From Rima Shore, *Rethinking the Brain: New Insights into Early Development* (New York: Families and Work Institute, 1997). Courtesy of Harry T. Chugani, MD, Children's Hospital of Michigan, Wayne State University, Detroit.

a six-year-old, and a fourteen-year-old. When a child feels good, loved, and cared for, the brain produces higher levels of serotonin, which in turn enhances the connections.

Children ages three to ten have three times as many synapses as an adult. As a child grows, there are fewer synapses, but they are more organized. Some of the synapses are pruned. What makes some synapses stay and some be pruned away? *Repetition!* The synapses that are used repeatedly are the ones that are kept, and the ones that are little used get pruned.

A PET scan measures activity in the brain by scanning the brain's use of glucose. PET scans comparing the level of activity in Romanian orphans who had little stimulation in their first two years of life to the level of activity of a child who had been raised in a healthy, interactive environment showed a *physical* difference in the architecture of the brain.[5]

Emotions boost memory by creating a release of chemicals that act as a memory fixative.[6] When emotions are engaged, the brain is activated. Early interactions have a long-lasting impact on how people develop. High levels of stress have a deleterious effect. Cortisol, a hormone, is elevated in stressful situations. When it is elevated for long periods of time, it inhibits the transmission of serotonin in the brain, which inhibits the connections needed for learning.

WHAT DOES IT MEAN?

Babies are able to respond from birth. They have the innate ability to mimic. They imitate our facial expressions even when they are a day or two old! Make faces at them! Talk to them! Smile at them! Early experiences not only affect later development but have a decisive affect on the architecture of the brain; a baby stops babbling if not spoken to for six months. It is not just "nice" to have a happy, engaging learning environment. When a child is curious and engaged, it is actually easier for his or her brain to take in information and for the child to learn. The stimulation we offer our children—by talking with them, responding to them, reading with them, and exposing them to a variety of experiences—is not just "a good thing to do." These experiences at an early age make a difference in the way that the brain develops and how it can continue to develop.

At birth, an infant's vision is blurry. The infant appears to focus in the center of the visual field during the first few weeks after birth. Peripheral vision is not well developed. Near vision is better developed than far vision. Infants focus on objects held eight to fifteen inches in front of them. As their vision develops, infants show preference for certain objects and will gaze longer at items patterned with checks and stripes rather than solid colors. Studies also show that infants prefer bold colors to pastels. They show visual preference for (gaze longer at) faces more than objects. By two months, an infant will show preference for a smiling face over a face without expression.[7] Because emotions boost memory, having a child emotionally involved in what is going on, and building on the child's interests, makes learning easier.

When a child wants a book read for the fiftieth time, the book is becoming part of his or her memory and him- or herself. Repetition is not just something they want; it is something they need in order to learn.

APPLICATION

New research on the brain becomes available continuously, affecting what we know about child development and, in turn, what we do with our children. It shapes what we communicate to parents and caregivers. Sharing this research with adults who care for children helps them understand their children's actions better and can therefore have an impact on their behavior with their children.

Other Key Factors Influencing a Child's Reading Development

Physiology is not the only factor affecting a child's reading development. Research shows that other factors affect children's learning. Below are synopses of some key research findings.

SHARED READING

An often-quoted report, *Becoming a Nation of Readers: Report of the Commission on Reading*, underscores the role of the parent in laying the foundation for children learning to read. The commission noted, "The single most important activity for building the knowledge required for eventual success in reading is reading aloud to children."[8] The commission also noted the importance of parents and caregivers:

> Parents play roles of inestimable importance in laying the foundation for learning to read. Parents should informally teach preschool children about reading and writing by reading aloud to them, discussing stories and events, encouraging them to learn letters and words and teaching them about the world around them. These practices help prepare children for success in reading.[9]

Preventing Reading Difficulties in Young Children notes that children with limited exposure in certain areas, such as shared reading, will start school at a disadvantage. "Children who are particularly likely to have difficulty learning to read in the primary grades are those who begin school with less prior knowledge and skill in certain domains, most notably letter knowledge, phonological sensitivity, familiarity with the basic purposes and mechanisms of reading, and language ability."[10]

The age at which shared reading begins has consistently been shown to be a strong predictor of individual differences in young children's language abilities. One study found a significant correlation between the reported age of the beginning of shared reading and language scores at four years of age.[11] The age at which parents started to read to their child is associated with their child's interest in and enjoyment of reading activities. In turn, a child's interest in reading activities is an important predictor of his or her later reading achievement. The earlier we start, the better.

ATTITUDE OF THE PARENT/CAREGIVER

A report from *Preventing Reading Difficulties in Young Children* stressed the influence adults can have on the quality and quantity of their children's early literacy experiences. "A wide range of factors in turn affects the nature of these interactions, including the parents' attitudes and beliefs about reading and literacy, the children's motivation for reading, the opportunities parents provide their children and their actual behaviors with them, and the parents' own reading and literacy abilities."[12] Some researchers have found that parents who believe that reading is a source of entertainment have children with a more positive view about reading than do parents who emphasize the skills aspect of reading development.[13]

Parents and caregivers are in the best position to support early literacy. They know their children's moods. Children learn best when they are awake and alert, not too tired, but not so active that they cannot focus.

Children learn through their senses. They enjoy doing activities with their parents or caregivers. They learn through repetition. The adult who cares for the child can incorporate appropriate activities during the course of the day, making the learning experiences informal and pleasurable.

TELEVISION/VIDEO VIEWING

According to a study by the Kaiser Foundation, one-third of all children from newborns to six-year-olds (36 percent) have a TV in their bedrooms, more than one in four (27 percent) have a VCR or DVD, one in ten have a video-game player, and 7 percent have a computer. Thirty percent of children from newborns to three-year-olds have a TV in their rooms, as do 43 percent of four- to six-year-olds. Children who have a TV in their bedrooms or who live in heavy TV households spend significantly more time watching than other children do and less time reading or playing outside. Those with a TV in their room spend an average of twenty-two minutes more per day watching TV and videos than other children. Those living in heavy TV households are more likely to watch every day (77 percent versus 56 percent) and to watch for longer when they do watch (an average of thirty-four minutes more per day). They are also less likely to read every day (59 percent versus 68 percent), and they spend less time reading when they do read (six minutes less per day). In fact, they are less likely than other children to be able to read at all (34 percent of children ages four to six from heavy TV households can read, compared to 56 percent of other children that age). "These findings definitely raise a red flag about the impact of TV on children's reading," says Victoria Rideout, of the Henry Kaiser Family Foundation.[14]

FAMILY ECONOMICS AND EARLY LITERACY

The socioeconomic circumstances of a child's world can have an impact on a child's literacy development in many ways. According to *America's Kindergartners*, a report from the National Center for Education Statistics, children from families who did not receive welfare services were more likely to pass reading proficiency levels one (letter recognition), two (beginning sounds), and three (ending sounds) than kindergartners from families who did receive public assistance. Children whose families did not receive public assistance are more likely than children whose families received public assistance to have all three print familiarity skills (knowing that print reads left to right, knowing where to go when a line of print ends, and knowing where the story ends).[15]

Poorer preschool children and those from working-class homes are also less likely to have children's books in their homes; are less likely to be read to frequently, and at an early age; are less likely to have opportunities to talk about books with an adult; and are less likely to have opportunities to engage in imaginative storytelling.[16]

Research has shown that mothers from lower income groups engage in less shared picture book reading and produce fewer teaching behaviors during that time than mothers from middle-class groups. One estimate is that the typical middle-class child enters first grade with 1,000 to 1,700 hours of one-on-one picture book reading, whereas a child from a low-income family averages just 25 hours. These kinds of experiential differences, which are a reflection of social-class differences, are clearly important in accounting for differences in academic outcomes and point to the importance of adopting approaches for preschoolers that prevent later difficulties in reading, writing, and other tasks of formal schooling.[17]

Lois Bloom points out in her foreword to Betty Hart and Todd Risley's *Meaningful Differences in the Everyday Experiences of Young American Children*:

> For example, race/ethnicity doesn't matter; gender doesn't matter; whether a child is the first in the family or born later also doesn't matter. But what does matter, and it matters very much, is relative economic advantage. First, . . . children living in poverty, children born into middle-class homes, and children with professional parents all have the same kinds of everyday language experience. They all hear talk about persons and things, about relationships, actions, and feelings, and about past and future events. And they all participate in interactions with others in which what they do is prompted, responded to, prohibited, or affirmed. The differences between the families . . . were not in the kinds of experience they provided their children, but in the differing amount of those experiences. The basic finding is that children who learn fewer words also have fewer experiences with words in interactions with other persons, and they are also children growing up in less economically advantage homes. . . . It turns out that frequency matters.[18]

INDIVIDUAL RISK FACTORS

As individuals, children at risk for reading difficulties

> have gained less knowledge and skill regarding literacy during their preschool years;
>
> lack age-appropriate skills in the cognitive processing related to literacy, especially phonological awareness, naming of objects, sentence or story recall, and general language;
>
> have been diagnosed with an early language impairment;
>
> are hearing impaired or have another medical diagnosis with reading problems occurring as a secondary symptom;
>
> have parents with a history of reading problems.[19]

The relationship between the skills children possess when entering school and their later academic performance is remarkably stable. Research has shown that there is nearly a 90 percent probability that a child who is a poor reader at the end of the fourth grade started out a poor reader at the end of first grade. Knowing alphabet letters when beginning kindergarten is a strong predictor of reading ability in the tenth grade.[20]

So, what can be done to break the cycle, to help support families no matter what the reading level of the adults, to strengthen the child's foundation for learning to read? There is a lot that library staff and parents/caregivers can do to support early literacy development! A good place to start is by learning more about the six early literacy skills: print motivation, phonological awareness, vocabulary, narrative skills, print awareness, and letter knowledge.

Research Regarding Early Literacy Skills

PRINT MOTIVATION

Print motivation is having an interest in and an enjoyment of books.

D. F. Lancy and C. Bergin found that children who are more fluent and positive about reading came from parent-child pairs who viewed reading as fun and encouraged questions and humor while reading. Children who learn from their parents that literacy is a source of enjoyment may be more motivated to persist in their efforts to learn to read despite difficulties they may encounter. Having pretend reading sessions, attempting to identify words and letters on T-shirts and cereal boxes, and playing with educational toys were reported by parents as important activities in which their children engaged with print.[21]

A family's influence on a child's literacy involves far more than merely providing books or engaging in leisure-time reading. A study of parents reading with toddlers found that when the interaction with the parent is negative, it carries over to the activity of reading. Children feel aversion to the activity, reading, when the experience is not pleasant.[22] A positive experience is one where the adult is focused on the child without distractions. The adult allows the child to participate and ask questions as she or he reads the book, relates what is happening in the book to the child's experience, and follows the child's lead.

While this is not surprising, it shows us that just saying "Read with your child every day" or "Read with your child fifteen minutes a day" is not sufficient. We must make sure that the adult knows *how* to make the reading experience a pleasant one. Keeping the interaction around reading and sharing books positive and stress-free creates an environment where a child can learn more easily. As noted earlier, chronic stress can impair brain development and the ability to learn. We can model positive reading behaviors, but we can also offer parents/caregivers specific tips on making the experiences positive, for example, by finding a comfortable spot to read a book related to the child's interests.

PHONOLOGICAL AWARENESS

Phonological awareness is the ability to hear and play with the smaller sounds in words. It includes activities that work with rhyme, words, syllables, and initial sounds.

Some other definitions that may be helpful follow:

> *Phoneme*—the smallest part of spoken language that makes a difference in the meaning of words. English has about forty-one phonemes. The word *as* has two phonemes (/a/ /s/); *chick* has three phonemes (/ch/ /i/ /k/).

> *Grapheme*—the smallest part of written language that represents a phoneme in the spelling of a word. It can be just one letter, such as *k, b, l,* or *r,* or two letters, such as *br* or *ch.*

> *Phonemic awareness*—the ability to hear, identify, and manipulate the individual sounds, or phonemes, in spoken words.

Phonics—the understanding that there is a predictable relationship between *phonemes* (the sounds of the spoken language) and *graphemes*
(the letters and spellings that represent those sounds in written
language).[23]

One of the hallmarks of poor readers is poor phonological processing skills. Children who are better at noticing rhymes, syllables, and phonemes are quicker to learn to read. This relationship continues even after variables like IQ, vocabulary, memory, and social class are made statistically insignificant.[24] In other words, phonological awareness is one of the key skills that children need to possess on the road to becoming fluent readers. It is also something that can be taught and encouraged through picture book reading and wordplay.

According to Susan Hall and Louisa Moats, in their book *Straight Talk about Reading*, phonological awareness is

> necessary, but not sufficient to become a good word reader. Besides being able to notice, think about, and manipulate sounds in words, a prospective reader also needs to use that knowledge to read words, recall extensive vocabulary, re-member background knowledge about the word, and use strong thinking skills. For most children who have difficulty reading, phonological awareness can be stimulated through direct training. This is great news because it means that even for children who enter school with deficiencies in their understanding of speech sounds, appropriate kindergarten and first grade curricula can develop this key skill for reading readiness for most children.[25]

VOCABULARY

Vocabulary is knowing the names of things.

Infants learn vocabulary quickly. Research findings by Janellen Huttenlocher and others of the University of Chicago show that this growth is clearly linked to the extent their parents converse with them.[26]

Not only is the amount of speech between parent and child important but so is how we speak with young children. Speaking in "parentese" has been shown to hold a baby's attention longer than plain adult speech. "Parentese" is speech with a singsong or up-down quality, a slightly higher pitch, and a slower pace than normal adult speech.[27]

A child with a large listening and speaking vocabulary has an enormous advantage in learning to read. Reading comprehension depends more than any other single skill on knowing the meanings of the individual words in the passage. In addition, the process of relating the printed word to a spoken word is faster and more accurate when that word is already in the child's speaking vocabulary.

NARRATIVE SKILLS

Narrative skills is the ability to describe things and events and to tell stories.

There is a strong relationship between spoken language and written language. Once printed words are recognized, text comprehension depends heavily on the reader's oral language abilities. Language development in preschoolers is related to later reading achievement.[28] A number of studies support these conclusions by demonstrating a positive correlation between oral skills and reading. In short, the children who have larger vocabularies and a better understanding of spoken language have higher reading scores.[29]

Mealtime conversation provides an opportunity for children to acquire knowledge about narrative when family members recount the day's activities, thus giving children an experience that is of well-documented value in learning about language and communication.[30] Developing narrative skills is a focal point of dialogic reading. See chapter 3, "Dialogic Reading: *How* We Read with Children Makes a Difference," for more information.

PRINT AWARENESS

Print awareness is noticing print in the environment, knowing how to handle a book, and understanding how to follow the words on a page.

Print awareness refers to a general understanding of how print is used rather than to knowledge about specific letters. It has been shown to have a moderate correlation with reading ability in the primary grades and is just one of the types of information a child needs to know to be ready to read. Print awareness includes the following:

Awareness that print has meaning.

The knowledge that people read the text, not just look at the pictures.

Awareness of how to read a book—right side up, starting with the first page and continuing to the end. In English, the left page is read first and the text is read from left to right.

Understanding that words are units separated by white spaces.

Print is all around us.[31]

Print awareness is an important part of knowing how to read and write. Children who know about print understand that the words they see in print and the words they speak and hear are related. They will use and see print a lot, even when they're young—on signs and billboards, in alphabet books and storybooks, and in labels, magazines, and newspapers. They see family members use print, and they learn that print is all around them and that it is used for different purposes.[32]

LETTER KNOWLEDGE

Letter knowledge is knowing that letters are different from each other, that the same letter can look different, and that each letter has a name and is related to specific sounds.

Among the skills that are traditionally evaluated, the one that appears to be the strongest predictor of reading success on its own is letter identification.[33] In writing systems like ours, which is alphabetic, children learn to decode written words by connecting units of print, called graphemes, to units of sound, called phonemes. (See definitions under "Phonological Awareness," above.) Writing reverses the process and involves translating units of sound, phonemes, to units of print, graphemes. In both cases, children must be able to recognize the differences in letters, to understand that letters are different from each other. A child who is learning how to read and cannot recognize and tell one letter in the alphabet apart from another will have a hard time learning the sounds that those letters represent, or make.[34]

Other studies indicate that letter knowledge might play an important role in the development of phonological awareness. S. R. Burgess and C. J. Lonigan found that preschool children's letter knowledge was a unique predictor of growth in phonological sensitivity across one year.[35]

Letter knowledge alone is not enough, as studies indicate that programs designed to promote lasting early literacy skills are most effective when letter knowledge and phonemic awareness are combined.[36] Children become familiar with the way letters look before they attach a sound to the letter. Appendix D covers the order in which children learn the sounds of letters.

What Does This Mean for Those Who Serve Children and Their Families?

One goal of most parents and caregivers is that their children become good readers. The research is strong; we know the risk factors, and we are learning more about early literacy. As we become familiar with the research and specific activities that help adults support their child's early literacy development, we can share this information with parents and caregivers, keeping it fun as we help them on the road to a lifelong love of reading and books.

Chapter 2 takes some of the research noted above, as well as the work of the researchers who worked on the "Every Child Ready to Read @ your library" project, and looks at specific ways to incorporate and explain aspects of early literacy to the adults and ways to strengthen what we already do with children.

NOTES

1. *National Reading Panel: Teaching Children to Read: An Evidence-Based Assessment of the Scientific Research Literature on Reading and Its Implications for Reading Instruction: Reports of the Subgroups* (Bethesda, MD: National Institute of Child Health and Human Development, National Institutes of Health, 2000). Available at http:// www.nifl.gov.

2. International Reading Association and National Association for the Education of Young Children, *Learning to Read and Write: Developmentally Appropriate Practices for Young Children: Position Statement* (Washington, DC: NAEYC, 1999), 4.

3. Ibid.

4. I Am Your Child Foundation, *The First Years Last Forever: The New Brain Research and Your Child's Healthy Development* (Los Angeles: I Am Your Child Foundation, 1997).

5. Constance Holden, "Small Refugees Suffer the Effects of Early Neglect," *Science Magazine* 274, no. 15 (November 1996): 1076–77.

6. Pam Schiller, *Start Smart! Building Brain Power in the Early Years* (Beltsville, MD: Gryphon House, 1999), 128.

7. Kathleen Berger, *The Developing Person through Childhood and Adolescence* (New York: Worth, 1991).

8. National Academy of Education, *Becoming a Nation of Readers: The Report of the Commission on Reading* (National Academy of Education, 1985), 23.

9. Ibid, 57.

10. Committee on the Prevention of Reading Difficulties in Young Children, *Preventing Reading Difficulties in Young Children* (Washington, DC: National Academy Press,1998), 137.

11. Adam Payne, Grover Whitehurst, and Andrea Angeli, "The Role of Home Literacy Environment in the Development of Language Ability in Preschool Children from Low-Income Families," *Early Childhood Research Quarterly* 9, nos. 3–4 (1994): 422–40.

12. Committee on the Prevention of Reading Difficulties in Young Children, 138.

13. L. Baker, D. Scher, and K. Mackler, "Home and Family Influences on Motivations for Reading," *Educational Psychologist* 32, no. 2 (1997): 69–82.

14. Victoria Rideout, Elizabeth Vandewater, and Ellen Wartella, *Zero to Six: Electronic Media in the Lives of Infants, Toddlers and Preschoolers: A Kaiser Foundation Report* (Washington, DC: Henry Kaiser Family Foundation, 2003).

15. Kristin Denton and Elvira Germino-Hausken, U.S. Department of Education, National Center for Education Statistics, *America's Kindergartners* (Washington, DC: 2000), 16.

16. J. M. Mason and B. M. Kerr, "Literacy Transfer from Parents to Children in the Preschool Years," in *The Intergenerational Transfer of Cognitive Skills: Volume II: Theory and Research in Cognitive Science*, ed. T. G. Sticht, M. J. Beeler, and B. A. McDonald, 49–68 (Norwood, NJ: Ablex, 1992).

17. Marilyn Jager Adams, *Beginning to Read: Thinking and Learning about Print* (Urbana-Champaign: University of Illinois, Reading Research and Education Center, 1990), 85.

18. Betty Hart and Todd R. Risley, *Meaningful Differences in the Everyday Experiences of Young American Children* (Baltimore: P. H. Brookes, 1995), x–xiii.

19. Committee on the Prevention of Reading Difficulties in Young Children, 132.

20. G. Reid Lyon (testimony, U.S. Senate, Committee on Labor and Human Resources, April 28, 1998).

21. Committee on the Prevention of Reading Difficulties in Young Children, 143.

22. A. G. Bus and others, "Attachment and Bookreading Patterns: A Study of Mothers, Fathers, and Their Toddlers," *Early Childhood Research Quarterly* 12 (1997): 81–98.

23. Bonnie Armbruster, *Put Reading First: The Research Building Blocks for Teaching Children to Read, Kindergarten through Grade 3* (Jessup, MD: National Institute for Literacy, 2001).

24. Susan B. Neuman and David K. Dickinson, eds., *Handbook of Early Literacy Research* (New York: Guilford, 2001), 16.

25. Susan Hall and Louisa Moats, *Straight Talk about Reading: How Parents Can Make a Difference during the Early Years* (Chicago: Contemporary Books, 1999), 173–74.

26. Janellen Huttenlocher and others, "Early Vocabulary Growth: Relation to Language Input and Gender," *Developmental Psychology* 27, no. 2 (1991): 236–48.

27. Craig Ramey, *Right from Birth: Building Your Child's Foundation for Life* (New York: Goddard, 1999), 93.

28. Neuman and Dickinson, 19.

29. Ibid.

30. C. E. Snow and P. O. Tabors, "Language Skills That Relate to Literacy Development," in *Language and Literacy in Early Childhood Education*, ed. B. Spodek and O. N. Saracho, 1–20 (New York: Teachers College Press, 1993).

31. Hall and Moats,163–65.

32. Bonnie Armbruster, *A Child Becomes a Reader: Birth through Preschool* (Washington, DC: National Institute for Literacy, 2003).

33. Committee on the Prevention of Reading Difficulties in Young Children, 113.

34. Neuman and Dickinson, 16.

35. S. R. Burgess, and C. J. Lonigan, "Bidirectional Relations of Phonological Sensitivity and Pre-reading Abilities: Evidence from a Preschool Sample," *Journal of Experimental Child Psychology* 70 (1998): 117–41.

36. L. Bradley and P. E. Bryant, *Rhyme and Reason in Reading and Spelling* (Ann Arbor: University of Michigan Press, 1985).

2

Incorporating and Explaining Key Early Literacy Concepts

How is the early literacy enhanced storytime similar to and different from our traditional storytimes? Storytimes remain a warm, inviting activity that open the world of books to young children. Storytimes offer young children and their parents/caregivers exposure to a variety of skills, small and large motor development, social and early literacy skills. Through modeling, we offer adults an opportunity to observe how they can support their children's early literacy development outside the library.

Early literacy enhanced storytimes take them a step further by *explaining* to the adults how the elements of storytime support early literacy. In this way, we can help parents/caregivers become more fully aware of the key role they play in the development of their child's early literacy skills and the importance of early literacy as part of overall child development. In addition, adults learn specific ways to support their children's continued development of these skills.

This chapter offers both general suggestions and specific examples of ways to plan storytimes to incorporate early literacy skills and to convey them to parents and caregivers. (Sample storytimes that incorporate early literacy skills and messages as asides to the adult participants can be found in chapters 7 through 9.) In many ways, these storytimes are like traditional storytimes, with social skills and motor skills development; however, they go a step further. Specific examples of ways to explain the basic concepts of early literacy and the role the parents and caregivers play as their child's first teacher are presented by directly speaking to the adults during the storytime. This is one of the main differences between an early literacy enhanced storytime and its more traditional counterpart. Let's look at how to incorporate early literacy information for adults into storytimes by examining the storytime planning process.

Relating Developmental Stages to Storytimes

Children's developmental stages help us determine the approaches to take during story-time. Early talkers are the youngest children up until the point they have more than fifty words of expressive (talking) vocabulary. At this point, they are called talkers. Once they have a firmer grasp of language and can answer more involved questions, they are called prereaders. Note that there are no firm and fast rules governing when each child can do any given activity. Some of the activities for prereaders would work just as well with older children, and some prereaders will not be able to fully do some of the activities. Each presenter needs to be sensitive to the ability of each group and, within each group, to each child.

Each developmental stage has a place in storytime and an appropriate program to go with it. For example, babies see objects best when they are about twelve inches away from their faces. There is no way the storytime presenter can be twelve inches away from each infant. So, the *presenter* becomes the *facilitator* between the adult and the child. With babies, storytime largely consists of rhymes and songs, with relatively few print materials being used. Rhymes and songs strongly support the skill of phonological awareness. The goal here is to encourage talking and positive interactions between the baby and the adult. The warm sharing of a board book can be a baby's first positive experience with print.

Talkers are no longer a captive audience. The presenter is an object of interest but not for long! As these children learn to interact with the storytime presenter, they become less tentative and more willing to try new things, as new people become familiar ones. Storytime is full of rhyme and song, and now, short books. Remember, parents need to know that although reading to their children is important, even more important is *how* they read to their children.

Prereaders are increasingly independent. Their speech is more advanced. They can listen to longer stories and fully participate. At this age, it is common for parents and caregivers to become more concerned about how well their children are prepared for school. Storytime for this age includes finger plays, rhymes, and more complex, longer books. The presenter's messages to the adults encompass the full range of early literacy skills while stressing the importance of keeping learning fun.

Not every element, whether book, finger play, creative dramatics, song, craft, flannel board, or musical activity, lends itself equally well to each skill. Because storytimes already are literacy based, adding early literacy information for the adults and making the storytime components more intentional can be fairly easily accommodated. It takes a little more thought initially. Early literacy enhanced storytimes require more time to prepare than traditional ones at first. Once you get the hang of it, it will feel natural.

Let's look at each format (the picture book; rhymes, songs, and finger plays; flannel board or magnet board; action or movement; activity time, crafts, and writing; and home activities) to see how early literacy skills can be incorporated into each one.

Bringing Early Literacy into Common Storytime Components

Our storytimes already include components that support early literacy skills. This chapter takes each storytime component and highlights ways to incorporate early literacy skills. However, not all the skills—or even all aspects of one skill—should be discussed in one storytime. The following suggestions allow you to keep your basic storytime format and style and build on it. You can decide for any one storytime what you want to highlight. The idea is *not* to bring in all new things but rather to reexamine the storytimes you are comfortable with and enhance them. Pick and choose and use the parts that appeal to you, adapt them, and make them yours.

Storytime Introduction

The storytime introduction is the time for you to gather the children and adults together, welcome them, introduce yourself, and help get them settled. Some presenters address behavior, such as what to do when a child is disruptive to the group. This is also the time to address the adults' behavior. They may be used to sitting and chatting with each other or in other ways not giving you and their children their attention. This is the time to draw their attention to the fact that you are highlighting early literacy skills that researchers have determined are important for their children's early literacy development. Be sure to acknowledge and express in a positive way the key role the adult plays in the child's early literacy development.

In the early literacy enhanced storytime, the introduction can also be used to describe or briefly explain the early literacy skill you will be highlighting during the program. One or two sentences are fine. For example, if you use name tags, they can be used to explain *print awareness*, which is, in part, noticing print; *print motivation*, which is being interested in and enjoying print (what child doesn't love his or her own name!); and *letter knowledge*, which is knowing letters are different from each other, knowing their names, and that they are related to sounds. Some children may be able to write their names. Others can spell their names to you as you write them. Others may recognize their name when it is written. They are making the connection between the spoken and the written word, with a word that is most important to them—their names!

You may find it helpful to have a poster of the six skills (see appendix D) or of the skill you are highlighting. Explain what you are doing and why a couple of times during the storytime. To help ease yourself into doing this, have the phrases you want to share with the adults ready ahead of time. Make a note, on paper or mentally, of what you plan to say and at what points in the storytime, or write brief paragraphs that you can read aloud. The sample storytimes in chapters 7 through 9 contain examples to get you started.

What Do I Tell the Adults?

> "The early literacy skill I'll be highlighting today is *vocabulary*. It is knowing the names of things. Children need this skill for two reasons: to be able to understand what they read and to recognize words when they try to sound them out."

> "Today I'll be highlighting the early literacy skill *print awareness*. Children with print awareness know how to handle a book, to follow the words on a page, and to recognize print when they are out and about."

The Opening

You may choose to leave your storytime opening as is. If you decide to enhance it, what you do will depend on what kind of activity or song you choose. Look at how you normally open a storytime, and think about how to make it more playful. Keeping the same welcoming song throughout your storytimes gives children a sense of security, and they are happy to start with something familiar.

Examples

Literacy skills can be added to this part of your storytime in a variety of ways. For example, if you do or say something with the children's names, after saying each child's name correctly, play around with the sounds in their names. Pronounce each name with the same first-letter sound. If you plan to talk about the letter *m* and its sound, /m/, *Joshua* becomes *Moshua*; *Keshawn* and *Desiree* become *Meshawn* and *Mesiree*, respectively.

If you go around the circle asking children's names, you could play a clapping game. Say, "We are going to say our names, and we are going to clap out how many parts, or syllables, there are in each name." For example, say *Cristina* (*Cris-ti-na*) as you clap once for each of the three syllables. Repeat this with each child's name. This could be done as you hand out name tags, too. Another time, you could point out the different beginning letters and letter sounds of the children's names, and then clap out the parts of their names. This breaking down of words into parts is called *segmentation* and is part of phonological awareness.

You might decide to sing or say your song or poem through once and then make a change the second time through. Introduce the change by telling the children exactly what you are going to do. If you sing a "hello" or "pleased to see you" song, after singing it the regular way, tell the children you are going to change the first sound of each word, and have them start with /b/.

For example, for prereader storytimes, after singing, "The More We Get Together," say, "Now we are going to sing the song again, only in a different way. We are going to start every word with the /b/ sound instead of the real first sound. It will sound like this:

> Be bore be bet bogether, bogether, bogether,
>
> Be bore, be bet bogether
>
> Be bappier be'll be."

Then ask, "Now, can you sing it with me that way?" The children will think it is silly and fun. At each storytime you can do different beginning sounds.

What Do I Tell the Adults?

Intermittently, you need to explain to the adults what you are doing and why. Here are some sample phrases.

> "Breaking words into parts will help the children later when they are sounding out or decoding words."
>
> "Children who know words are made up of smaller parts have an easier time tackling new words when they are reading."
>
> "Research tells us that children who can play with the sounds in words have an easier time learning to read than those who can't."

The Theme

If you have a theme, take a little time to discuss it in your storytimes for the older children. Many of us take this opportunity to give information or background about the topic. In an early literacy enhanced storytime, allow time for children to talk about the topic as well. We are often concerned that children will start talking and won't listen or that we will not be able to keep their attention. By allowing them to talk about what they know, however, we are helping them develop their narrative skills and use their vocabulary. We also are modeling for the adults how to encourage conversation around the topic of a book before reading it together. You can use a preestablished hand signal, instrument sound, or simple clapping rhythm to bring the group back together again.

Examples

Consider also the way that you talk about books depending on the theme. For example, when *Blue Sea*, by Robert Kalan, is grouped with other books on size, you would talk about it using that concept. When it is grouped with stories about fish or the sea, you would focus more on the fish aspect of the story. If you grouped it with Paul Galdone's *The Gingerbread Boy*; *Jump, Frog, Jump*, also by Robert Kalan; and *The Gunniwolf*, by Wilhemina Harper, with a theme of "Catch Us If You Can," you would be talking about *Blue Sea* from yet another perspective. Each perspective pulls in new or familiar experiences. Each theme exposes children to different vocabulary as well.

When you include this interactive time, you may find yourself asking some questions about the theme and relating it to the children's experiences. Sometimes when we ask a question, the adults chime in with a reply before the children even have a chance to respond. Here is a perfect time to explain that it takes more time for children to reply than it does for adults. Ask the parents to give them a good five seconds to respond first.

So often prereaders clamor to tell us something they know about the topic, and we do not have time to listen to all their comments. Shyer children, who are often the ones who could use the talking practice, listen and do not speak. Try this: first, establish a sound signal to bring their attention back to you. Then say, "Children, tell the person who brought you today something about (the topic)." Then use your signal. Now have the adults tell their children something about the topic. Draw their attention back with your sound signal.

What Do I Tell the Adults?

"Allowing your child to talk about the book or the picture on the cover or the topic of the book before you read it develops narrative skills. It may also allow your child to listen to the story more continuously once she or he has talked about his or her experiences relating to what is happening in the book."

"Think about the many perspectives or concepts in the books you read. When you read them again and again, you can bring up different topics and talk about different things. You can offer words that your child might not know. This develops vocabulary."

"One thing I learned is hearing a question and formulating a response involves at least three different parts of the brain. You may have noticed that it takes children longer than adults to respond to questions because they have not had as much practice at it as we have. Try to wait about five seconds to give your child time to respond to what you say." *[Count off on your hand, slowly raising one finger at a time to show five seconds.]* "We can even try this now as I ask you all to think of some things about our theme today."

The Picture Book

Picture books are the underpinning of storytimes. Even when fewer books are included in storytimes for early talkers (newborns to twenty-four months), we still know that children and their families will take from storytime the joy of reading books. Sharing books is the part of the storytime that is most obviously related to early literacy.

Regardless of the kind of book being used, certain simple yet important things can be done to encourage the development of early literacy skills. All six skills can be demonstrated with just about any book! That means you can use your favorite books no matter which skill you choose to discuss. In fact, you could use the very same book for six story-times (children love repetition) and then model for and explain to the adults how any book they read supports each of the skills, highlighting a different skill each time. It is too much to bombard the adults with information about all six skills at one storytime.

PRINT MOTIVATION

Print motivation is an interest in and enjoyment of books. Here are some suggestions for demonstrating print motivation during storytime:

> Share books *you* enjoy.
>
> Convey your love of books and reading in the way you share the books.
>
> Model reading books in a cheerful voice, putting expression into your reading.
>
> When appropriate, have children and adults join in at certain parts.
>
> For the youngest children, adults can do choral reading (everyone reading the book aloud together) with you so that they get the rhythm and fun of reading the book. The baby tunes in to the parent's voice.
>
> Use nonfiction books that might capture the interest of the children.
>
> Have a comfortable setting where adults and children can share books together, as part of storytime or before and after it.

> Children learn by doing. They learn best when they are actively engaged in an activity, and this includes the sharing and reading of books.

What Do I Tell the Adults?

> "Choose a time when you and your child are in a good mood to share books."
>
> "Even if your child is interested for only a short time, that's OK. Keep it fun. You can try again later."
>
> "It is more important for the interaction around a book to be positive than for it to be long."

PHONOLOGICAL AWARENESS

Phonological awareness is the ability to hear and play with the smaller sounds in words and includes the following: the ability to

> break words into parts or segments (what is *mon-key* without the *mon*?);

say the initial sound (what sound does *bear* start with? What other words start with the same sound as *bear*?); and

say whether two words rhyme (do *dog* and *cat* rhyme? Do *cat* and *hat* rhyme?).

For many of us, sharing rhyming books is a standard part of any storytime. However, there are things that we can do to extend the children's exposure to and appreciation of rhyme and other parts of phonological awareness.

Examples

Phonological awareness can be highlighted with any picture book. Without changing the books you use in your storytime, you can highlight phonological awareness in any of the following ways:

Read a book that rhymes.

Read a book that has alliteration; talk about that first sound; what other words start with the same sound? For example, *Turtle Splash*, by Cathryn Falwell, contains the phrases "rabbit rustling" and "lounging in a line."

Use a songbook.

Take a word from the book (whether it's a rhyming book or not) and play with the word; notice what rhymes with it or what sound it starts with.

After reading a book, go back through the book and play with its words. For example, clap out the number of syllables in the names of vegetables, people, or places mentioned in the story, or change the initial sound of the refrains that you are saying as a group. The same kinds of attraction that children have for silly songs and rhyme can be developed from many storybooks, regardless of whether or not they rhyme. For example, with the book *Caps for Sale*, by Esphyr Slobodkina, take the word *cap* and say, "What rhymes with *cap*? Perhaps someone says *map*. (A silly word that has no meaning, like *fap, quap*, or *vap*, is fine, too.) Then sing a rhyming song to the tune of "Skip to My Lou."

> *Cap, map*, these words rhyme
>
> *Cap, map*, these words rhyme
>
> *Cap, map*, these words rhyme
>
> So rhyme along with me.

What Do I Tell the Adults?

"Making up rhyming words, even making up silly nonsense words that rhyme, is one good way to develop phonological awareness, one of the early literacy skills."

"Playing with words, especially words that are interesting to your child, is a fun way to develop phonological awareness. It helps children later when they are trying to sound out words."

"Songs are a wonderful way to build phonological awareness because there is a different note for different syllables. Babies are learning the rhythm of language, and young children are hearing parts of words."

VOCABULARY

Vocabulary is knowing the names of things (also of emotions, concepts, ideas). Books offer us so many opportunities to expand vocabulary!

Examples

Review a book you are using to see if there are words that might be unfamiliar to your group or an interesting word you may want to bring to their attention.

Many books for younger children have one or a few pictures per page. Model naming the pictures and relating them to the real thing. Talk about the picture, adding information.

Take an unfamiliar word from the book, and talk about it before you start reading. This will ensure that the children understand the book and acquire some new words. You can also explain an unfamiliar word in a book by giving a simple explanation before going on. Some words can be confusing, especially those with multiple meanings. For example, in *Caps for Sale*, a cap is a hat, but it could also be the top to a soda bottle or a small firecracker. In books where all the words are familiar to the children, you might introduce a less-familiar synonym.

Use nonfiction books. They often help adults figure out what unfamiliar words mean and can be a real source of information and new vocabulary words.

What Do I Tell the Adults?

"Research shows that it is easier for children to read words they have already heard. Try to expose them to as many words as you can. Talking about the words in books is one way to do this."

"Children with a strong vocabulary can understand what they read better than children with a smaller vocabulary."

"Books have many words that are not often used in normal conversation or on television. By reading books with children, you expand their vocabulary."

"Research shows that talking with your child even from birth makes a difference later in his or her overall vocabulary. Don't worry about whether or not children understand. Talk with them, and leave time for them to talk back, too!"

NARRATIVE SKILLS

Narrative skills is the ability to describe things and events and to tell stories.

Picture book sharing can play a huge role in a child's ability to describe things and events and to tell stories. Reading storybooks helps children gain a sense of story structure: a beginning, a middle, and an end in some stories, or a beginning, a problem, and a resolution in others.

Examples

To help strengthen *narrative skills*, try the following:

> Ask children and adults to repeat phrases along with you as you read the book.
>
> Have children do a motion and repeat a phrase along with you as you read the book.
>
> Expand the book using flannel boards, puppets, creative dramatics, and props, using them as ways to help children retell the story.
>
> Ask children some questions before, during, or after reading the book. Be responsive to all their replies. Do not expect one "right" answer. Because conversation about the book is so important, chapter 3, "Dialogic Reading: *How* We Read with Children Makes a Difference," is devoted to this topic.

What Do I Tell the Adults?

> "It is critically important that we encourage the children to participate and to talk! This is more easily done one-on-one than in a group."
>
> "When we share books in different ways, we develop different skills. When we read a book straight through, children are getting the continuity of the story and are developing listening skills. When we encourage them to retell the story or to relate something in the story to their lives, we help their narrative skills, one of the early literacy skills researchers have identified to help with reading and comprehension."
>
> "Be patient when you are having your child talk back to you. It takes them time to organize their thoughts. Conversations use three different parts of the brain, and they need time to coordinate them!"

PRINT AWARENESS

Print awareness is noticing print everywhere, knowing how to handle a book, and understanding how to follow the words on a page.

Children need to know the mechanics of how books and words work, that we read from left to right in English, and that we start from the front of the book, turning pages from right to left. Reading picture books in storytime gives us lots of opportunities to enforce these concepts.

Examples

> Run your finger under the title and the names of the author and the illustrator when you start the book as well as under repeated phrases as you read the book.
>
> Play around with the physical attributes of the book by holding it upside down or backward as you start to read it. See what reactions you get from your prereaders. Make a game out of it by asking, "Is *this* the right way to start a book?"
>
> Many books have interesting endpapers. Talk about them and what they might tell you about the story.

What Do I Tell the Adults?

> "I am running my finger under the words occasionally so that the children see that it is the text I am reading, not the pictures. This is part of print awareness. It helps them realize that the spoken word can be written."
>
> "There are many things you can do during the day to help your child with print awareness: point out signs as you are walking or driving—like labels at the grocery store and stop signs. When you make lists, say the words aloud as you write them down."
>
> "Let your child turn the pages of a book while you read."
>
> "Research tells us that children who know that print has meaning understand quickly how words work in reading and writing."
>
> "Babies will put books in their mouths and bite them. This is how they explore their world. Let the baby have some books that you don't mind getting messed up. This is how they learn about books!"

LETTER KNOWLEDGE

Letter knowledge is knowing letters are different from each other, that the same letter can look different, and that each letter has a name and relates to specific sounds.

Examples

Try the following to encourage the acquisition of this skill during storytime.

> Point out the beginning letter of a word in the title that would have meaning to the child and to what you are doing. For example, if you are talking about bears and the word *bear* is in the title, you could point to the letter *b* and say its name and sound.

Use an alphabet book.

Use a book with alliteration and talk about the letter. Have the children draw the letter in the air. Shape a long rope into a letter on the ground, and march around it.

For the younger children, talk about shapes, and the concept of same and different.

What Do I Tell the Adults?

For younger children: "Young children learn best through their senses. Letters are made of shapes. Let young children explore real things that are round (like a ball), that are straight (like blocks), and that have holes in them. In this way, they will have a better understanding of shapes when they see them on paper."

"Children learn best when what they are learning relates to them. When exposing them to letters, start with their name or with a topic that interests them."

"Children can learn about letters in different ways—by noticing them all around. They can make their bodies or fingers into letters, use magnetic letters, or make letters out of play dough."

Rhymes, Songs, and Finger Plays

Rhymes, songs, and finger plays make up the largest part of storytimes for newborns to two-year-olds and contribute significantly to the storytimes for two- through five-year-olds. By making posters or flip charts of the words to the rhymes, songs, and finger plays you do in storytime, you allow the participants to become more of a group and to hear each other as they all follow along together. This also supports print awareness.

Phonological awareness, the ability to play with the smaller sounds in words, is the early literacy skill that is most directly and naturally linked to rhymes, songs, and finger plays.

Babies become acquainted with language by listening to its rhyme and rhythm. For children who are speaking, repeating rhymes and songs is the introduction to becoming able to make rhymes themselves. Songs, by their very nature, have a different note for each syllable. Subconsciously, young children are hearing individual words being broken down into parts.

One aspect of phonological awareness, as noted in the "Picture Book" section above, is recognizing words that rhyme and being able to make words that rhyme. You can leave out a word that rhymes and let children fill it in.

Recognizing rhymes and starting sounds is easier than producing them. For example, it is easier to say whether two words rhyme than to think of a word to rhyme with one given. It is easier for a child to respond to, "Does *fun* rhyme with *cat*?" than for a child to respond to, "What rhymes with *fun*?"

Rhyming and hearing starting consonants are easier than games that take words apart and mix up the parts. Be aware of the stages and language experiences of your participants. Help parents become aware of their own child's stage of development by explaining what is easier and what is harder.

Examples

Let's look at some songs and finger plays and see how we can add even more early literacy value to them. As with the other elements in storytimes, we are limited only by our imaginations.

Let's try "Twinkle, Twinkle, Little Star" as an example.

> Twinkle, twinkle, little star
>
> How I wonder what you are.
>
> Up above the world so high
>
> Like a diamond in the sky.
>
> Twinkle, twinkle, little star
>
> How I wonder what you are.

Note the words that rhyme, and have children think of other words that rhyme. In our example, *star* and *are* rhyme. You might ask the children, "What other words rhyme with *star* and *are*?" The words can be silly nonsense words as long as they rhyme. If the child makes a mistake, try to find a way to minimize it. For example, if a child says *star* rhymes with *bright*, you might say, "*Star* and *bright* don't rhyme, but a star *is* bright. *Bright* rhymes with *light*."

For four- and five-year-olds, see if they can hear parts of words by breaking them apart. This is another element of phonological awareness, called *segmentation*. You can take each word of a song and have the children jump, stomp, clap, or nod for each different part of the word. Use one clap or action for the number of syllables in *star* and two for *twinkle*!

The children can also be asked to leave the first, or last, sound off of words. For example, say, "What happens if we leave the last sound off a word? What is *twinkle* without the *kle*?" *[You can hold up one hand for twin and the other hand for kle.]* "Take away the *kle* and what do we have? *Twin*!"

Certain kinds of songs and poems lend themselves more easily to manipulation than others. Over time, and with practice, you will develop a sense of what works and what doesn't. The sample storytimes in chapters 7 though 9 offer many examples of activities to encourage wordplay.

> It is much easier for children to read a word when they are familiar with it. Take advantage of every opportunity to introduce children to new words and new contexts for the words they already know. This is one way we help them to develop vocabulary.

Rhymes and poems are often rich in vocabulary. To help children increase their vocabulary, ask them for a synonym for a word. For example, ask them what else twinkles. You could also ask for other words that mean the same thing as *twinkle*. *Shine* is similar to *twinkle*. How does it sound to say, "Shining, shining, little star"?

Letter knowledge can be enhanced through finger plays as well. Incorporate the manual alphabet (see appendix A). Or, if you are highlighting letter knowledge during a storytime, you could choose *w* as a letter and show the children the letter from the manual alphabet. Then point to your *w* when you sing the words *wonder* and *world* from "Twinkle, Twinkle, Little Star."

Narrative skills could be highlighted by asking them to retell the song. For three- to five-year-old children, ask them to tell you in words what happens. Ask, "What is the song about? That's right, it's about a star that is up in the sky." You could ask them what it looks like: does it *shine, glow, wink*? All of this is helping them think and respond to questions about what they have heard. Some rhymes are too nonsensical and might not lend themselves to a narrative retelling.

It is helpful for both the adults and the children to have the words to songs written on a flip chart so all can follow. Print awareness includes being able to follow words on a page. From time to time, run your finger under the words to show children that you are following the words that are written.

Would you do this with every poem, song, and finger play? Definitely not. Would you do all these activities for one poem or song during one storytime? Definitely not. These are just some ideas of things that can be done. Start with what feels most comfortable.

Flannel Board or Magnet Board

A flannel board or magnet board is often used to tell stories from books while adding variety to the presentation. It is particularly warranted when small books bear enlarging and when the movement in the story is enhanced or can be better understood through the use of the flannel board.

The flannel or magnet board offers another opportunity to retell a story and to have the children help you retell it, thereby supporting their narrative skills. It allows for more flexibility in the retelling as well. Children often like to come up after the storytime to retell the story or make up a new one using the felt pieces.

The flannel board is also used with songs that repeat (countdown songs) and with songs like "B-I-N-G-O." Again, the flannel board allows more creative interaction by the children.

Action or Movement

There are often a number of action and movement activities during the storytime. Some are part of the story itself. Others are body stretches that get the wiggles out between stories.

During an action-packed song or story, if you use gestures to help tell a story, include some vocabulary in the tale. For example, if you are using the book *The Great Big*

Enormous Turnip, by Alexi Tolstoy, you could say, "Was it little, tiny, and small? No, it was *enormous*, *gigantic*, and *humongous*," stretching your arms out as you say the synonyms, making the turnip's size change in relationship to the words. By doing this, you incorporate movement or action into the stories, making them more instructive and, more important, more engaging.

Helping children remember a story so that they can retell it supports narrative skills. It may be easier for them to remember the story if you give them gestures to accompany the story. The classic example of this is any version of *We're Going on a Bear Hunt*. Other stories lend themselves to actions. Just think of the fun that could be had if every time a certain animal name was said, a corresponding gesture or sound—or both—went with it!

If you do a story break or stretch, try asking the children how to make their bodies into a particular letter. Ask them to think of things with the first sound of /k/, like *kitten* or *kite*. Become the animals, or turn into the object.

Activity Time, Crafts, and Writing

We can wrap up storytime for the youngest children with a time for the adults to interact with one another while including playtime with the young child. Bring out your assortment of developmentally appropriate toys to encourage this kind of activity.

Crafts have been dropped as part of storytime at some libraries, often because of the amount of time craft preparation takes or a lack of funds to buy materials. Crafts, however, can be a vehicle for the retelling of stories. They can help the child internalize stories and can offer a means of communication among children, and between adults and children. If making crafts as part of storytime is not possible, consider a take-home sheet (see appendix B) with patterns and names of the characters or the order in which a story took place. This kind of activity works best with prereaders.

The crafts we choose can enhance early literacy skills. This is best achieved by steering clear of coloring sheets and activities where children are given things to cut out and paste on paper. Crafts should encourage a child's personal and creative expression. The more predictable the craft, the more difficult it is to encourage thought and creativity. For example, instead of giving a child a cutout of a cow to color, let the child draw the cow him- or herself. If you can't tell what the picture is, ask, and the child will tell you.

Writing is clearly linked to early literacy. Conventional wisdom used to be that children couldn't write until they could read. Research indicates that reading and writing develop concurrently and are interrelated.

Writing can be integrated into crafts in a number of ways. Perhaps the clearest and most direct activity is to include story dictation in storytime. At the end of the storytime,

> Connecting writing to crafts strengthens the connection between the written and spoken word. It can help children understand that their words have meaning and can be written down for others to read.

give the children paper and crayons or any kind of writing instrument. Ask them to draw or write something about the story. It could be their favorite character, scene, or what they think the story is about. Once they have finished their drawings, have them tell the adult with them what their picture is. The adult writes down their words, as they say them, trying not to change what they say. It is important for the children to see that what they say can be written down, that their words have meaning and value. Children should also always be encouraged to sign their work with their names. Now, have the parents read their words back to them. It can be very empowering for children to see their words written on paper and hear them read aloud. This activity is clearly related to print awareness and to narrative skills.

Home Activities

As mentioned under "Activity Time, Crafts, and Writing," some activities can be done at home to extend the storytime experience and to encourage parents and caregivers to enrich language at home. Appendix B provides samples of activity sheets that can be used as handouts at storytimes.

Our Storytimes: Same and Different

Although the overall storytime may look similar to what you have done in the past, we cannot minimize the changes that may be taking place. The following aspects may look different, and you will surely develop others as well.

Use fewer books but more involvement and development of each with children and adults.

Allow more time for children to talk or interact or both.

Exercise less "control," but still maintain a structure and a way to bring the group together.

Speak to adults before, during, and after the storytime program.

Adults become more attentive and see themselves as important to their children's early literacy development.

Adults participate more in storytimes.

Use planning time differently, especially initially. Focus on the adult links, figuring out wording to address parents with and ways that activities and crafts can include parents without taking away the child's initiative.

Give some explanations of what you are doing and why.

Offer suggestions of ways to continue early literacy activities in a positive way at home.

Do the same craft, but explain or do it in a different way.

Devote what used to be craft time to activity time, supporting interaction between adults and children.

Recognize the full importance of the significant adults in children's lives as key to their development and to their early literacy development.

While keeping the joy in our storytimes, we build on what we already do. We recognize the key role the parent or caregiver—who is with the child every day—has in supporting early literacy. Research shows there are skills young children need to have before they are ready to read. By saying what we do and why and by offering ideas to the parents and caregivers, we can have a positive influence on their children's development.

3

Dialogic Reading
How We Read with Children
Makes a Difference

In this book's sample storytimes (chapters 7 through 9) and discussions of vocabulary and narrative skills, the term *dialogic reading* is used. With dialogic reading, normal book reading roles change—the adult becomes the listener/questioner/audience, and the child becomes the teller of the story. Children are not told to be quiet and listen; instead, dialogues using the pictures are encouraged. Because dialogic reading has been found to make a difference in children's expressive language development, this chapter is devoted to explaining it.

Basically, the dialogic reading method promotes dialogue or conversation between the adult and the young child. Best of all, it can be learned and taught, so all participants can benefit from it. Research has shown that it is not enough to just read to a child. *How* adults read with children is as important as *whether* and *how often* adults read to them. Children learn most from books when they are actively involved. With dialogic reading, they *are* involved.

Dialogic reading is not the only way to share a book with a child. It improves *vocabulary and narrative skills*, while reading a book in the traditional way develops listening skills. In tests of language development, children who have been read to dialogically are substantially ahead of children who have been read to traditionally. Dialogic reading has been proven to have a greater effect on the oral language skills of children from middle- and upper-middle-class families than a similar amount of reading in the more traditional way. Studies conducted with children from low-income families who were in child-care centers also witnessed positive changes in the development of their language. A large-scale longitudinal study of the impact of dialogic reading over a year on a Head Start program for four-year-olds showed that the gains were maintained through the end of kindergarten.[1]

Dialogic reading can be taught. Library staff can learn how to teach people for whom book sharing is not intuitive how to use books and stories in a comfortable way as a basis for conversation and learning. Dialogic reading can start when the child has about fifty words of expressive (speaking) vocabulary, when a child can respond to you with at least a short phrase. (For more information, the "Every Child Ready to Read @ your library" workshop for parents and caregivers of two- and three-year-olds explains and demonstrates how to teach adults to do dialogic reading with their children. Go to http://www.pla.org/earlyliteracy.htm.)

Think about the active, engaging, interactive experience that an adult, a young child, and a book involves. The child must listen to answer questions. He must be able to speak, at least to some extent, to respond to questions. He must be able to repeat appropriate responses, remember them, and use them if asked. He is learning that the information in books is something worth talking about. He is seeing that it is praiseworthy to ask and respond to questions and that his opinion counts. All this from reading a picture book! The adult is learning, too, as he gets a peek into the workings of a young mind. Just what can a young child understand about a story? How much can he predict what is going to happen? To what extent can he relate what goes on in a book to what he has experienced?

Dialogic reading is not the typical way in which an adult reader shares books with a young child. Rather than encouraging the dynamic of the adult as the storyteller, the child is encouraged to become an active participant or storyteller or both. As an active listener, the adult asks questions, adds information, encourages responses, and challenges the child to expand his commentary through probing questions. The child's responses are encouraged, and the child is praised, while the adult reformulates questions and urges the child on to more sophisticated responses. For two- and three-year-olds, who are just building vocabulary, questions concentrate on naming objects ("What's this?") and asking "what" action questions ("What is happening here?") and are directly related to the pictures in the book. The adult adds information and repeats the child's answer: "What's that?" "A truck." "Yes, a truck, a big red fire truck." For children who speak more, adults can add questions about feelings ("How do you think the boy is feeling?" or "When have you felt scared?"). For older children, such as four- and five-year-olds with more verbal skills, questions first relate to what is happening in the picture and can then be expanded ("How do you think the boy got down from the tree?" or "I wonder what would happen if . . .?" or "What would you do if . . .?").

Some adults have always read this way to their children. They use expression and are fluent and fluid readers. They ask questions and engage their children in the stories of the books. For other adults, however, sharing books this way does not come naturally. One of the strongest features of dialogic reading is that it can be taught. Adults can learn how to effectively share books with children. They do not need to be good readers or gifted storytellers to help their children develop skills that will help them later with reading. By explaining and modeling this behavior, we can make this kind of book interaction and the strengthening of vocabulary and narrative skills accessible to all.

Incorporating Dialogic Reading in Storytime

The real benefit to the child in terms of expressive language development comes when the child is talking with an adult, one-on-one, *not* in a group situation. The child gets the adult's undivided attention, the adult then responds promptly and directly to the child's comment or question, and no one is excluded from the dialogue. The child gets more speaking time; her ideas are specifically responded to. It is often the shyer child who does not respond in a group situation who needs this kind of interaction the most. In a group situation, the number of responses necessitates choosing a line of questioning to follow, which means another line of discussion is not taken, and children must compete for the adult's attention.[2]

Does it make sense to use dialogic reading as part of storytime? If so, how? Briefly demonstrating dialogic reading with one page of a book you read shows the adults both the technique and the value of dialogic reading. They can then share books with their children at home or in the child-care setting using dialogic reading. To many, we are the experts in how and what to read to children. By demonstrating dialogic reading in each storytime for two- through five-year-olds, we show adults how much importance we place on it. Dialogic reading is valuable in any language, and it particularly develops vocabulary and narrative skills, all of which support the child at this stage of early literacy development.

The Steps to Dialogic Reading

Dialogic reading can be learned, and thus easily taught, using the steps that follow. First, choose a book that lends itself to dialogic reading. What kinds of books work best? The best books for dialogic reading have the following characteristics:

- ■ Clear pictures
- ■ A simple story
- ■ Not too long
- ■ Pictures of things that are familiar to your child or the children
- ■ Action and detail in the pictures
- ■ Interesting to your child or the children

One book that works well with dialogic reading is *Jump, Frog, Jump*, by Robert Kalan. Using Kalan's book, take the following eight steps.

1. Read the book through as you normally would, having the children chime in with "Jump, frog, jump." Although you are basically reading the story straight through, encourage participation as children name the next animal or wonder what may come next from picture clues. (Some books contain unfamiliar words. Either before or during the story, explain the words to the children, and have them repeat them, so the children become more comfortable with the new vocabulary.)

2. Choose a page that lends itself to dialogic reading, that is, a page where something is happening. In Kalan's book, the page where the goldfish jumps out of the pond is one good choice.

3. Say to the adults, "What I am doing now is dialogic reading, having a conversation with the children around the book. Studies show this is most effective when you do this one-on-one with your child. It develops vocabulary and narrative skills."

4. Once you have read the page, ask "what" questions: point to the fish and ask, "What's this?" Children will say a fish or a goldfish. You'll respond and say, "Yes, a fish, a big orange fish" or "Yes, a goldfish that's jumping out of the pond. Let me hear you say that." Then the children repeat your phrase.

Tips to Build Vocabulary

Ask "what" questions.

Follow answers with another question.

Repeat what your child says.

Give an answer, and have the child repeat it.

Help your child as needed.

Praise and encourage your child.

Follow your child's interest.

Enjoy!

---

5. As you turn to another page, say to the adults, "Children learn best when they are actively involved. Here are some examples of open-ended questions that can help your child develop expressive language. These are harder than 'what' questions."

6. On the page where the turtle is trapped in the net, you can say, "Look at the turtle. What happened to him?" "He's under a net." "Yes, that's right; he is caught in the net. How do you think he feels?" "I think he is sad," says one child. Another might say, "He looks angry." Respond to the children: "Yes, I could see where he could feel both sad and angry. When have you felt sad or angry?"

Tips to Build Sentence Skills

Ask open-ended questions:

   What's going on here?

   I wonder how . . .

   What do you see on this page?

   What do you think . . .?

   What if . . .?

Follow answers with another question (What else do you see?)

Expand what your child says.

Add another piece of information.

Help your child repeat your longer phrases.

Enjoy!

---

7. Note that we don't ask "Where's the frog?" because all a child has to do is point. He doesn't have to say anything. *You* can point when you ask a "what" question. We also do not ask questions that can be answered yes or no. Again, not enough language is required. Instead of asking, "Have you ever felt sad?" ask, "When have you felt sad?" so that the child will be able to respond with some words.

8. It takes a long time for some children to think about the question and respond. Give them time! If the child clearly doesn't have a response, help out by providing one or rephrasing the question.

Helpful Hints

Ask questions that *cannot* be answered yes or no.

Give your child plenty of time to answer, but help out when he or she does not know what to say.

You can point to a picture and ask "What's that?" or "What's happening here?" But don't ask "Where's the rabbit?" because it allows your child to point and not say anything.

HOW DOES DIALOGIC READING CHANGE THE STORYTIME?

Explaining and demonstrating to the adults what you are doing and how it supports early literacy are part of the early literacy storytime approach. It is simply one more way to show parents and caregivers how they can support their children's early literacy development.

Because dialogic reading is a highly interactive way to share a book, interactive group dynamics become a more prominent part of storytime. Build up to more participatory storytimes by having children join in with books that are designed for a group response. Use books with phrases that are supposed to be repeated. Use chants, rhymes, and songs to help all of you become more comfortable with that kind of response. Understand that the dialogic demonstration will be a less formal time where children can call out answers. If necessary, ask them to take turns. Have a song or quieting finger play ready to help transition to the next book or activity.

Sharing a book using dialogic reading takes more time than the more conventional use of picture books, where you tell the story in a straightforward manner. Plan to read one less book than usual. You can show a video, such as *Hear and Say: Reading with Toddlers* (see appendix E) after storytime or publicize a workshop you will present using the "Every Child Ready to Read @ your library" workshop script (go to http://www.pla.org/earlylit.htm). Distribute the dialogic reading bookmark to parents after the storytime (see appendix D for a copy of the bookmark).

Dialogic reading helps children expand their expressive vocabulary and their narrative skills, and it keeps them engaged in the book by relating the story to their own experiences. When children listen to a book with a few questions and interactions, they learn listening skills and understand the continuity of story. All are valuable and help in the child's early literacy development.

Children should have the benefit of sharing the stories in books in different ways. Dialogic reading is *one* way to share a book, not the *only* way. Including dialogic reading in your storytime will get easier and more natural to both you and the children, given time. It is fun to see and hear the children's responses to a book. The other adults in the room will also be engaged by the children's creativity and ideas. Giving adults an additional way to help their children become fluent readers makes it even more worthwhile. The key is to relax and enjoy the story and the children. While supporting early literacy skills, dialogic reading heightens an appreciation of books, stories, and words for the presenter, the adults, and their children.

NOTES

1. G. J. Whitehurst and others, "A Picture Book Reading Intervention in Daycare and Home for Children from Low-Income Families," *Developmental Psychology* 30 (1994): 679–89.

2. Colleen Huebner, "Emergent Literacy: Creating Public Value for Our Youngest Customers!" (preconference, Public Library Association Conference, Seattle, WA, February 24, 2004).

4

Making Storytime Meaningful to All Learners

Just as there are multiple kinds of intelligences, there are multiple kinds of learning styles. Ideally, storytime can offer enough variety that all kinds of learners can participate in it in a meaningful way. Early literacy skills and activities can be used to encourage the development of different kinds of learning styles while strengthening and encouraging the children's innate styles.

Thomas Armstrong, in his book *In Their Own Way*, urges adults to use different kinds of activities to fit a variety of learning styles. Basing his work on Howard Gardner's theories, he identifies eight main kinds of learners, as follows:

1. The *linguistic* learner does well with words—saying, hearing, and seeing them.
2. The *logical-mathematical* learner creates concepts and searches for abstract patterns and relationships.
3. The *spatial* learners are best taught through the use of images, pictures, and color.
4. The *kinesthetic* learner needs to move, touch, and manipulate things.
5. The *musical* learner learns best through rhythm and melody.
6. The *interpersonal* learner needs others with whom to work and play.
7. The *intrapersonal* learner does best when able to select his own activities.
8. The *naturalist* learner needs to be outside rather than cooped up indoors.[1]

It is interesting to note that learning styles are often made manifest in personality types, too. Think of the highly talkative, sociable child—the one who just has to talk. It helps to realize that all of that sociability is part of how she learns, how she relates to her world in a meaningful way.

Most children seem to be noticeably stronger in one of three main styles—linguistic, spatial, or kinesthetic. Let's look at how our storytimes accommodate different kinds of learners, how what we do can be adapted, and how much of what we do is already a good fit for many.

A traditional storytime outline contains the following elements:

- Opening greeting or song or both
- Picture book
- Finger play
- Picture book
- Movement song or activity
- Picture book
- Closing song
- Arts and crafts/activity/writing

The traditional storytime already touches a few learning styles. The musical learner enjoys the songs and finger plays, the linguistic learner is thriving with the word sounds in picture books, the kinesthetic learner is on the edge of his rug waiting for the movement song or activity, and the spatial learner has her crayons sharpened in anticipation of the craft activity. The naturalist learner thrives on the many stories that include animals and the outdoors. This is terrific if, in fact, every element is included every time, and the youngsters don't mind waiting for the parts they can relate to! We can shake things up a bit by using early literacy strategies to incorporate some of the learning styles. This can be achieved by asking yourself some simple questions while developing storytime programs.

Can the opening greeting or song incorporate movement for the kinesthetic learner? Can we initiate movements to emphasize phonological awareness, like jumping when a certain sound is said or rhyme made? When reading picture books, wouldn't working on narrative skills by acting out the picture book help both the kinesthetic, interpersonal, and spatial learners? Even the mathematical learner would enjoy helping tell the story in sequence!

> Use early literacy strategies to help create story-times that are meaningful to children with all kinds of learning styles.

The three main categories of learners—the linguistic, spatial, and kinesthetic—are the easiest to attend to because they are easiest to identify. Focusing on these three will see to the needs of the majority of children. We most often favor linguistic learners in storytime. Because most of the children can't read, we count on them to hear and remember stories, songs, finger plays, and poems. Certainly, finger plays have endured in part because they do include movements that help us to remember the words. It might be helpful if we added still more movements to songs and poems that we use on a regular basis as an assist to those who don't have good auditory memories.

Spatial learners soak up their information from the pictures in the books we share with them. They find storytime a comfortable fit as they can learn by seeing the books and the movements.

The kinesthetic learner fares less well than the other two. It is annoying to try to share books with children when the squirmers won't sit still! The key here could well be to get all of the children moving together, throughout storytime, rather than trying to squelch them as they learn the way they do best.

There is no contradiction between storytime and learning styles when we open ourselves up to the possibility that we can engage the children in many different ways. We have a strong urge to make storytime fun for all. By being sensitive to all kinds of children and how they learn, we greatly increase the probability that they will all stay engaged.

NOTE

1. Thomas Armstrong, *In Their Own Way: Discovering and Encouraging Your Child's Multiple Intelligences*, rev. and updated ed. (New York: Penguin Putnam, 2000), 69–71.

5

Early Literacy and Speakers of Languages Other than English

Many of the concepts of early literacy can be transferred from one language to another. Spanish, the second most common language spoken in the United States, shares many of the mechanics of English. It is read from left to right, shares most of an alphabet with English, and is phonetic, even more so than English.

It is vital for adults who are not fluent English speakers to understand the importance of sharing books with their children, regardless of the language they use.[1]

> Research indicates that children with a strong literacy base in their first language have an easier time learning to read in English.

Parents need to know that their home language is a source of comfort and joy to their children. When children see and participate in early literacy behaviors (in any language), they develop a strong language base. Reading with their children in their native language will *help*, not hinder, their children's ability to read in English when they go to school. By instilling in their children a love of books, parents and caregivers are establishing a firm desire in their children to be able to read. In short, they are creating children with print motivation. Pointing out to children the letters or symbols in their native language corresponds to print awareness and letter knowledge. Phonological awareness can be developed through the traditional songs and rhymes in any language. Gaining fluency in any language is the basis for fluency in a new language. Speaking with children in the language most comfortable for the parent/caregiver allows a stronger development of vocabulary and narrative skills in their children than if they speak in English, where they are speaking with more limited vocabulary and are less able to express ideas and offer information.

> We need to help parents see that their own literacy skills are valuable and that sharing their culture and language with books will help their children become literate in English.

To encourage picture book reading in the families' home language, we can use bilingual picture books. We can also display books-on-tape and bilingual books for them to take home. Presenters who are fluent in just one language and who depend on a translator for help must be trained in using storytimes to help develop early literacy skills.

For many families, storytimes are a place to introduce their children to English—to hear the lilt of the English language, how the rhymes are said, and how books are read in fluent English.

Demonstrating and allowing time for dialogic reading provide adults from any language background with the opportunity to understand how they can support early literacy.

The following outline of a storytime for English-language learners capitalizes on what is known about early literacy and on the fact that the opportunity to learn English will draw people who do not currently use the library. Again, adapt this plan in any way you believe will support your group.

English-Language-Learner Storytimes

Newborns to Five-Year-Olds and Their Parents

OPENING

Welcome everyone.

OPENING SONG

1. On the flip chart, follow the text with your finger.
2. Repeat the same song every time, something like "Hello, and how are you?" with names. Choose a song or rhyme with wording used in regular conversation, too. For example:

> Hello, hello.
> Hello, and how are you?
> I'm fine, thanks.
> I'm fine, thanks.
> I'm hoping you are, too.

BIG BOOK

1. Read it once, pointing to the text.
2. Choral read it, pointing to the text.
3. Choral read it again for rhythm or fluency.
4. In future storytimes, read the same story again.

SONG OR RHYME

(Write song or rhyme on the flip chart ahead of time.)

1. Explain the importance of rhyme.
2. Reinforce to parents/caregivers that rhymes and songs in their own language are important! Have them share some of their own childhood rhymes. Other options: have rhymes in other languages already recorded and play them; ask patrons to record and bring songs or rhymes to the storytimes (if they like), and then play them. Then, if participants are shy, you can play a rhyme in a different language. When audience members hear a familiar rhyme, they really enjoy it!

(Stress that songs allow children to hear words broken into parts because of different notes for each syllable or part. Point out that rhyme is not a concept in all languages, but it can be done in any language, and that the rhyme can be a nonsense word.)

BOOK FOR DIALOGIC READING

1. Open to one page of a book, something with a familiar scene or situation.
2. Demonstrate "what" questions.
3. Urge participants to ask questions, in English or their own language.
4. Ask open-ended questions, or save them for another session, depending on the group.
5. Pass out a book to each family. Have adults practice dialogic reading in English. Then have them try dialogic reading in their native language. They will see the child can get a lot more vocabulary and information from the language they are most fluent in.

HEARING SOUNDS

1. To emphasize phonological awareness, choose a sound to talk about. (Choose the sounds that are most easily heard and those letters that have only one sound.) Show the letter and say the sound. Be aware that the sounds that come most easily in English may be different from those that come most easily in other languages.
2. Ask what words start with that sound. The words they respond with can be in English, their native language, or made-up words. The main thing is hearing the beginning sound. Make a game of it, or play "I Spy" with realia you have brought in. Bring things like empty cereal boxes, food items, or clothing. Name the items in English so participants learn the vocabulary.

TALK TIME

1. Try general conversation.
2. Talk about common situations with children, and simulate the actions (e.g., waking up and getting breakfast; talking with a child who wants to stay up late;

sitting at the dinner table, etc.). Say phrases in English; then ask participants to repeat them.

GOOD-BYE SONG

1. On the flip chart, follow the text with your finger. (Use the same song or rhyme each time.)
2. Talk about ways English speakers say good-bye (Come again; See you soon; Thanks for coming; I'm glad you came).

Other suggestions

1. Make a handout with vocabulary from one of the books you have chosen. Write words in English and have pictures so participants can understand.
2. Try a rebus book—in the middle of a story, a word would be a picture. After you say the word in the picture, participants repeat it.
3. Offer the same program several times; repetition is beneficial.
4. Use lots of repetition from storytime to storytime.
5. Invite English-speaking volunteers to interact and talk with participants after the storytime.

NOTE

1. Patton Tabors, *One Child, Two Languages: A Guide for Preschool Educators of Children Learning English as a Second Language* (Baltimore, MD: Paul H. Brookes, 1997).

Doing It!

6
Planning Your Early Literacy Enhanced Storytimes

The next three chapters present basic storytime planning suggestions and aids for three age levels: early talkers (newborns to twenty-four months), talkers (two- and three-year-olds), and prereaders and early readers (four- and five-year-olds). Although some books and resources go into more depth on planning storytime programs for these age groups, *Early Literacy Storytimes* focuses on how to highlight different early literacy skills in storytimes and explain them to parents and caregivers.

The sample storytimes in chapters 7 through 9 offer ideas on how to incorporate early literacy information into storytimes. Use these storytimes as is or as a guide and jumping-off point for creating your own storytimes.

Following the sample storytimes, chapter 10 offers tips and tools for developing your own early literacy enhanced storytimes. Appendix C includes a template to build your own storytimes, a summary of ways that storytime elements support each skill, and a sampling of presenter-caregiver messages to help you in your planning.

Storytime Basics

Whether you use the sample storytimes as they are, or use them as a planning tool to build your own storytimes, keep the following points in mind.

> *The length of the sample storytimes is about thirty minutes.* Each presenter is different, and each group is different. Flexibility is the key! Do what is fun for you, and respond as best as you can to the group you have.

> *Storytimes at different levels may include the same books or rhymes.* This is a *good* thing! Repetition is good because it helps children remember. In addition, at different ages or stages, children understand the same story on different levels and internalize the story, song, or rhyme in different ways. In the sample storytimes for early talkers,

many different rhymes and songs are included so that you can get as many ideas as possible. When you do the storytimes, however, you not only do each song or rhyme at least twice but you repeat about two-thirds of the songs or rhymes from one storytime to the next. In this way, both the adults and the children become familiar and comfortable with them. The same philosophy applies to opening and closing rhymes. Although you'll find several examples, choose *one* of each that you like, and use it every time. Then participants get used to them and have something familiar each time.

Print the words to the rhymes and songs on a flip chart for all to see. This is easier than having adults try to follow from a handout. They can glance up and then focus on their children more easily. It also supports print awareness. You can still offer the rhymes and songs on a handout for them to take home.

Consider demonstrating the rhymes and songs on a doll or stuffed animal of your own. For one rhyme or song, show ways to do the actions for a baby and for a toddler. Developing these actions is part of the way you spend your planning time.

Following the storytime, allow time for parents and children to mingle and talk. Put out some toys that encourage play and interaction, talk with the adults, and model the behaviors that support children's development. Think about how the activities support the early literacy skill you have emphasized. Try out some new activities or new ways of using familiar activities, too.

Early Literacy Enhanced Storytime Formats

As you think of ways to adapt the sample storytimes (or create your own), keep these guidelines in mind.

Storytimes for early talkers consist largely of rhymes and songs, with a few books and movement activities. All the rhymes and songs contribute to the development of phonological awareness. Because we are already speaking with the adults, it is easy to add information on early literacy during storytimes for this age level. This is also the age level where adults are *least* likely to realize how important what they do is to supporting early literacy development.

Storytime Structure for Early Talkers

Based on Multnomah County (OR)
Public Library's Youth Services Manual

The following storytime structure for early talkers is suggested, not mandated. Adapt this format to fit your personality and the group's needs.

1. Storytime introduction (welcome, early literacy comment)
2. Opening song or rhyme (same each time)
3. Set the stage: "Today we'll be talking about . . ."
4. Three or four rhymes or songs or both, each one done two or three times. Clap in between each rhyme. One or two should be repeated from the previous storytime. *[To keep their attention, use large stick puppets.]* Based on the group, mix bounces and action rhymes and songs with quieter ones.
5. Big book—all read together
6. Three or four rhymes or songs, each one done two or three times. Clap in between each rhyme. Repeat some from previous storytime. *[To keep their attention, use large stick puppets.]* Based on the group, mix bounces and action rhymes and songs with quieter ones.
7. Activity with music—scarves, instruments, etc. (optional)
8. Closing song (same each time)
9. Closing to adults, including some aspect of early literacy support at home
10. Playtime with toys or activity

Add to these components or adapt them according to what flows well for you and according to the responses from the participants.

Within the storytime, in addition to the opening and closing, include one or two statements to parents and caregivers. You may already be talking with parents and caregivers about information on child development as part of your storytimes (such as talking about object permanence following a peek-a-boo activity). That information may not be directly related to early literacy, but it does support child development. It also helps the adults understand their children. Keep that information in! The early literacy information that you explain to the adults is *not* meant to take the place of other important information for the adults but rather to add to it.

Storytimes for talkers include books, flannel boards, puppets, finger plays, songs, and music or movement activities or both. At this age level, in addition to sharing the joy of books, reading, and language, it is especially important to help adults see ways they can elicit expressive language from their children and ways to play with sounds and words. *Receptive language* or *vocabulary* is what the child can understand. *Expressive language* or *vocabulary* is what the child can say or speak.

Storytime Structure for Talkers

Based on Multnomah County (OR)
Public Library's Youth Services Manual

The following storytime structure for talkers is suggested, not mandated. Adapt this format to fit your personality and the group's needs.

1. Storytime introduction (welcome, early literacy comment)
2. Opening song or rhyme (same each time)

3. Set the stage: "Today we'll be talking about . . ." (may include theme talk)
4. Book (usually the longest of those selected)
5. Stretch based on previous book, a movement activity that extends the book (or action stretch below, or both)
6. Action stretch large motor activity: rhyme or song involving standing up and moving. Repeat until children and adults are comfortable. The action rhyme or song may be a repeat from previous storytime.
7. A shorter book or alternative format (flannel board, story cards, puppet, big book, etc.) story; also consider nonfiction book
8. Stretch based on previous book, a movement activity that extends the book (or action stretch below, or both)
9. Action stretch large motor activity: rhyme or song involving standing up and moving. Repeat until children and adults are comfortable. The action rhyme or song may be a repeat from previous storytime.
10. Book to read and then demonstrate dialogic reading with one page
11. Craft or activity time (optional). Presenters who do not prepare a craft activity for their storytimes often provide stickers or hand stamps for the toddlers.

    It is not sufficient to just *do* a craft activity. Explain to the adults and model for them ways to make the activity more language rich.

    If you do not do a craft, consider handing out instructions for one they can do at home. At the end of storytime, show a sample of it and demonstrate how to make it and *use* it to encourage and enhance language development.
12. Closing song (same each time)
13. Closing to adults, including some aspect of early literacy support at home

Storytimes for prereaders reflect the fact that prereaders are developmentally much more capable than their younger counterparts. Storytimes for them can contain not only more components but more in-depth treatment. Because prereaders' attention spans are getting longer, we can use longer and more complex stories.

Storytime Structure for Prereaders

Based on Multnomah County (OR)
Public Library's Youth Services Manual

The following storytime structure for prereaders is suggested, not mandated. Adapt this format to fit your personality and the group's needs.

1. Storytime introduction (welcome, early literacy comment)
2. Opening song or rhyme (same each time)
3. Set the stage: "Today we'll be talking about . . ." (may include theme talk)
4. Book (usually the longest of those selected)
5. Stretch or activity based on previous book

6. Action stretch large motor activity: rhyme or song involving standing up and moving. Repeat until children and adults are comfortable. The action rhyme or song may be a repeat from previous storytime.

7. A book or alternative format (flannel board, story cards, puppet, big book, etc.) story; also consider nonfiction book

8. Children retell story with flannel board or stretch based on previous book

9. Finger play

10. A book to read and then demonstrate dialogic reading with one page; also consider nonfiction book

11. Finger play, song, or rhyme

12. Book (optional)

13. Craft or activity time (optional). Presenters who do not prepare a craft activity for their storytimes often provide stickers or hand stamps.

> It is not sufficient to just *do* a craft activity. Explain to the adults and model for them ways to make the activity more language rich.
>
> If you do not do a craft, consider handing out instructions for one they can do at home. At the end of storytime, show a sample of it and demonstrate how to make it and *use* it to encourage and enhance language development.

14. Closing song (same each time)

15. Closing to adults, including some aspect of early literacy support at home

No matter what age-level storytime you are planning, the basic steps remain the same:

1. Choose books, songs, finger plays, and activities that are appropriate for your group and that you enjoy.

2. If you wish, give the storytime a theme.

3. Look over your plan, and think of one or, at most, two early literacy skills you would like to highlight.

4. You may want to add a song or activity related to the skill.

5. Decide upon a couple of points regarding early literacy to make to the adults. They can be part of an introduction as you are gathering the group, given during the storytime, related to something specific you are doing, or form part of your closing. (Examples of early literacy tips can be found in the sample storytimes, chapters 7 through 9; in chapter 10, "Build Your Own Early Literacy Storytimes"; and in appendix C, "What Can I Say? From Skill to Parent/Caregiver.")

No matter what the age level of the storytime, it is *not* necessary to revamp your whole storytime to conform to the structure in the examples. Use the storytime structure that works for you. Use *your* books, songs, and activities. If you want to use just a couple of the components in combination with your own material, that's fine.

> The goal in giving you examples in the sample storytimes is to help you gain the level of confidence you need to take the early literacy skills with the adult focus and apply them to your programs.

What Do the Symbols Mean?

The sample storytimes contain the following symbols, which correspond to each of the early literacy skills. Beside appropriate components in the sample storytimes are the symbols for the early literacy skills they support. For example, if you are looking for an element that supports a certain skill, just look for the symbol at the right. The "To the adults" messages are set off between lines, so they are easy to see. Apply the comments related to a particular skill to the element of your own program that is highlighting that same skill.

Print motivation is an interest in and enjoyment of books.

Phonological awareness is being able to hear and play with the smaller sounds in words. It includes being able to recognize and say rhymes, phonemic awareness, and alliteration.

Vocabulary is knowing the names of things.

Narrative skills is being able to describe things and events and to tell stories.

Print awareness is noticing print, knowing how to handle a book, and understanding how to follow the words on a page.

Letter knowledge is knowing that letters are different from each other, that the same letter can look different, and that each letter has a name and relates to specific sounds.

Notes to and instructions for the storytime presenter are presented in bold italic type.

Go for it!

7

Sample Storytimes
for Early Talkers

(Newborns to 24 Months)

The fun of storytime, of stories, of books, of language, its rhymes and rhythms, the wonder and joy of the experiences that boks and reading offer; all these form the foundation of storytime and are key to what we share with families. Keep this in mind as you enrich your storytimes.

OVER AGAIN

Storytime Introduction

Welcome to Cuddle-Up storytime. My name is _____. I am so glad you could all be here today.

To the adults:

While we are sharing rhymes, movement activities, and books, please participate as much as you can, following along with the movements I do. If your child is not happy, feel free to leave and come back when your child is calmer.

As we go along, I'll be pointing out some things you can be doing with your children at home to support their early literacy development.

Let's start with Peek-a-Boo.

| Print Motivation | Phonological Awareness | Vocabulary | Narrative Skills | Print Awareness | Letter Knowledge |

Opening Song

"Peek-a-Boo"

(Sing to the tune of "Frère Jacques")

Peek-a-boo, peek-a-boo	*Cover face with hands two times*
I see you! I see you!	*Point to children*
I see your button nose.	*Point to nose*
I see your tiny toes.	*Point to toes*
I see you! Peek-a-boo!	*Cover face with hands two times*

Repeat the song two times.
Clap together!

To the adults:

Peek-a-Boo is a game young children love. It helps them learn *object permanence*, the concept that even if something (you, for instance) cannot be seen, you are still there. When your baby is under ten months old, it is good to cover your own eyes while playing Peek-a-Boo. As your baby gets older, you can cover his or her eyes. There are many books that play with the idea of Peek-a-Boo.

Try *Where's the Baby?* by Cheryl Christian for a great Peek-a-Boo book.

Read Together Book

Where's the Baby?

By Cheryl Christian

Hand out one copy of Where's the Baby? *per family.*

To the adults:

We're going to read this book together. We'll start with the cover and read a couple of pages together. Then you'll read the rest at your own pace with your child. *[Read the words and do one or two pages.]*   When you read with your child, as you'll do now, don't *just* read the words. Talk about the pictures. Describe what is going on. Leave time for your child to say something back. *[Demonstrate.]* This type of inter- action sets the stage for increased *vocabulary*, which is knowing the names of things; and *narrative skills*, which is the ability to tell a story. Research has shown that these are both skills your child will need to get ready to read. Go ahead and start reading the rest of the book now. Keep it cozy and fun. If your child gets tired of the book, just stop and do something else.

Now let's do an action song.

Action Song

"Roll Your Hands"

From *Toddlers on Parade*, by Carol Hammett

(Sing to the tune of "Row, Row, Row Your Boat")

You can demonstrate using a doll, puppet, or stuffed animal.
Suit your actions to the words of the song.

To the adults:

For babies, roll their hands for them, with the baby in a comfortable position. For toddlers, let them imitate you, or help them along if they need it. You know your child best. Don't force your toddler to do it. If you do the actions, they're likely to join in.

Roll, roll, roll your hands
As fast as fast can be.
Do it now, let me see
Do it now with me.

Repeat with these substitutions:

Clap, clap, clap your hands
As loud as loud can be . . .

Tap, tap, tap your feet
As softly as can be . . .

Shake, shake, shake your feet
As quickly as can be . . .

Roll, roll, roll your hands
As fast as fast can be . . .

Repeat one or two times.
Clap together!

To the adults:

This is a good rhyme to do as you are bathing or diapering your child. Use different parts of the body and words for different actions to help increase your child's vocabulary. Even though your baby does not understand everything you say, it is important for her to hear you speak. The wider variety of words that your child hears, the larger her vocabulary will be, and the more easily she will later be able to read.

Now let's try "Grand Old Duke of York." I'll show you one way you can sing it with your babies and toddlers.

Action Song

"Grand Old Duke of York"

Traditional, as sung by Carol Hammett
on *Toddlers on Parade*

O, the Grand Old Duke of York	*Bounce baby on knees; toddlers march in place*
He had ten thousand men.	*Same*
He led them up to the top of the hill	*Hold baby in air; toddlers reach high*
And led them down again.	*Hold baby down low; toddlers reach low*
And when you're up you're up	*Hold baby in air; toddlers reach high*
And when you're down you're down	*Hold baby down low; toddler can reach low*
And when you're only halfway up	*Go halfway*
You're neither up nor down.	*Up, then down*

Repeat once slowly, then once quickly.
Clap together!

Next, let's all read a book together—grown-ups, too!

Big Book

Polar Bear, Polar Bear, What Do You Hear?

By Bill Martin Jr.

To the adults:

This book has a nice rhythm to it. We are going to read it all together. If your child likes it, you can bounce him to the rhythm of the words.

Hearing the rhythm of language and making the sounds of animals both contribute to *phonological awareness*, or the ability to hear sounds in words, one of the skills that researchers have found helps with reading later on.

As the adults read along with you, they will feel the rhythm of the language. This does not come naturally for many adults.

Here is an activity to help children hear rhythm.

Musical Activity

Hand out bells and/or rattles/shakers. Have adults and children shake the bells and bounce to "Bumpin' Up and Down in My Little Red Wagon," from Songs and Games for Toddlers, *by Bob McGrath, or another song with a strong beat.*

Great job! Listen to all those sounds. Let's put the instruments away now. Thank you.

Now let's try a tickle rhyme. Ready?

Action Rhyme

'Round and 'Round the Garden

'Round and 'round the garden	*Hold child's hand palm-up*
Goes the little mouse.	*Draw circles on child's palm with your finger*
Up, up, up he creeps	*Crawl fingers up child's arm*
Up into his house.	*Tickle under child's arm*

'Round and 'round the garden	*Hold child's hand, palm up*
Goes the teddy bear.	*Draw circles on palm with your finger*
One step, two steps	*Bounce fist up child's arm*
Tickle you under there.	*Tickle under child's arm or neck*

??

Repeat two times.

Clap together!

And now a huggy rhyme!

Action Rhyme

See Saw Margery Daw

Suit actions to words.

See saw Margery Daw
Baby loves when we hug him [her].
Baby has all the hugs in the world
Because he [she] knows we love him [her].

Repeat two times.

Clap together!

And now for our last song for today. Everybody stand up, please.

Closing Song

"Clap, Clap, Clap Your Hands"

From *Lively Songs and Lullabies*,
by Carol Rose Duane

Suit actions to words.

Clap, clap, clap your hands
Clap your hands together.
Clap, clap, clap your hands
Clap your hands together.

Repeat with these substitutions:

Jump, jump, jump up high . . .
Spin, spin around . . .
Give, give, give a hug . . .
Blow, blow, blow a kiss . . .
Wave, wave, wave good-bye . . .

To the adults:

See you next time. Thank you for coming. Be sure to do these rhymes and books with your children at home. Next time, on _____, we'll do some of these and some new ones too. Enjoy the fun of language with your children.

There is a display here of some parenting books you can check out and some information on early literacy if you'd like to pick some up.

Before you begin, remember to thank everyone for being with you. Everyone appreciates being appreciated! A sincere greeting and a smile set the stage for enjoyment.

'ROUND AND 'ROUND WE GO

Opening Song

"Come Right In"

(Sing to the tune of "Skip to My Lou")

Come, come, come right in	*Beckoning motion*
Come, come, come right in	
Come, come, come right in	
Joshua, Tamika, and Nikki.	*Substitute children's names*
Sit, sit, sit right down	
Sit, sit, sit right down	
Sit, sit, sit right down	
Sonya, Maya, and Jordan.	*Substitute adults' names*

Storytime Introduction

Welcome to Cuddle-Up storytime. My name is _____. I am so glad you could all be here today.

To the adults:

While we are sharing rhymes, movement activities, and books, please participate as much as you can, following along with the movements I do. If your child is not happy, feel free to leave and come back when your child is calmer.

As we go along, I'll be pointing out some things you can be doing with your children at home to support their early literacy development.

Let's start with a tickle rhyme. Ready?

Print Motivation	Phonological Awareness	Vocabulary	Narrative Skills	Print Awareness	Letter Knowledge

Action Rhyme

These Are Baby's Fingers

Suit actions to words

These are baby's fingers
These are baby's toes
This is baby's belly button
'Round and 'round it goes!

Repeat two times.

Clap together!

Okay, for the next song, please stand up. We're doing to do "Ring around the Rosie."

Form large circle or do actions individually.

Action Song

"Ring around the Rosie"

Ring around the rosie	*Adult and child stand; adult holds baby*
A pocket full of posies	*Adult and child turn around and*
Ashes, ashes	*around; can change direction*
We all fall down.	*Kneel or sit on the floor*

Cows are in the meadow
Eating buttercups
Ashes, ashes

We all stand up!	*Stand up!*

Ring around the rosie	*Adult and child turn around and around;*
A pocket full of posies	*can change direction*
Ashes, ashes	
We all fall down.	*Kneel or sit on the floor*

Repeat two or three times.

Clap together!

Music Activity

Use egg-shakers you purchase or make shakers using ping-pong balls. Slit them open and put in small bells, rice, or split peas and seal with tape. Have enough shakers to give to adults and children.

Okay, let's shake together to some music!

> *Shake the shakers to the rhythm of "New Way to Walk" from* Hot! Hot! Hot! Dance Songs, *or another song with a strong beat.*
>
> *Collect the shakers.*

Great! Let's put the shakers away now.

Next we have a book, *The Wheels on the Bus.* You may know this as a song.

Big Book

The Wheels on the Bus

(any version)

> *Point to the pictures or do motions, according to what works best.*

Now let's do a tickle rhyme.

Action Rhyme

'Round and 'Round the Garden

'Round and 'round the garden   *Draw circles with finger on child's tummy*
Goes the teddy bear

One step, two steps   *Fingers jump up the front of child*
Tickle you under there.   *Tickle under arm*

> *Repeat two times.*
>
> *Clap together!*

Let's say this rhyme together. Feel free to follow the words on this flip chart.

Action Rhyme

Old King Cole

> *Use props or stick puppet.*

Old King Cole
Was a merry old soul
And a merry old soul was he;
He called for his pipe
And he called for his bowl
And he called for his fiddlers three.

Now every fiddler had a fine fiddle
And a very fine fiddle had he;
Twee tweedle dee, tweedle dee
Went the fiddlers
Oh, there's none so rare
As can compare
With King Cole and his fiddlers three!

> *Repeat two times.*
>
> *Clap together!*

Great! Now get ready for a bounce.   *Demonstrate using a doll or puppet.*

Action Song

"Horsey, Horsey"

From Lively Songs and Lullabies, by Carol Rose Duane

Horsey, Horsey on our way
We've been together for many a day.
So let your ears stick up
    and your tail hang down
Giddy up, we're homeward bound.
[Instrumental music]

Bounce child on knees

Lift child up
Lower child
Bounce child on knees
Bounce to rhythm of music

Repeat.

Way to go!

Clap together!

To the adults:

With this song, children are hearing rhythm, fast and slow. As you bounce them, they hear and feel the rhythm in music and in the words. This is the beginning of *phonological awareness*, the ability to hear the smaller sounds in words. Also, because each part of a word, or syllable, has a different note when sung, children begin to hear parts of words just by hearing songs and rhymes!

Now, let's try this bounce together.

Action Rhyme

Rickety Rickety Rocking Horse

Rickety, rickety, rocking horse
Over the fields we go.
Rickety, rickety, rocking horse
Giddy up, giddy up
WHOA!

Bounce child on knees

Stop bouncing

Repeat two times.

Clap together!

Here comes a tickle for the babies and a stretch for the older children. Watch as we go along.

Book

Share a book you enjoy and that parents will too, such as

Baby Knows Best

By Kathy Henderson

To the adults:

You may often hear the phrase, "Read with your child fifteen minutes a day," or "Read with your child twenty minutes a day." No one expects young children to sit and be read to that long at one sitting. Even thirty seconds at a time is fine. It is more important for the interaction between you and your child to be a positive one than for it to be a long one. Researchers have found that if the interaction around books is a negative one with impatient words or negative feelings, then the child associates reading with a negative feeling. So . . . the more you share books and talk together, the better, but do it when it can be a positive experience for you and your child. If your child is not in the mood, look for a few minutes when your child is quietly alert, not too tired and not too active.

Now let's do "Pop Goes the Weasel."

Action Song

"Pop Goes the Weasel"

All around the cobbler's bench   *Bounce baby on knees*
The monkey chased the weasel
The monkey thought 'twas all in fun
POP goes the weasel!   *Raise child above head*
     Older child: jump up

A penny for a spool of thread   *Bounce baby on knees*
A penny for a needle
That's the way the money goes
POP goes the weasel!   *Raise child above head*
     Older child: jump up

Repeat two or three times.

Clap together!

Now we are ready for our good-bye song.

Closing Song

"Clap, Clap, Clap Your Hands"

From Lively Songs and Lullabies,
by Carol Rose Duane

Suit actions to words.

Clap, clap, clap your hands
Clap your hands together.
Clap, clap, clap your hands
Clap your hands together.

??

Repeat with these substitutions:

Jump, jump, jump up high . . .
Spin, spin around . . .
Give, give, give a hug . . .
Blow, blow, blow a kiss . . .
Wave, wave, wave good-bye . . .

To the adults:

See you next time. Thank you for coming. Be sure to do these rhymes
and books with your children at home. Next time, on _____, we'll do
some of these and some new ones too. Enjoy the fun of language with
your children.

There is a display here of some information on early literacy you can
take, and there are also some books and music CDs for young children,
if you'd like to check them out.

Take a moment to remember why you are doing this! You want everyone to love books as much as you do, so try to convey this idea with your enthusiasm.

YUM! YUM!

Storytime Introduction

Welcome to Cuddle-Up storytime. My name is _____. I am so glad you could all be here today.

To the adults:

We are going to be sharing rhymes, movement activities, and books. Please participate as much as you can, following along with the movements I do. We expect some degree of chaos. However, if your child is not happy, feel free to leave and come back when your child is calmer.

   As we go along, I'll be pointing out some things you can be doing with your children at home to support their early literacy development.

Let's start with our Peek-a-Boo game.

Opening Song

"Peek-a-Boo"

(Sing to the tune of "Frère Jacques")

Peek-a-boo, peek-a-boo	*Cover face with hands two times*
I see you! I see you!	*Point to children*
I see your button nose.	*Point to nose*
I see your tiny toes.	*Point to toes*
I see you! Peek-a-boo!	*Cover face with hands two times*

   Repeat two times.

   Clap together!

Print Motivation   Phonological Awareness   Vocabulary   Narrative Skills   Print Awareness   Letter Knowledge

To the adults:

Children learn by repetition. Infants and young children have the most active brains. The more stimulation they receive from their environment—what they see, hear, touch, taste, and smell—the more connections are made between brain cells. After a while there are so many connections that the ones that are not used are pruned. It is repetition that keeps these connections between brain cells and makes them strong. So at home or in the car, do these rhymes and songs over and over again.

Now we're ready for Pat a Cake.

Action Rhyme

Pat a Cake

Pat a cake, pat a cake, baker's man	*Clap baby's hands*
Bake me a cake as fast as you can.	*Clap faster*
Pat it and prick it and mark it with B	*Pat hands together, draw a "B" with finger*
And put it in the oven for Baby and me.	*Two hands extended, hug baby*

Now have adults say child's name instead of "Baby."

Repeat two times.

Clap together!

Now let's try "The Muffin Man."

Song Bounce

"The Muffin Man"

Oh, do you know the muffin man	*Bounce child on your knees*
The muffin man, the muffin man?	
Oh, do you know the muffin man	
Who lives in Drury Lane?	
Oh, yes I know the muffin man	
The muffin man, the muffin man.	
Oh, yes I know the muffin man	
Who lives in Drury Lane.	

Repeat once or twice.

Clap together!

So, we've had a cake, a muffin, and now it's time for a pancake. Ummm good!

Action Rhyme

Mix a Pancake

Demonstrate motions for baby and older child.

Mix a pancake	*Baby: rub baby's back in circle motion*
	Older child: moves fist in circle
Stir a pancake	*Baby: pat baby's back in rhythm*
Pop it in a pan.	*Older child: extends hands*
Fry a pancake	*Baby: hold baby flat, supporting head*
	Older child: circular motion with hand
Toss a pancake	*Baby: lift high*
	Older child: flings hands up
Catch it if you can.	*Baby: hold baby close*
	Older child: claps hands

Repeat two times.

Great!

Clap together!

To the adults:

Rhyming is one way that children hear parts of words. This aspect of phonological awareness helps them later in sounding out words.

Here's a nice little bounce.

Rhyme with Stick Puppet

Sippity Sup

Sippity sup, sippity sup
Bread and milk from a china cup.
Bread and milk from a bright silver spoon
Made of a piece of the bright silver moon!
Sippity sup, sippity sup
Sippity, sippity sup!

Repeat two times.

Clap together!

You may remember this rhyme. You can follow the words on the flip chart.

Action Rhyme

Sing a Song of Sixpence

Use stick puppets or flannel board.

Sing a song of sixpence
A pocket full of rye;
Four-and-twenty blackbirds
Baked in a pie!
When the pie was opened
The birds began to sing;
Wasn't that a dainty dish
To set before the king?

The king was in the counting house
Counting out his money;
The queen was in the parlor
Eating bread and honey.
The maid was in the garden
Hanging out the clothes;
When down came a blackbird
And snapped off her nose!

Repeat one or two times.

Clap together!

Now let's read a book about three bears. This version by Byron Barton is one of the simpler versions.

Book

Three Bears

By Byron Barton

To the adults:

We'll read this big book together. Look how your child loves the sound of your voice and responds to it.

That sounded good all together.

Okay, now we're ready for a tickle rhyme.

Action Rhyme

Hot Cross Buns

Bounce baby on your knees or use the actions below.

Hot cross buns   *Cross on child's back or palm of hand*
Hot cross buns
One a penny   *One finger up*
Two a penny   *Two fingers up*
Hot cross buns.   *Cross on child's back or palm of hand*

Repeat two or three times.

Clap together!

To the adults:

Some children like this kind of play on their bodies. Others can be extremely sensitive, and they don't enjoy it. See how your child responds. If he doesn't like it, just recite the rhyme to him in a cheerful voice.

Here's a little bounce with different sounds and feelings.

Action Rhyme

Pudding on a Plate

Pudding on a plate, pudding on a plate   *Rock from side to side*
Wibble wobble, wibble wobble
Pudding on a plate!

Candies in a jar, candies in a jar   *Bounce up and down*
Shake 'em up, shake 'em up
Candies in a jar.

Candles on a cake, candles on a cake
Blow 'em out, blow 'em out   *Baby: adult blows on baby*
                                               Older child: blows
Candles on a cake.

Repeat two times.

Clap together!

To the adults:

Here's a book with lots of sounds to play with. Some will sound familiar! You can read along with me if you like, and join in saying the sounds.

Book

The Baby Goes Beep

By Rebecca O'Connell

Read through the book once with the sounds, emphasizing the rhythm of the sounds and helping them capture the rhythm as they join in. Then read through it a second time.

To the adults:

We just read the book from start to finish, feeling the rhythm of the text and noticing the sequence of actions. Now let's go through it again. This time we'll read it but also talk about what is happening in the pictures. This helps your child develop *vocabulary*, which is knowing the names of things; and *narrative skills*, which is the ability to describe things. These skills are the foundation for your child's understanding of what she will later read. You may not get through the whole book when you share a book like this. That is just fine!

Demonstrate using a doll or stuffed animal: pick one of the pictures and talk about what is happening. Label some of the things in the picture and talk about the child's experience. Leave time for the child to talk, too.

Let's try this rhyme.

Action Rhyme

Here's a Cup

Here's a cup	*Form cup with one hand*
And here's a cup	*Form cup with other hand*
And here's a pot of tea.	*Form pot with both hands*
Pour a cup	*Pouring motion*
Pour a cup	*Pouring motion*
Have a cup with me.	*Pretend to drink*

Ummmmm. Yummy. Tastes good. Let's do it again.

> *Repeat two times.*
>
> *Clap together!*

Now we are ready for our last song for today.

Closing Song

"Clap, Clap, Clap Your Hands"

From *Lively Songs and Lullabies*,
by Carol Rose Duane

Suit actions to words.

Clap, clap, clap your hands
Clap your hands together.
Clap, clap, clap your hands
Clap your hands together.

Repeat with these substitutions:

Jump, jump, jump up high . . .
Spin, spin around . . .
Give, give, give a hug . . .
Blow, blow, blow a kiss . . .
Wave, wave, wave good-bye . . .

To the adults:

See you next time. Thank you for coming. Be sure to do these rhymes
and books with your children at home. Next time, on _____, we'll do
some of these and some new ones too. Enjoy the fun of language with
your children.

There is a display here of some information on early literacy you can
take, and there are also books and music CDs for young children, if
you'd like to check them out.

Since many adults imitate what we do, remember to keep book sharing fun.

LITTLE ADVENTURES

Storytime Introduction

Welcome to Cuddle-Up storytime. My name is _____. I am so glad you could all be here today.

To the adults:

We are going to be sharing rhymes, movement activities, and books. Please participate as much as you can, following along with the movements I do. We expect some degree of chaos. However, if your child is not happy, feel free to leave and come back when your child is calmer.

As we go along, I'll be pointing out some things you can be doing with your children at home to support their early literacy development.

Ready! Let's start with Peek-a-Boo.

Opening Song

"Peek-a-Boo"

(Sing to the tune of "Frère Jacques")

Peek-a-boo, peek-a-boo	*Cover face with hands two times*
I see you! I see you!	*Point to children*
I see your button nose.	*Point to nose*
I see your tiny toes.	*Point to toes*
I see you! Peek-a-boo!	*Cover face with hands two times*

Repeat two times.

Clap together!

 Print Motivation   Phonological Awareness   Vocabulary   Narrative Skills   Print Awareness Letter Knowledge

Let's start with a Mother Goose rhyme. I have a candle here, and a rhyme to go with it! Don't worry, we're not lighting the candle.

Point to flip chart of rhyme.

Action Rhyme

Jack Be Nimble

Have a candle or a cutout of one.

Jack be nimble
Jack be quick
Jack jump over the candlestick!

Baby: lift from left to right overhead
Older child: jump!

Repeat two or three times.

To the adults:

Even though young children do not understand the meanings of the rhymes, it is important for them to hear them. By six months babies are already able to recognize the sounds of the languages they hear. They are also losing those sounds they don't hear, even though they were born able to learn to make them.

Let's say this rhyme together.

Rhyme

Jack and Jill Went up the Hill

Use large stick puppets.

Jack and Jill went up the hill
To fetch a pail of water.
Jack fell down and broke his crown
And Jill came tumbling after.

Repeat two times.

Clap together!

Okay, get ready for "Row Your Boat." At the end you'll be a submarine.

Action Song

"Row, Row, Row Your Boat"

Traditional, as sung by Bob McGrath
on Songs and Games for Toddlers

Row, row, row your boat	*Rock forward and backward, child facing you*
Gently down the stream	
Merrily, merrily, merrily, merrily	
Life is but a dream.	
Rock, rock, rock the boat	*Sway side to side*
Over rapids we will go	
Merrily, merrily, merrily, merrily	
Hope we don't need a tow.	
Row, row, row your boat	*Rock forward and backward*
Underneath the stream	
Ha-ha, fooled you!	
You're a submarine!	*Lean child backward and bring back up again*

Repeat two or three times.

Clap together!

Next comes a rhyme about someone who falls off a wall.

Rhyme

Humpty Dumpty

Use large stick puppets or flannel board.

Humpty Dumpty sat on a wall.	*Toddlers can form a circle by holding their hands together and touching fingers*
Humpty Dumpty had a great fall.	
All the king's horses	
And all the king's men	*Pull two hands apart*
Couldn't put Humpty together again.	

Repeat two times.

On the last time, say:

But I can.	*Form the circle with hands again*

Now we're ready for a bounce.

Bounce

Ride a Cockhorse

First time slowly, then faster and faster.

Ride a cockhorse to Banbury Cross
To see a fine lady upon a white horse;
With rings on her fingers and bells on her toes
She shall have music wherever she goes.

    Repeat two times.

    Clap together!

Now let's all read a book together—grown-ups too!

Read Together Book

Tom and Pippo Go for a Walk

By Helen Oxenbury

Hand out one copy of Tom and Pippo Go for a Walk *per family.*

To the adults:

We're going to read together. We'll start with the cover and read a couple of pages together. Then you'll read the rest at your own pace with your child. *[Read the words and do one or two pages.]* When you read with your child, as you'll do now, don't JUST read the words. Talk about the pictures. Describe what is going on. Leave time for your child to say something back. *[Demonstrate.]* Keep it cozy and fun. If your child gets tired of the book, just stop and do something else.

As you collect the books:

To the adults:

When children are young, they treat books as they would any other toy. This means they put them in their mouths and explore them by pushing and pulling and sometimes tearing them. Sometimes people keep books out of reach of young children. Of course, there are going to be some books that are special that will need to be kept out of reach, but allowing children to explore books is how they learn about books and how to handle them. This is part of *print awareness*. Keep some in their toy box. If you have a bookshelf, keep some face out, not spine out, so they can see the pictures on the covers. They'll be more likely to crawl up to them. By doing these things you help your child develop *print motivation*, which is the enjoyment of books. You also help them develop *print awareness*, which is learning how books work, with pages that turn. These are two skills that are important in becoming ready to read.

Okay, now how about a little bounce?

Rhyme Bounce

Diddle, Diddle, Dumpling

Diddle, diddle, dumpling, my son John
Went to bed with his knickers on;
One shoe off, and one shoe on
Diddle, diddle, dumpling, my son John.

> *Repeat two times.*
>
> *Clap together!*

Now let's see what this child sees when going for a walk.

Big Book

I Went Walking

By Sue Williams

Read the book together.

To the adults:

One way you can help increase your child's vocabulary is by "narrating your day." This simply means to say what you are doing while you are doing it. Or you can say what your child is doing as he or she is doing it. You might even add little stories about when you were a child. By doing this, you are exposing your child to lots of language! When you leave your child time to respond, even if you cannot understand what he is saying, you are setting the stage for good *narrative skills*, or being able to describe what is going on.

Let's do a wiggly rhyme.

Action Rhyme

These Little Fingers

These little fingers go
Wiggle wiggle wiggle
Wiggle wiggle wiggle
Wiggle wiggle wiggle.
These little fingers go
Wiggle wiggle wiggle
And now they're on my _____ .

Start using some commonly mentioned parts of the body.

To the adults:

To build vocabulary, when you do this rhyme at home add on parts of the
body that we may not often mention, such as elbow, wrist, or eyebrow.

?.?

Now do another verse using a less common part of the body.

Here's a fun wobbly bounce.

Bounce

Mother and Father and Uncle John

Mother and father and Uncle John	*Bounce child on knees*
Went to town, one by one.	
Mother fell off!	*Tip child to one side*
Father fell off!	*Tip child to other side*
But Uncle John went on and on and on.	*On lap, bounce faster*

?.?

Repeat two or three times.

Clap together!

Let's see how you can be a squirrel climbing up a tree. It's a tickle for the babies and a
stretch for the older children.

Rhyme with Puppet

Furry, Furry Squirrel

Furry, furry squirrel
Hurry, hurry hop

Baby: do as a tickle up and down body
Older child: crouch like a squirrel and grow
tall, hands up, then come down again

Scurry up the tree trunk
To the very top.
When you reach the branches
Hurry, turn around
Furry, furry squirrel
Scurry to the ground.

> *Repeat two times, faster each time.*

> *Clap together!*

And now it's time for our last song.

??

Closing Song

"Clap, Clap, Clap Your Hands"

From *Lively Songs and Lullabies,* by Carol Rose Duane

Suit actions to words.

Clap, clap, clap your hands
Clap your hands together.
Clap, clap, clap your hands
Clap your hands together.

> *Repeat with these substitutions:*

Jump, jump, jump up high . . .
Spin, spin around . . .
Give, give, give a hug . . .

Blow, blow, blow a kiss . . .
Wave, wave, wave good-bye . . .

??

To the adults:

See you next time. Thank you for coming. Be sure to do these rhymes and books with your children at home. Next time, on _____, we'll do some of these and some new ones too. Enjoy the fun of language with your children.

There is a display here of some parenting books and videos and some on reading with your child. *[You can display books such as Mem Fox's* **Reading Magic** *and Jim Trelease's* **Read-Aloud Handbook.***]*

Everyone responds to smiles and laughter. Make both a part of storytime.

ANIMALS

Storytime Introduction

Welcome to Cuddle-Up storytime. My name is _____. I am so glad you could all be here today.

To the adults:

We are going to be sharing rhymes, movement activities, and books. Please participate as much as you can, following along with the movements I do. We expect some degree of chaos. However, if your child is not happy, feel free to leave and come back when your child is calmer.

As we go along, I'll be pointing out some things you can be doing with your children at home to support their early literacy development.

Let's do a name game for starters.

Opening Rhyme

"My Name Is . . ."

Traditional, as sung by Bob McGrath
on *Songs and Games for Toddlers*

My name is _____, that's my name.
My name is _____, always the same.
My name is _____, all the time.
My name is _____, isn't that fine.

Repeat with children's names.

Now let's try Hey Diddle Diddle.

Print Motivation	Phonological Awareness	Vocabulary	Narrative Skills	Print Awareness	Letter Knowledge

Rhyme
Hey Diddle Diddle

Use stick puppets or flannel board.

Hey diddle diddle
The cat and the fiddle
The cow jumped over the moon.
The little dog laughed
To see such sport
And the dish ran away
With the spoon.

To the adults:

As you can see, nursery rhymes expose children to a variety of words that
are not used in everyday conversation. They expand a child's *vocabulary*.
Children also hear rhyming words, which helps develop *phonological
awareness*. Research shows that children who know rhymes find it easier
to learn to read.

Let's try this song with all kinds of animal sounds.

Song with Stick Puppets

"I Had a Little Rooster"

*Traditional, as sung by Pete Seeger
on Birds, Beasts, Bugs and Fishes*

I had a little rooster and he pleased me
And I fed my rooster by yonder tree
And my little rooster went cockle doodle doo
Eeoodle, eeoodle, eeoodle, eeeoooo.

I had a little cat and the cat pleased me
And I fed my cat by yonder tree
And my little cat went meow, meow, meow
And my little rooster went cockle doodle doo
Eeoodle, eeoodle, eeoodle, eeeoooo.

I had a little sheep and the sheep pleased me
And I fed my sheep by yonder tree
And my little sheep went baa, baa, baa
And my little cat went meow, meow, meow
And my little rooster went cockle doodle doo
Eeoodle, eeoodle, eeoodle, eeeoooo.

Clap together!

To the adults:

Hearing and learning animal sounds helps children hear different kinds of sounds. Did you know animals make different sounds in different languages?

And what sound does a clock make? Tick tock!

Action Rhyme

Hickory Dickory Dock

Hickory dickory dock	*Baby: swing or rock baby* *Older child: raises one arm, bent at elbow, sways side to side*
The mouse went up the clock.	*Baby: raise baby above head* *Older child: fingers crawl up arm*
The clock struck one	*Baby: wiggle baby once* *Older child: holds up pointer finger*
The mouse ran down	*Baby: bring baby down to you* *Older child: fingers crawl down arm*
Hickory dickory dock.	*Baby: swing or rock baby* *Older child: arm sways side to side*

Hickory dickory dock
The mouse ran up the clock.
The clock struck two
The mouse said, "Boo!"
Hickory dickory dock.

Hickory dickory dock
The mouse ran up the clock.
The clock struck three
The mouse said, "Whee!"
Hickory dickory dock.

Hickory dickory dock
The mouse ran up the clock.
The clock struck four
The mouse said, "No more!"
Hickory dickory dock.

Repeat one time.

Clap together!

Okay, let me see you put your two hands together so they look like a fish.
Now let me see how you make them swim.

Song

Did You Ever See a Fishy?

(Sing to the tune of
"Did You Ever See a Lassie")

Did you ever see a fishy, a fishy, a fishy

Baby: sway back and forth together
Older child: holds palms together and
wiggles them

Did you ever see a fishy
Swim this way and that?
Swim this way and that way
And this way and that way?
Did you ever see a fishy
Swim this way and that?

Yes, I've seen a fishy, a fishy, a fishy
Yes, I've seen a fishy
Swim this way and that
Swim this way and that way
And this way and that way
Yes, I've seen a fishy
Swim this way and that.
Good!

Clap together!

Now, let's see what these jellyfish do on the rock.

Story with Flannel Board

Three Jellyfish

Three jellyfish, three jellyfish
Three jellyfish sitting on a rock.
One fell off.

Two jellyfish, two jellyfish
Two jellyfish sitting on a rock.
Another fell off.

One jellyfish, one jellyfish,
One jellyfish sitting on a rock.
It fell off.

No jellyfish, no jellyfish
No jellyfish sitting on a rock.
ZOOP! One jumped on!
ZOOP! Another jumped on!
ZOOP! ANOTHER jumped on! Yay!

Three jellyfish, Three jellyfish
Three jellyfish sitting on a rock! Hooray!
Let's count them: one . . . two . . . three!

Repeat one time.

Clap together!

To the adults:

The language used in storybooks is different from what we use when we are speaking, so children hear different words, which builds *vocabulary*. Stories also have a certain structure, with a beginning, a middle, and an end. By exposing your children to storybooks, you help them become familiar with the way language is written. Reading and sharing stories with children is fun. It also will help them to know what to expect when they read stories themselves.

Listen to all the interesting words in this book.

Big Book

Mr. Gumpy's Outing

By John Burningham

Read the book.

To the adults:

Toddlers often have short attention spans, but they can follow shorter stories. Storybooks offer them one way to try to make sense of their world. Follow their interests by reading them stories that build on their own experiences.

Let's sing this song together as I put the frogs on the flannel board.

Song with Flannel Board

"Three Little Speckled Frogs"

Three little speckled frogs   *Hold up three fingers*
Sat on a speckled log
Eating some most delicious bugs
Yum yum!   *Rub tummy*
One jumped into the pool   *Hold up one finger*
Where it was nice and cool
Now there are two speckled frogs.

Two little speckled frogs . . .

> *Count down to none.*
>
> *Repeat one time.*
>
> *Clap together!*

Here's a rhyme playing Peek-a-Boo with your fingers.

Rhyme with Stick Puppets

Two Little Blackbirds

Or use a pointer finger on each hand and suit your actions to the words.

Two little blackbirds
Sitting on a hill
One named Jack and
The other named Jill.
Fly away Jack
Fly away Jill.
Come back Jack
Come back Jill.

Two little blackbirds
Sitting on a hill
One named Jack and
The other named Jill.

Repeat two or three times.

Clap together!

Now it's time for our good-bye song.

Closing Song

"Clap, Clap, Clap Your Hands"

From *Lively Songs and Lullabies,* by Carol Rose Duane

Suit actions to words.

Clap, clap, clap your hands
Clap your hands together.

Clap, clap, clap your hands
Clap your hands together.

Repeat with these substitutions:

Jump, jump, jump up high . . .
Spin, spin around . . .
Give, give, give a hug . . .

Blow, blow, blow a kiss . . .
Wave, wave, wave good-bye . . .

To the adults:

See you next time. Thank you for coming. Be sure to do these rhymes and books with your children at home. Next time, on _____, we'll do some of these and some new ones too. Enjoy the fun of language with your children.

There is a display here of some parenting books you can check out and some information on early literacy if you'd like to pick some up. I also pulled some books of rhymes for young children, if you'd like to check them out.

Take a moment and look around you. This is a good time to remember how much you love books and children.

HOORAY FOR ME!

Storytime Introduction

Welcome to Cuddle-Up storytime. My name is _____. I am so glad you could all be here today.

To the adults:

Please participate as much as you can as we share rhymes, songs, music, and books. If your child is not happy, feel free to leave and come back when your child is ready.

As we go along, I'll be pointing out some things you can be doing with your children at home to support their early literacy development.

Let's start with our first song.

Opening Song

"Come Along and Sing"

(Sing to the tune of "London Bridge")

Come along and sing with me
Sing with me, sing with me.
Come along and sing with me
It's time for storytime.

??

Repeat with these substitutions:

. . . clap . . .   . . . stretch . . .
. . . bounce . . .   . . . sing . . .
. . . pound . . .

 Print Motivation   Phonological Awareness   ?? Vocabulary   Narrative Skills   Print Awareness   Letter Knowledge

To the adults:

Your children love to hear the sound of your voice. They also pick up on the rhythm of language, so we'll try some rhymes and songs together. As you repeat them at home, notice what your child does as he or she responds to different ones. As they get older and more familiar with them, children start to clap or do the motions to a rhyme or song they recognize.

Let's start with dancing fingers.

Action Song

"Dance Your Fingers Up"

(Sing to the tune of "Looby Loo")

Dance your fingers up and	*Baby: wiggle your fingers on baby's body.*
Dance your fingers down.	*Older child: wiggles own fingers over his body*
Dance your fingers in and out	
All around the town.	
Dance them on your shoulders	*Suit actions to words.*
Dance them on your head.	
Dance them on your tummy	
Tuck them into bed.	*Baby: cross baby's arms over tummy*
	Older child: tucks fingers into armpits

> *Repeat two times.*
>
> *Clap together!*

Here's a rhyme using our fist, our fingers in a ball, and then out they come, one by one. For babies, you can wiggle each finger.

Action Rhyme

Five Little Peas

Five little peas in a pea pod pressed	*Make a fist*
One grew, two grew, so did all the rest.	*Fingers come out one by one*
They grew and they grew	*Fingers out wide*
And they did not stop	*Raise hand high*
Till all of a sudden	
The pod went POP!	*Loud clap*

> *Repeat two or three times.*
>
> *Clap together!*

To the adults:

I'd like to read a book called *I'm a Baby, You're a Baby*. The refrain is
also "I'm a baby. You're a baby." Say that part along with me. Then we'll
find out what baby animals are called. By using specific names for things,
like *cat* and *kitten*, you help your child learn new words, which develops
vocabulary. You also help them understand the differences between
similar things. This sets the stage for them seeing differences in many
things, including later on in the way letters look, too.

I'll read the book and you join in with "I'm a baby, you're a baby."

Book

I'm a Baby, You're a Baby

By Lisa Kopper

Read the book.

Let's do this rhyme showing different parts of the body.

Action Rhyme

One Finger

Hold baby on outstretched legs.

One finger   *Show on your hand or on child's hand*
One thumb
One arm
One leg
One nod of the head
And fall into bed!   *Pick baby up and bring down to your legs*

Repeat two or three times.

Clap together!

And another one using baby's legs! Older children can stand up and dance.

Action Rhyme

Charlie Chaplin

Lay baby on back.

Charlie Chaplin went to France
To teach the ladies how to dance.

First he did the rumba	*Move baby's knees back and forth*
Then he did the kicks	*Move baby's legs in kicking motion*
Then he did the samba	*Put baby's legs together and move up and down*
Then he did the splits.	*Gently move baby's legs apart and back together*
Great!	

Repeat two or three times.

Clap together!

Let's read a book together about Spot, a puppy.

Big Book

Spot's Birthday

By Eric Hill

To the adults:

This book, *Spot's Birthday,* is a lift-the-flap book. It is well suited to children who are able to lift up the flaps, which is one way to engage them in the book.

Children of different ages need different kinds of books. An infant's vision is blurry. They need pictures with bright colors and stark contrast between the background and the object. As they get a little older, they focus better and enjoy looking at pictures of things that are familiar to them, especially faces. As they become toddlers, they enjoy the predictability of repeated words and actions in a book and can focus on pictures that have detail. Feel free to ask us to help you choose books for your children.

Read the book.

It's time for another tickle rhyme.

Tickle Rhyme

Pizza Pickle Pumpernickel

Pizza, Pickle, Pumpernickel
My little girl [boy] shall have a tickle.   *Tickle child's tummy*
One for her [his] nose, and one for her [his] toes,   *Touch nose, toes, and tummy*
And one for her [his] tummy where the cracker goes!

> *Repeat two or three times, then again with child's name.*
>
> *Clap together!*

And now it's time for an action song.

Action Song

"Roll Your Hands"

From *Toddlers on Parade*, by Carol Hammett

(Sing to the tune of "Row, Row, Row Your Boat")

> *Suit actions to words.*

Roll, roll, roll your hands
As fast as fast can be
Do it now, let me see
Do it now with me.

> *Repeat with these substitutions:*

Clap, clap, clap your hands   Shake, shake, shake your feet
As loud as loud can be . . .   As quickly as can be . . .

Tap, tap, tap your feet   Roll, roll, roll your hands
As softly as can be . . .   As fast as fast can be . . .

> *Clap together!*

___

To the adults:

Okay! Let's have some fun with instruments. Take a shaker or bells and
we'll shake them to the rhythm of the music.

Musical Activity

Ask group to stand (if suitable in your space). Hand out bells or shakers. Have adults and children shake instruments and bounce to "Doing the Penguin" from Hot! Hot! Hot! Dance Songs *or some other song with a strong beat.*

Collect the instruments.

Now a couple of tickle rhymes.

Tickle Rhyme

'Round and 'Round the Garden

'Round and 'round the garden	*Circle child's tummy with finger or walk in circle*
Goes the teddy bear.	
One step, two step	*Move finger up child's body*
Tickle him under there.	*Tickle child's neck*

??

'Round and 'round the garden	*Circle child's tummy with bottom of your fist*
The little bunny goes	
Hippity-hop, hippity-hop	*Light bounce fist up child's body*
I'm gonna get your nose!	*Rub child's nose*

Repeat two or three times.

Clap together!

Here's a song that's fun to do as you diaper your baby.

Tickle Rhyme

"Little Flea"

From *Wee Sing for Baby*,
by Pamela Beall

Creeping, creeping little flea	*Crawl fingers up baby's body*
Up my leg and past my knee	
To my tummy on he goes	
Past my chin and to my nose	
Now he's creeping down my chin	

??

To my tummy once again
Down my leg and past my knee
To my toe that little flea.
GOTCHA!   *Tickle tummy*

    Repeat two times.

    Clap together!

And now our good-bye song for today.

Closing Song

"Clap, Clap, Clap Your Hands"

From *Lively Songs and Lullabies,*
by Carol Rose Duane

    Suit actions to words.

Clap, clap, clap your hands
Clap your hands together.
Clap, clap, clap your hands
Clap your hands together.

    Repeat with these substitutions:

Jump, jump, jump up high . . .
Spin, spin around . . .
Give, give, give a hug . . .
Blow, blow, blow a kiss . . .
Wave, wave, wave good-bye . . .

To the adults:

See you next time. Thank you for coming. Be sure to do these rhymes
and books with your children at home. Next time, on _____, we'll
do some of these and some new ones too. Enjoy the fun of language
with your children.

    There is a display here of books about different stages of develop-
ment. Feel free to check them out if you like. There are also some books
that talk about reading with young children.

Bring everyone into your storytime before you begin. Remind them, and yourself, that you are about to enter the magical world of books.

BOUNCE ABOUT

Opening Song

"Come Right In"

(Sing to the tune of "Skip to My Lou")

Come, come, come right in	*Beckoning motion*
Come, come, come right in	
Come, come, come right in	
Joshua, Tamika, and Nikki.	*Substitute children's names*
Sit, sit, sit right down	
Sit, sit, sit right down	
Sit, sit, sit right down	
Sonya, Maya, and Jordan.	*Substitute adults' names*

Storytime Introduction

To the adults:

Welcome to Cuddle-Up storytime. I am so glad you could all be here today. We are going to be sharing rhymes, movement activities, and books. Please participate as much as you can, following along. We expect some degree of chaos. However, if your child is not happy, feel free to leave and come back when your child is calmer.

As we go along, I'll be pointing out some things you can be doing with your children at home to support their early literacy development.

Let's start with an action song.

Print Motivation	Phonological Awareness	Vocabulary	Narrative Skills	Print Awareness	Letter Knowledge

Action Song

"Hello Song"

(Sing to the tune of
"Here We Go 'Round the Mulberry Bush")

Suit actions to words.

This is the way we wave hello
Wave hello, wave hello.
This is the way we wave hello
So early in the morning.

Repeat the same or use other motions.

Clap together!

Let's sing a lively action song to the tune of "Row, Row, Row Your Boat."

Action Song

"Clap, Clap, Clap Your Hands"

(Sing to the tune of "Row, Row, Row Your Boat")

Suit actions to words.

Clap, clap, clap your hands
Clap them just like me.
Do it now, let me see
Do it now with me.

Repeat with these substitutions:

Touch, touch, touch your shoulders . . .
Roll, roll, roll your hands . . .
Tap, tap, tap your knees . . .
Shake, shake, shake your hands . . .
Nod, nod, nod your head . . .
Wave, wave, wave good-bye . . .

Good! What other actions can you think of?

Ready for a bouncing rhyme!

Action Rhyme

I'm Bouncing

I'm bouncing, bouncing everywhere	*Bounce child on your knees*
I bounce and bounce into the air	*Lift child above you*
I'm bouncing, bouncing like a ball	*Bounce child on your knees*
I bounce and bounce and then I fall.	*Let child down to floor gently*

Repeat two times.

Clap together!

Board Book

Choose a board book that has pictures of things commonly found around the house: food, toys, etc.

To the adults:

When you are selecting books for young children, choose ones that have pictures of things that are familiar to them. So, here is one with a picture of an apple. You can talk about the apple in the picture, its color. Then get a real apple and show it to your child. Talk about how it tastes—sweet; how it feels—round and smooth; how it feels when you bite it—crunchy. "It's too hard for you to eat because you don't have teeth yet, but you eat applesauce, which is made from apples!" By showing the child the real object, you are helping them realize that pictures *represent* real things. Later they will also understand that printed words represent real things.

Read the book.

Let's sing a teddy bear song together.

Action Rhyme

Three Brown Teddies

You can also use this as a flannel board rhyme.

Three brown teddies sitting on the wall	*Baby: bounce on knees*
Three brown teddies sitting on the wall	*Older child: hold up three fingers and move hand up and down rhythmically*
And if one brown teddy should accidentally fall	*Baby: lower gently to floor*
	Older child: hold out both hands palms up; clap on fall
There'd be two brown teddies sitting on the wall.	*Baby: repeat as above*
	Older child: hold up two fingers

Two brown teddies . . .

One brown teddy . . .

There'd be no brown teddies sitting there at all.

> *Repeat two times.*
>
> *Clap together!*

Here's an activity that young children, even babies, enjoy.

Bubble Play

Bubbles

Blowing bubbles every day
I blow them all around
I like to watch them float up high
Or POP upon the ground!

To the adults:

Blowing bubbles is lots of fun. Babies watch them, following their movement with their eyes, while older ones reach for them. Even older children run after them. I'll blow some bubbles now. Let's see how the children react. You can talk about the shape of the bubbles, the size, the colors. By giving your children these words, they will learn to describe things in detail. This helps with *narrative skills*, which is being able to describe things.

To the adults:

We are going to read this book together. Don't worry about whether or not your child can see this big book. Your child loves the sound of your voice. We use a slightly higher-pitched voice and speak more clearly and slowly than we do when speaking with adults. This is called *parentese*. Researchers find that speaking in parentese keeps your child's attention longer than using your regular voice. Your child will respond to your voice and to the rhythm of language. Watch your child's reactions as we read the book together.

Big Book

Five Little Monkeys Jumping on the Bed

By Eileen Christelow

Read the book together.

Let's try a bouncing rhyme to "Trot, Trot, Trot to London."

Bounce

Trot, Trot, Trot to London

Trot, trot, trot to London; trot, trot, trot to Dover	*Bounce baby on your knees*
Look out, Baby, or you might fall OVER!	*Bounce, then lean baby back on over*
Trot, trot, trot to Boston; trot, trot, trot to Lynn	*Bounce baby on your knees*
Look out, Baby, or you might fall IN!	*Allow baby to fall between knees*

Repeat two times.

Clap together!

Here's a song with the sounds that different animals say.

Action Rhyme with Puppets

When Ducks Get Up in the Morning

When ducks get up in the morning
They always say good day.

When ducks get up in the morning
They always say good day.
Quack-quack, quack-quack
That is what they say.
Quack-quack, quack-quack
That is what they say.

Repeat with these substitutions:

. . . cows . . . / Moo-moo . . .   . . . pigs . . . / Oink-oink . . .

. . . fish . . . / Glub-glub . . .   . . . chickens . . . / Pock-pock . . .

. . . birds . . . / Tweet-tweet . . .

What other animals can you think of?

Clap together!

And now for our good-bye song. Ready!

Closing Song

"Clap, Clap, Clap Your Hands"

From *Lively Songs and Lullabies,*
by Carol Rose Duane

Suit actions to words.

Clap, clap, clap your hands   Clap, clap, clap your hands
Clap your hands together.   Clap your hands together.

Repeat with these substitutions:

Jump, jump, jump up high . . .   Blow, blow, blow a kiss . . .

Spin, spin around . . .   Wave, wave, wave good-bye . . .

Give, give, give a hug . . .

To the adults:

See you next time. Thank you for coming. Be sure to do these rhymes
and books with your children at home. Next time, on _____, we'll
do some of these and some new ones too. Enjoy the fun of language
with your children.

There is a display here of some information on early literacy, and
there are also some books you might enjoy sharing with your children
and would like to check out.

8

Sample Storytimes for Talkers

(Two- and Three-Year-Olds)

The fun of storytime, of stories, of books, of language, its rhymes and rhythms, the wonder and joy of the experiences that books and reading offer; all these form the foundation of storytime and are key to what we share with families. Keep this in mind as you enrich your storytimes.

OVER AND OVER AGAIN

Storytime Introduction

Welcome to storytime. My name is _____. I am so glad you could all be here today.

To the adults:

We are going to be sharing books, rhymes, songs, and movement activities. Please participate as much as you can, following along. We expect some degree of chaos. However, if your child is not happy, feel free to leave and come back when your child is calmer.

    Today I'll be pointing out some activities we are doing that support early literacy in the areas of *vocabulary*, which is knowing the names of things; and *narrative skills*, which is the ability to describe things and to tell stories. *[Point to poster if you have one in the room.]* Both of these are skills that researchers say will help your child be ready to read. Today

Print Motivation	Phonological Awareness	Vocabulary	Narrative Skills	Print Awareness	Letter Knowledge

we are going to share books and songs that have repeated phrases.
Children love repetition, and in fact, need it in order to learn.

    I'll also be suggesting some activities you can do throughout the day.

Opening Rhyme

Open, Shut Them

Suit actions to words.

Open, shut them, open, shut them
Give a little clap.
Open, shut them, open, shut them
Put them in your lap.

Creep them, crawl them, creep them, crawl them
All the way to your chin.
Open wide your little mouth, ahhhhh
And do not let them in.

Repeat the rhyme a little faster, then again even faster!

Clap together!

The first book I'll share with you today is *Brown Bear, Brown Bear, What Do You See?*
by Bill Martin Jr.

Book

Brown Bear, Brown Bear, What Do You See?

By Bill Martin Jr.

Have them say the repeated phrase.

Read again together if they need to get more comfortable with it.

Let's sing this song together. Everyone stand up. We'll have a stretch.

Action Song

"If You're Happy and You Know It"

If you're happy and you know it, clap your hands. *Clap twice*
If you're happy and you know it, clap your hands. *Clap twice*
If you're happy and you know it, then your face will surely show it.
If you're happy and you know it, clap your hands. *Clap twice*

> *Repeat with these substitutions:*

. . . stomp your feet   . . . shout hooray

. . . jump up high   . . . sit right down

. . . turn around

> *Clap together!*

Good job! Get settled in now, so you can see.

Story with Flannel Board

Too Much Noise

By Ann McGovern

This story is about an old man who has so many animals in his house, that his house is "toooo noisy." Let me hear you say that, "Tooooo noisy!" That's what Peter, the old man, says. One of the animals is a donkey. What sound does a donkey make? Right! Hee-hawww, heeee-hawww.

> *Go through each animal, letting them practice saying the animal sounds.*
>
> *As you read the story, when you come to the words "wise man" you can say: "A wise man is someone who is smart and can help people figure out what to do."*

To the adults:

You can help children understand words they may not know by offering a little explanation as you go along, as I did with *wise man*. If you prefer, you can explain these words before you start the book. Researchers note that the more words your children know and understand, the more vocabulary they have, the easier it will be for them when they begin to read.

Let's do a countdown song with frogs. Frogs like to jump in the water.

Song with Flannel Board

"Five Green and Speckled Frogs"

Do using five fingers of your hand or a flannel board.

Five green and speckled frogs
Sat on a speckled log
Eating some most delicious bugs.
Yum! Yum!
One jumped into the pool
Where it was nice and cool
Then there were four green speckled frogs.

Repeat with these substitutions:

Four green and speckled frogs . . .

Three green and speckled frogs . . .

Two green and speckled frogs . . .

One green and speckled frog . . .

Then there were no green speckled frogs.

Now let me see you all jump like frogs. How does a frog jump? He makes a big hop. Let's get down on the floor. Let me see you be a frog and hop around. Good! Now, let me see you fall into a pool of water. Good! Now up you go and hop around some more. You're like those speckled frogs!

OK, gather round now for our next story, *Lisa Can't Sleep*. Sometimes I have trouble falling asleep. What do you do when you can't sleep?

Allow time for replies.

Activity with Story

Lisa Can't Sleep

By Kaj Beckman

After reading the story, use props for Lisa's toys and let the children retell the story with you.

To the adults:

Narrative skills, the ability to retell stories, is one of the early literacy skills that researchers say children need in order to understand what they read. Using things you have around the house as props can help children remember a story and retell it.

Now it's time for our last song.

Closing Song

"The More We Get Together"

The more we get together, together, together
The more we get together, the happier we'll be.
For your friends are my friends, and my friends are your friends
The more we get together, the happier we'll be.

The more we sing together, together, together
The more we sing together, the happier we'll be.
For your songs are my songs, and my songs are your songs
The more we sing together, the happier we'll be.

The more we read together, together, together
The more we read together, the happier we'll be.
For your books are my books, and my books are your books
The more we read together, the happier we'll be.

The more we get together, together, together
The more we get together, the happier we'll be.
For your friends are my friends, and my friends are your friends
The more we get together, the happier we'll be.

To the adults:

See you next time. Thank you for coming. Be sure to talk about and act out stories with your children at home.

There is a display here of some parenting books and some information on early literacy if you'd like to pick some up. I have also pulled some books that have repetition in them. They are good ones for your child to try to tell back to you after you have read them together a few times. Feel free to check them out.

Remember, when you have fun, the children and adults will too!

I WANT TO . . .

Storytime Introduction

Welcome to storytime. My name is _____. I am so glad you are all here today.

To the adults:

We are going to be sharing books, rhymes, songs, and movement activities. Please participate as much as you can. If your child is not happy, feel free to leave and come back when your child is calmer.

Researchers have noted that one of the six areas of early literacy is *print motivation*, which means having an interest in and an enjoyment of books. Children are more likely to develop print motivation when they are involved with the story. As I share the books today, you'll see different ways you can keep your children interested as you read with them.

Opening Rhyme

Open, Shut Them

Suit actions to words.

Open, shut them, open, shut them
Give a little clap.
Open, shut them, open, shut them
Put them in your lap.

Creep them, crawl them, creep them, crawl them
All the way to your chin.
Open wide your little mouth, ahhhhh
And do not let them in.

Repeat the rhyme, a little faster, then again even faster!

Print Motivation	Phonological Awareness	Vocabulary	Narrative Skills	Print Awareness	Letter Knowledge

The first book I'll read with you is about an animal called a *llama*.

Book

Is Your Mama a Llama?

By Deborah Guarino

Today our books talk about wanting to do something. What do you sometimes want to do? *[Give some time for responses.]* In our first book, a baby llama wants to find his Mama Llama. The book is called *Is Your Mama a Llama?* by Deborah Guarino.

A llama is an animal. *[Open to the second-to-last page and show them a picture of the llama.]* What animal do you think a llama looks like? *[Let different children give their opinions.]*

> *If the adults are giving responses to your questions before the children have a chance to reply, you can tell them the following:*

To the adults:

It is interesting to know that hearing a question and formulating a response involve at least three different parts of the brain. You may have noticed it takes children longer than adults to respond to questions because they have not had as much practice at it as we have. Try to wait about five seconds to give your child time to respond to what you say. *[Count off on your hand, slowly raising one finger at a time to show five seconds.]* We can even try this now as I ask you all to think of some things about our theme today.

In this story the baby llama is always asking, "Is your mama a llama?"
Can you say that—"Is your mama a llama?"

Let me hear you say that. *[Practice a few times.]* Good!

> *Read the book and have them say the sentence.*

To the adults:

Having your child say a repeated phrase with you throughout the book keeps him or her involved, so they will enjoy the book more. This supports *print motivation*.

Here's a rhyme about six kittens. They wanted to jump in a box of paint!

Rhyme with Flannel Board

Rainbow Kittens

Line up the kittens in a row, the colors of a rainbow.

Six little kittens found a box of paint.
They jumped right in . . . their mother will faint!
The first little kitten came out all red.
"I'll be orange," the second one said.
The third little kitten turned bright yellow.
"I'll be green," said the next little fellow.
The fifth kitten said, "My favorite is blue."
"Purple for me," said the sixth with a mew.
Dancing home the little kittens go
To show their mother a KITTEN RAINBOW!

You can put up a felt rainbow, if you want

Repeat so they can say along with you the words on the flip chart.

Clap for all the colors in the kitten rainbow.

Now let's read another book. This one is about Choco, who is trying to find his mother.

Book

A Mother for Choco

By Keiko Kasza

Read the book together.

Now let's do a rhyme about five monkeys who want to jump on the bed.

Rhyme

Five Little Monkeys

Five little monkeys jumping on the bed	*Five fingers up as hand moves up and down*
One fell off and bumped his head.	*Hit head with hand, gently*
Mama called the doctor and the doctor said	*Hold phone to mouth*
"No more monkeys jumping on the bed."	*Wag finger*

Repeat for four, three, two, and one monkey.

One little monkey jumping on the bed
He fell off and bumped his head.
Mama called the doctor and the doctor said
"No more monkeys jumping on the bed."

Our last book today is *Happy Birthday, Sam,* by Pat Hutchins. Sam wants to do things by himself. Let's see how he finds a way.

Book

Happy Birthday, Sam

By Pat Hutchins

Read the book.

And now for our last song.

Closing Song

"Saying Good-bye"

(Sing to the tune of "Mulberry Bush")

This is the way our hands say good-bye
With a clap clap-clap
Clap clap-clap.
This is the way our hands say good-bye
With a clap clap-clap, clap-clap.

This is the way our knees say good-bye
With a tap tap-tap
Tap tap-tap.
This is the way our knees say good-bye
With a tap tap-tap, tap-tap.

This is the way we wave good-bye
Wave good-bye, wave good-bye
This is the way we wave good-bye
Good-bye until next time.

To the adults:

See you next time. Thank you for coming. Enjoy reading together with your children. If you would like some book suggestions, I'd be happy to help you find some you and your child might enjoy.

There is a display here of some parenting books and some information on early literacy if you'd like to pick some up.

Since many adults imitate what we do, remember to keep book sharing fun.

ON THE FARM

Storytime Introduction

Welcome to storytime. My name is _____. I am so glad you could all be here today.

To the adults:

We are going to be sharing books, rhymes, songs, and movement activities. Please participate as much as you can, following along. You who are with your children every day are in the best position to help your child learn. You know your children's routines and their moods best. So take advantage of little times during the day when they are ready to learn. During the storytime I'll be sharing some ideas and activities you can do to support some of the six early literacy skills that researchers have determined are necessary to help your child be ready to read.

Let's start with Ten Little Fingers. Ready?

Opening Rhyme

Ten Little Fingers

I have ten little fingers	*Hold up ten fingers*
They all belong to me	
I can make them do things	
Would you like to see?	*Wiggle fingers*
I can shut them up tight	*Make fist*
Or open them all wide	*Open hands wide*
I can put them all together	*Interlock fingers*
Or make them all hide.	*Hide behind back*
I can make them jump high	*Reach over head*
I can make them jump low	*Down to the floor*
I can fold them quietly	*Fold hands together*
And hold them just so.	*Put hands in lap*

That was great!

		??			
Print Motivation	Phonological Awareness	Vocabulary	Narrative Skills	Print Awareness	Letter Knowledge

Theme Talk

Today we'll be talking about farms and animals on the farm. You might already know something about a farm. Think for a minute about what you know. Now turn to the adult who brought you to storytime and tell her or him something you know about farms. When I play this triangle, it's time to stop talking. *[They talk.]*

Good! Now listen while your Mom or Dad or whoever brought you today tells you something about farms. *[Use the triangle or whatever signal you want to bring the attention back to you.]* Good! It is good to learn from each other.

The first book I'll read to you today is *Big Red Barn*, by Margaret Wise Brown.

Book or Big Book

Big Red Barn

By Margaret Wise Brown

Read the book.

Have a look at some of the shapes in the pictures. In this picture *[choose one in which they can see the barn well]* you can see that the windows are rectangles. They have four straight lines.

> *After showing the shape in the picture, show the shape in flannel board or foam so that it is very clear.*

Now let's see how you can make shapes using your hand in the air.

Action Rhyme

Draw a Shape

Use flannel board pieces or foam shapes.

Draw a rectangle, draw a rectangle	*Draw a rectangle in air with finger*
Shaped like a window.	
Draw a rectangle, draw a rectangle	
With corners four.	

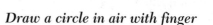

Draw a circle, draw a circle	*Draw a circle in air with finger*
Round as can be.	
Draw a circle, draw a circle	
Just for me.	*Point to self*

Draw a triangle, draw a triangle
With corners three.
Draw a triangle, draw a triangle
Just for me.

Draw a triangle in the air

Point to self

To the adults:

Before children learn actual letters, they are aware of shapes. Before
they have the coordination to hold a crayon and write, they can move
their whole arms and bodies.

Everybody stand up now. Let's see you make a circle shape with your whole body. Good!
Now a circle with your fingers. Good!

Repeat for the square and triangle.

Our next book is one with flaps. You can help me with this one.

Flap Book

Who's in My Bed?

By Helen Piers

Read the book.

Next comes a song about ducks, one of the farm animals. What sound does a duck make?
. . . Right! Follow along with me for "Five Little Ducks."

Song

"Five Little Ducks"

Traditional, as sung by Raffi on *Rise and Shine*

Five little ducks went out one day
Over the hills and far away.
Mother Duck said, "Quack, quack,
    quack, quack!"
But only four little ducks came back.

Hold up hand
Move hand in circle motion
Four fingers bend to thumb

Hold four fingers up

Count down to "none of her five little ducks came back."

？？

Sad mother duck went out to play
Over the hills and far away.
Mother Duck said, "Quack, quack, quack, quack!"
And all of her five little ducks came back.

Slow down here; she's sad

Repeat and sing all together.

Okay! Everybody have a seat for an alphabet book. It's an alphabet book of things around a farm.

Book

Farm Alphabet Book

By Jane Miller

You may not want to read this whole book. You can choose certain letters that talk about things that would interest the children.

To the adults:

You need not read all the pages of an alphabet book. You can let your child choose the pages she or he wants you to read or talk about.

To the adults:

Researchers have noted one of the six areas of early literacy as *letter knowledge*. This means being able to recognize letters and to know their names. Alphabet books are one way to help children become aware of letters and how they look. It is best not to quiz your child on the letters. Just point them out as you are reading through the book. The letter your child is likely to be most interested in is the first letter of his or her name. Make sure you point out that letter when you come to it. You may even want to start with that letter in the book.

On some farms, the farmers grow fruit, like apples. These farms are called *orchards*. Here's a rhyme about Farmer Brown.

Rhyme with Flannel Board

Five Green Apples

Traditional, as sung by Lois and Bram Sharon
on *Mainly Mother Goose*

Farmer Brown had three green apples hanging on the tree.
Farmer Brown had three green apples hanging on the tree.
Then he plucked one apple and ate it hungrily
Leaving two green apples a-hanging on the tree.

Count down to "Leaving no green apples a-hanging on the tree."

Have each child come up and put a felt apple on the tree.
Clap for the full tree at the end.

Read or Sing Book

Cows in the Kitchen

By June Crebbin

Here's a songbook about a sleepy farmer. It goes to the tune of "Skip to My Lou." You can try it with me.

Demonstrate dialogic reading using a page from this book. For example, using the last page for "What" questions: point to an animal and ask, "What's this animal?" If you point to a sheep, and the children answer "sheep," say "Yes, a sheep, a smiling white sheep."

For open-ended questions, you can demonstrate with, "What do you see in this picture?" You will have to pick one child's reply. "A plate, yes, a broken plate. When was something broken at your home?" "How did you feel when something broke?" You are only demonstrating, giving adults the idea of how it works.

To the adults:

Dialogic reading is one way of sharing a book with a child. It supports vocabulary and narrative skills. I can only demonstrate it here. It works best one-on-one so you can follow the lead of your child. If you want more information, please talk with me after the storytime.

And now for our good-bye song.

Closing Song

"Saying Good-bye"

(Sing to the tune of "Mulberry Bush")

This is the way our hands say good-bye
With a clap clap-clap
Clap clap-clap.
This is the way our hands say good-bye
With a clap clap-clap, clap-clap.

This is the way our knees say good-bye
With a tap tap-tap
Tap tap-tap.
This is the way our knees say good-bye
With a tap tap-tap, tap-tap.

This is the way we wave good-bye
Wave good-bye, wave good-bye
This is the way we wave good-bye
Good-bye until next time.

To the adults:

See you next time. Thank you for coming. Enjoy reading together with
your children. If you would like some book suggestions, I'd be happy to
help you find some you and your child might enjoy. If you are interested
in alphabet books, I have displayed some that would be of interest to
this age group. When you look at alphabet books, you'll notice that
some of them are quite involved and are of more interest to older children and adults.

---

*You can put out large letters and shapes for the children to play with
after storytime. They can be magnet letters or be made out of foam,
flannel, or cardboard.*

Take a moment and look around you. This is a good time to remember how much you love books and children.

ALL ABOUT ME

Storytime Introduction

Hand out to adults the bookmark on dialogic reading; see appendix D.

Welcome to storytime. My name is _____. I am so glad you are all here today.

To the adults:

We are going to be sharing books, rhymes, songs, and movement activities. Please participate as much as you can, following along. If your child is not happy, feel free to leave and come back when your child is ready. Today I'll be pointing out some activities we are doing that support early literacy in the areas of vocabulary and narrative skills. Researchers have found that these are two of the skills that are part of a solid foundation for being ready to read. *Vocabulary* is knowing the names of things. *Narrative skills* are being able to describe things and events and to tell a story.

I'll be pointing out some things you can do at home, too.

Are you ready for Open, Shut Them? Let me see your hands.

Opening Rhyme
Open, Shut Them

Suit actions to words.

Open, shut them, open, shut them
Give a little clap.
Open, shut them, open, shut them
Put them in your lap.

Creep them, crawl them, creep them, crawl them
All the way to your chin.
Open wide your little mouth, ahhhhh
And do not let them in.

Repeat the rhyme, a little faster, then again even faster!

Print Motivation	Phonological Awareness	Vocabulary	Narrative Skills	Print Awareness	Letter Knowledge

Our first book follows Jesse Bear through his day. Let's see what he does.

Book

Jesse Bear, What Will You Wear?

By Nancy White Carlstrom

Read book. When you come to the words "moustache of white," point to the moustache in the picture or to your own upper lip. When you come to "water to float my bubble and boat," you can say, "See the boat floating on top of the water. It stays on top; it doesn't sink to the bottom."

To the adults:

From time to time you might explain a word using the pictures, as I did with *moustache*. Children like to hear books over and over again. We can point out different words or pictures at different readings.

Look at what you are wearing today. I am wearing blue pants and a white blouse. My shoes are black. Tell your mom or dad or whoever brought you today what you are wearing. *[Have a signal like an instrument or a clapping rhythm to draw their attention back to you.]* Okay now adults, you tell your child what you are wearing. *[Have a signal to draw their attention back to you.]*

Okay. Very good. Now let's see what Teddy is wearing.

Action Song

"Teddy Wore His Red Shirt"

Dress a teddy, optional.

Teddy wore his red shirt, red shirt, red shirt   *Point to clothing*
Teddy wore his red shirt all day long.

> *You can change "Teddy" to the names of children.*

> *Repeat with these substitutions:*

. . . blue pants . . .   . . . green socks . . .
. . . yellow hat . . .   . . . white shoes . . .

Our next book talks about things we can do with our hands. We can do so many things.

Book

Hands Can

By Cheryl Hudson

Read book. Talk with the children about what they can do with their hands. What can they think of? Examples could be waving, bending forefinger to say "come here," signaling "stop" with hand, clapping, snapping fingers, American Sign Language "I love you," and counting.

Now let's do a rhyme using our hands.

Action Rhyme

Humpty Dumpty

Written out on flip chart.

Humpty Dumpty sat on a wall.	*Forefingers and thumbs of both hands form a circle*
Humpty Dumpty had a great fall.	*Pull two hands apart*
All the king's horses and all the king's men	
Couldn't put Humpty together again.	*Shake head*
But IIIIIII can!	*Forefingers and thumbs of both hands form a circle*

Repeat once or twice.

Clap together.

And here's a rhyme about your hands. You can follow along on the flip chart.

Action Rhyme

Fee Fi Fo Fum

Written out on flip chart.

Fee fi fo fum	*Bounce hand as fist*
See my fingers	*Open out four fingers*
See my thumb.	*Hold up thumb*
Fee fi fo fum	*Bounce hand*
Good-bye fingers	*Fold fingers in*
Good-bye thumb.	*Stick thumb into fingers*

Repeat once or twice.

Clap together.

Now let's have some music playtime together.

Play Music Together

Choose music with a strong beat. Hand out musical instruments to each child and adult. Have children play instruments to the beat of the music, as best they can. They can do this while sitting or while walking around, depending on the group. If you like, you can stop the music and they stop playing; then they start when the music starts. They find it so much fun to not get fooled by the music!

Now it's time for a book about a bear named Sam who isn't feeling very well.

Book and Dialogic Reading

Don't You Feel Well, Sam?

By Ann Hest

Read the book all the way through, the way you normally would. Then choose a page to demonstrate dialogic reading.

To the adults:

I'll demonstrate for you now another way to share a book called *dialogic reading*. The bookmarks I gave you might help you. Here, you become the listener and the child becomes the teller. Don't worry about the story itself. Think more about ways that you can help relate what is happening in the picture to your child's experience. This helps them later to understand what they are reading. It is hard to do in a group. It is best done one-on-one.

For example, open to approximately page 23, where Mrs. Bear is holding Sam on her lap.

What's this?   *Point to the mouse*

That's right a mouse, a little white mouse.

What do you think the mouse is doing?

Yes, it looks like he is trying to drink from the cup.

Instruct adults to follow the child's lead.

What do you see in this picture?

Yes, a big bear.

What is the bear doing?

Yes, hugging baby bear.

How did you feel when you were sick?

Now it's time for our good-bye song.

Closing Song

"Saying Good-bye"

(Sing to the tune of "Mulberry Bush")

This is the way our hands say good-bye
With a clap clap-clap
Clap, clap-clap.
This is the way our hands say good-bye
With a clap, clap-clap, clap-clap.

This is the way our knees say good-bye
With a tap tap-tap
Tap tap-tap.
This is the way our knees say good-bye
With a tap tap-tap, tap-tap.

This is the way we wave good-bye
Wave good-bye, wave good-bye
This is the way we wave good-bye
Good-bye until next time.

Bring everyone into your storytime before you begin. Remind them, and yourself, that you are about to enter the magical world of books.

TASTES GOOD

Storytime Introduction

Welcome to storytime. My name is _____. I am happy to see you all here today.

To the adults:

We are going to be sharing books, rhymes, songs, and movement activities. Please participate as much as you can, following along. Feel free to take your child out and come back in if you need to.

Today I'll be pointing out some activities we are doing that support early literacy in the area of *print awareness*, which includes knowing how a book works, and how we follow the words on the page.

As you see what we do here in storytime, you may get some ideas of what you can do with your child throughout the day.

Ready! Let's start with Open, Shut Them.

Opening Rhyme

Open, Shut Them

Suit actions to words.

Open, shut them, open, shut them
Give a little clap.
Open, shut them, open, shut them
Put them in your lap.

Creep them, crawl them, creep them, crawl them
All the way to your chin.
Open wide your little mouth, ahhhhh
And do not let them in.

Repeat the rhyme, a little faster, then again even faster!

Print Motivation   Phonological Awareness   Vocabulary   Narrative Skills   Print Awareness   Letter Knowledge

---

Our storytime today is about things that taste good. What tastes good to you? . . .
Hmmmm! Good!

One of the things I love to eat is cake. Our first book is about Benny, who is helping to
bake his birthday cake.

Book

Benny Bakes a Cake

By Eve Rice

Read the book. Run your finger under the title as you say it.

To the adults:

You can run your finger under the words of the title as you say it.
This helps children understand that you are reading the text, not the
pictures. Do this only with the title or a repeated phrase, so it doesn't
get in the way of sharing the story.

Benny Bakes a Cake, *by Eve Rice, is a good book to use to demonstrate dialogic reading. Using the page where Benny is crying because
his cake is ruined allows you to not only ask questions about what is
in the picture but also to talk about Benny's feelings and relate it to
something in the child's own experience.*

To the adults:

Having a dialogue with your child about the pictures in a book is called
dialogic reading. I asked some questions about the pictures. I also talked
about Benny's feelings and related them to the children's experiences.
Dialogic reading helps develop vocabulary and narrative skills. Research
shows that the best effects come when you do it with one child at a time.

Now for a rhyme about making a pancake. Let's try it together.

Action Rhyme

Pancake

Suit actions to words.

Mix a pancake, stir a pancake   Fry a pancake, toss a pancake
Pop it in a pan.   Catch it if you can!

    Repeat two times.

    Clap together!

Let's read a book about Max, who needs something from the grocery store.

Book

Bunny Cakes

By Rosemary Wells

Read the book.

To the adults:

Bunny Cakes is a book where writing is important to the story. Encourage your child to draw pictures and "write" lists. Scribbling is fine. Research tells us that reading and writing are connected and support each other. This is part of *print awareness*.

Now it's time for a stretch for our whole body. Everyone stand up, please.

Action Rhyme

Head and Shoulders, Baby

Suit actions to words.

Head and shoulders, baby; one *[clap]*, two *[clap]*, three
Head and shoulders, baby; one *[clap]*, two *[clap]*, three
Head and shoulders
Head and shoulders
Head and shoulders, baby; one *[clap]*, two *[clap]*, three.

Repeat with these substitutions:

Shoulders and waist . . .
Waist and knees . . .
Knees and toes . . .

Clap together!

Very good. Everyone sit down now for our next story.

Cookies are a delicious food too. In this story a mouse wants a cookie. Let's see what happens when he gets one.

Book

If You Give a Mouse a Cookie

By Laura Numeroff

Use flannel board or props.

Read the book, running finger under text of title. Then retell with flannel board or props.

Sometimes people have cookies and drink milk as the mouse did. Sometimes adults drink tea. Let's do this rhyme together. You can follow along on the flip chart.

Action Rhyme

Cup of Tea

Written out on flip chart. You can do this rhyme as fingerplay or as a stand-up stretch.

Here's a cup	*Make cup with one hand*
And here's a cup	*Make a cup with other hand*
And here's a pot of tea.	*Make teapot with both hands*
Pour a cup	*Pour*
And pour a cup	*Pour*
And have a drink with me.	*Pretend to drink*

Repeat two times.

Animals in the zoo need to eat too. Let's see what they like to eat.

Book with Flannel Board

Sam Who Never Forgets

By Eve Rice

Read the book together.

Now it's time for our good-bye song.

Closing Song

"The More We Get Together"

The more we get together, together, together
The more we get together, the happier we'll be.
For your friends are my friends, and my friends are your friends
The more we get together, the happier we'll be.

The more we sing together, together, together
The more we sing together, the happier we'll be.
For your songs are my songs, and my songs are your songs
The more we sing together, the happier we'll be.

The more we read together, together, together
The more we read together, the happier we'll be.
For your books are my books, and my books are your books
The more we read together, the happier we'll be.

The more we get together, together, together
The more we get together, the happier we'll be.
For your friends are my friends, and my friends are your friends
The more we get together, the happier we'll be.

To the adults:

See you next time. Thank you for coming. As you read books with your child, take the time to let him or her turn the pages. It's part of *print awareness*.

There is a display here of some parenting books and some information on early literacy if you'd like to pick some up.

Before you begin, remember to thank everyone for being with you. Everyone appreciates being appreciated! A sincere greeting and a smile set the stage for enjoyment.

TIME FOR BED

Storytime Introduction

Welcome to storytime. My name is _____. I am so glad you could all be here today.

To the adults:

We are going to be sharing books, rhymes, songs, and movement activities. Please participate as much as you can, following along. We expect some degree of chaos. However, if your child is not happy, feel free to leave and come back when your child is calmer.

Today I'll be pointing out some activities we are doing that support early literacy in the area of *phonological awareness*. This is the term that researchers give to the ability to break words down into parts, to hear that words are made up of smaller parts.

You can see what we do here in storytime, and you may get some ideas of what you can do with your child throughout the day.

Let's start with Open, Shut Them.

Opening Rhyme

Open, Shut Them

Suit actions to words.

Open, shut them, open, shut them
Give a little clap.
Open, shut them, open, shut them
Put them in your lap.

Creep them, crawl them, creep them, crawl them
All the way to your chin.
Open wide your little mouth, ahhhhh
And do not let them in.

Repeat the rhyme, a little faster, then again even faster!

Print Motivation	Phonological Awareness	Vocabulary	Narrative Skills	Print Awareness	Letter Knowledge

Our storytime today is about bedtime, about going to bed.

Book

Z-Z-Zoink!

By Bernard Most

The first book we are going to read is about a pig that is looking for a good place to sleep. What does it sound like when someone snores? *[Either repeat their sound or demonstrate a snoring sound if they don't know.]* Let's all make that snoring sound together. Good!

When the pig in this story snores he goes Z-Z-ZOINK, he's snoring with oink at the end because he's a pig that says OINK.

Let's see what happens.

Read the book.

To the adults:

Having your child hear and make the sounds of the animals is one enjoyable way to help develop *phonological awareness*, to eventually be able to hear the smaller sounds in words.

The animals in our next book sleep quietly.

Book or Big Book

Time for Bed

By Mem Fox

If you use a big book, have the adults read along with you.

To the adults:

Reading rhyming books and sharing rhymes both help your child hear parts of words. You can play "I Spy" like this, too. First talk about some of the things in a picture, naming them and allowing your child time to repeat them.

Demonstrate the "I Spy" rhyming game. For example, open to the page with the fish.

Let's see what we see on this page. A big fish, a little fish, some bubbles, the ocean, deep water, etc. I spy with my little eye something on this page that rhymes with or sounds like *dish*. What could it be? . . . Right! *Fish!*

To the adults:

You can play these games with any book or picture, or even as you are walking or driving around.

Let's all stand now and do a stretch.

Action Song

"Teddy Bear"

Everyone stands up.

Teddy bear, teddy bear, turn around.	*Turn around*
Teddy bear, teddy bear, touch the ground.	*Touch the ground*
Teddy bear, teddy bear, show your shoe.	*Point to shoe*
Teddy bear, teddy bear, I love you.	*Hug yourself*

Teddy bear, teddy bear, climb upstairs.	*Pretend to climb stairs*
Teddy bear, teddy bear, brush your hair.	*Pretend to brush hair*
Teddy bear, teddy bear, turn out the light.	*Pretend to switch off light*
Teddy bear, teddy bear, say "Good-night!"	*Hands together and lean head on them*

Repeat.

Clap together!

Some children take a teddy bear or stuffed animal to bed with them. Let's see what happens to this child who has so many animals.

Book

Ten Little Animals

By Laura Coats

Read the book through once. Then read it again and have them sing or say it along with you.

To the adults:

Songs have different notes for different syllables. This is one way we help children hear the parts of words, and it's fun, too! Listen as we sing "Twinkle, Twinkle Little Star."

Action Song with Flannel Board

"Twinkle, Twinkle Little Star"

Talk about stars in the sky at night, when we are asleep. You can do the actions standing or sitting. When done, let each child put a felt star on the flannel board to make a beautiful sky. You can put up a moon and one star first, to start them off.

Twinkle, twinkle little star | *Hands open and shut*
How I wonder what you are.
Up above the world so high | *Raise twinkling hands*
Like a diamond in the sky. | *Make diamond shape with fingers*
Twinkle, twinkle little star | *Hands open and shut*
How I wonder what you are.

Let's read this book about a mother who is trying to make things quiet so her baby can go to sleep. This story takes place in Thailand. Some animal sounds are different from the ones we know here. As we go along, you can say them along with me.

Book

Hush! A Thai Lullaby

By Mingfong Ho

If you have children who speak different languages, talk about the sounds that animals make in their languages.

And now for our good-bye song.

Closing Song

"The More We Get Together"

The more we get together, together, together
The more we get together, the happier we'll be.
For your friends are my friends, and my friends are your friends
The more we get together, the happier we'll be.

The more we sing together, together, together
The more we sing together, the happier we'll be.
For your songs are my songs, and my songs are your songs
The more we sing together, the happier we'll be.

The more we read together, together, together
The more we read together, the happier we'll be.
For your books are my books, and my books are your books
The more we read together, the happier we'll be.

The more we get together, together, together
The more we get together, the happier we'll be.
For your friends are my friends, and my friends are your friends
The more we get together, the happier we'll be.

See you all soon!

To the adults:

Thank you for coming. Enjoy reading together with your children. Today we did a lot of books that rhyme, and we helped children hear the rhythm of language. I have displayed some books that rhyme and some books with rhymes in them, which help your child develop phonological awareness while you enjoy books together. Feel free to check them out.

   See you next time.

Take a second and remember why you are doing this! You want everyone to love books as much as you do . . . try to convey this idea with your enthusiasm.

BIG AND SMALL

Storytime Introduction

Hand out the bookmark on dialogic reading; see appendix D.

Welcome to storytime. My name is _____. It is great to see you all here today.

To the adults:

We are going to be sharing books, rhymes, songs, and movement activities. Please participate as much as you can, following along. Feel free to leave with your child if you need to and come back when your child is ready.

Today I'll be pointing out some activities we are doing that support early literacy in the areas of vocabulary and narrative skills. *Vocabulary* is knowing the names of all kinds of things. *Narrative skills* is being able to describe things and to tell stories. These skills help children to understand what they will read.

Here we go with Open, Shut Them. Ready?

Opening Rhyme
Open, Shut Them

Suit actions to words.

Open, shut them, open, shut them
Give a little clap.
Open, shut them, open, shut them
Put them in your lap.

Creep them, crawl them, creep them, crawl them
All the way to your chin.
Open wide your little mouth, ahhhhh
And do not let them in.

Repeat the rhyme, a little faster, then again even faster!

Print Motivation	Phonological Awareness	Vocabulary	Narrative Skills	Print Awareness	Letter Knowledge

Theme Talk

Today our stories are about big and small. *[Ask children some questions related to size. For example: "Let's think about some animals that are big and small. What can you think of that is very big? What can you think of that is very small?"]*

To the adults:

When you ask your children questions, give them extra time to think and to answer you. Talking back and forth uses four different parts of the brain, so it takes them some time to form their responses.

Here's a story about being too small to help, but then, sometimes being small is good!

Book

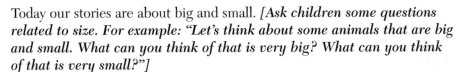

You're Too Small!

By Shen Roddie

Read the book.

Our next story is about fish that are big and small.

Book with Flannel Board

Blue Sea

By Robert Kalan

Read the book. Have children chime in with "Ouch." Have the children retell the story as you put up pieces on the flannel board.

To the adults:

Having your child retell stories is one way to develop your child's narrative skills. Having props or pictures helps your child to remember what comes next.

And now let's have a stretch.

Stretch

Pretend to be a little fish, a big fish, a bigger fish, the biggest fish. How does a little fish swim differently from a really big fish? Let's see!

To the adults:

Acting out stories or parts of them, having young children use their whole bodies, helps them internalize and understand what is happening in the story. They will be able to tell the story back to you, especially their favorites, which they like to hear over and over again.

Book and Dialogic Reading

Hi!

By Ann Scott

Read the whole book. Then turn to a page, for example, approximately page 11, where Margarita is leaning against her mother as three women go out the door.

What do you see on this page?

What is the girl doing?

How do you think she feels?

When have you felt that way?

To the adults:

I am demonstrating dialogic reading, which works best one-on-one with your child. With *dialogic reading*, which means having a conversation around a book, you encourage your child to use language. Ask questions according to what your child knows. If he or she doesn't know many words, just answer for him or her. That's the way your child will learn more words.

Okay, let's all stand up please and have a big stretch. We are going to shake different parts of our bodies.

Action Song

"Here We Go Looby Loo"

The first stanza of this song is the chorus.

Here we go looby loo
Here we go looby lie
Here we go looby loo
All on a Saturday night.

I put my right foot in
I put my right foot out
I give my right foot a shake, shake, shake
And turn myself about.

Repeat chorus.

I reach way up high
I reach way down low
I give my body a shake, shake, shake
And turn myself about.

Repeat chorus.

I put my left foot in
I put my left foot out
I give my left foot a shake, shake, shake
And turn myself about.

Repeat chorus.

I reach big and wide
I squinch up just so
I give my body a shake, shake, shake
And turn myself about.

Repeat chorus.

Our next book shows how something small turns into something big.

Book

Pumpkin, Pumpkin

By Jeanne Titherington

Read the book.

Things that are quite big often start from just a little seed, like this big pumpkin!

To the adults:

Ask us to help you find some nonfiction [true] books on things your child is interested in. Nonfiction books give us different vocabulary from the words we find in stories, and we can all learn new things together from these books!

And now for our good-bye song.

Closing Song

"Saying Good-bye"

(Sing to the tune of "Mulberry Bush")

This is the way our hands say good-bye
With a clap clap-clap
Clap clap-clap.
This is the way our hands say good-bye
With a clap clap-clap, clap-clap.

This is the way our knees say good-bye
With a tap tap-tap.
Tap tap-tap.
This is the way our knees say good-bye
With a tap tap-tap, tap-tap.

This is the way we wave good-bye
Wave good-bye, wave good-bye
This is the way we wave good-bye
Good-bye until next time.

To the adults:

See you next time. Thank you for coming. Enjoy reading together with your children. If you would like some book suggestions, I'd be happy to help you find some you and your child might enjoy.

I have displayed some books that work well for dialogic reading. They have clear pictures that children relate to and some action going on in the pictures.

We are also having an evening workshop on dialogic reading next month, if you'd like to learn more about it.

Remember, the books are the key. All of your messages to the adults should reinforce your love of books and words.

ALL KINDS OF ANIMALS

Storytime Introduction

Welcome to storytime. My name is _____. I am so glad you could all be here today.

To the adults:

We are going to be sharing books, rhymes, songs, and movement activities. Please participate as much as you can, following along.

Today I'll be pointing out some activities we are doing that support early literacy in the areas of knowing words and what they mean. Building vocabulary is important because it helps children understand what they read later on. It also helps them recognize words as they try to sound them out later when they begin to read.

Books use many words that we don't usually hear on television or in regular conversations.

Let's get ready for our first rhyme, Open, Shut Them. Hold up your hands.

Opening Rhyme
Open, Shut Them

Suit actions to words.

Open, shut them, open, shut them
Give a little clap.
Open, shut them, open, shut them
Put them in your lap.

Creep them, crawl them, creep them, crawl them
All the way to your chin.
Open wide your little mouth, ahhhhh
And do not let them in.

Repeat the rhyme, a little faster, then again even faster!

Print Motivation	Phonological Awareness	Vocabulary	Narrative Skills	Print Awareness	Letter Knowledge

Our stories today are about animals, all kinds of animals. Our first one is about a bear.

Let's see what happens when this bear comes out of his cave in the spring.

Book

Bear Wants More

By Karma Wilson

Read the book. Have the children say the repeated phrase with you.

To the adults:

Even in a fairly simple story like this one, there are many words that we don't use in everyday conversation, such as *waddle, shoots from the ground, nibble, blade of grass, tromp, hare* (instead of *rabbit*), and *wedged*. Even if you don't talk about the meaning of all these words, they hear the words in the story and get an idea of what they mean from hearing the story and from the pictures.

Bear Wants More *can be used to demonstrate dialogic reading. The page where the bear gets stuck gives several options for simple "What" questions as well as talking about how it feels to be stuck, and relating that to the child's own experience.*

To the adults:

Dialogic reading, which encourages *vocabulary* and *narrative skills*, works best when you choose a book that you and your child have already read together. Books with clear pictures with some action work well. We learn a lot about what your child thinks with dialogic reading.

Our next rhyme is also about a bear, but this time we are looking for a bear.

Action Story

Let's Go on a Bear Hunt

Let's go on a bear hunt.	*Slap thighs*
All right; let's go.	
Oh look I see a wheat field!	
Can't go over it	
Can't go under it	
Let's go through it.	
All right; let's go.	
Swish swish swish.	*Rub hands together*
Walk along.	*Slap thighs*
Oh, look. I see a lake!	
Can't go around it.	
Can't go over it.	
Let's swim across.	
All right; let's go.	*Swimming motion*
Walk along.	*Slap thighs*
Oh, look. I see a swamp!	
Can't go around it.	
Can't go under it.	
Let's go through it.	
All right; let's go.	*Feet up and down slowly*
Yuck, very muddy.	
Walk along.	*Slap thighs*
Oh, look. I see a tree!	
Can't go over it.	
Can't go under it.	
Let's go up it.	
All right; let's go.	*Climb tree, look around with hand to forehead*

Walk along.	*Slap thighs*
Oh, look. I see a bridge!	
Can't go around it.	
Can't go under it.	
Let's cross over it.	
All right; let's go.	*Stamp feet and click tongue*
Walk along.	*Slap thighs*
Oh, look. I see a cave!	
Can't go around it.	
Can't go under it.	
Let's go IN it.	
All right; let's go.	
Golly it's dark in here.	
Better use my flashlight.	
Oh, it doesn't work.	
I think I see something.	
It's big; it's furry!	
It's got a big nose!	
I think it's a bear.	
IT IS A BEAR!	
Let's go!!	

Repeat everything backward and fast

WHEW! We made it!

Clap together!

Our next story is about a turtle and other animals near a pond. It's also a counting book.

Book

Turtle Splash: Countdown at the Pond

By Cathryn Falwell

Read the book. Point out or read the information at the end of the book.

To the adults:

Here again you can see the richness of language, many words you would not use in conversation. Children's books have about thirty-one rare words per thousand words; that's three times more than in conversation and 25 percent more rare words than what is on television programs. The more rare words the children know, the easier it will be when it comes time for school and formal learning. *[You could display the* Read-Aloud Handbook, *by Jim Trelease.]*

??

Now let's do a rhyme about a turtle.

Finger Play

There Was a Little Turtle

There was a little turtle	*Fist with thumb sticking out*
He lived in a box	*Cup hands together*
He swam in a puddle	*Swimming motion with hands*
He climbed on the rocks.	*Fingers climb up other hand*
He snapped at a mosquito	*Snap fingers or make grabbing motion with one hand*
He snapped at a flea	*Snap fingers or make grabbing motion with one hand*
He snapped at a minnow	*Snap fingers or make grabbing motion with one hand*
And he snapped at me!	*Snap fingers or make grabbing motion with one hand*
He caught the mosquito	*Clap hands, gulp*
He caught the flea	*Clap hands, gulp*
He caught the minnow	*Clap hands, gulp*
But he didn't catch me!	*Shake head and smile, point to self*
Clap together!	

Our next book is about a lot of farm animals and one wild animal! Let see what happens when they meet.

Book or Big Book

Hattie and the Fox

By Mem Fox

Read the book.

And now for our good-bye song.

Closing Song

"Saying Good-bye"

(Sing to the tune of "Mulberry Bush")

This is the way our hands say good-bye
With a clap clap-clap
Clap clap-clap.
This is the way our hands say good-bye
With a clap clap-clap, clap-clap.

This is the way our knees say good-bye
With a tap tap-tap
Tap tap-tap.
This is the way our knees say good-bye
With a tap tap-tap, tap-tap.

This is the way we wave good-bye
Wave good-bye, wave good-bye
This is the way we wave good-bye
Good-bye until next time.

To the adults:

Thank you for coming. Enjoy reading together with your children. I'd be happy to help you choose books that are rich in language to share with your children.

See you next time.

9

Sample Storytimes for Prereaders

(Four- and Five-Year-Olds)

The fun of storytime, of stories, of books, of rich language, its rhymes and rhythms, the wonder and joy of the experiences that books and reading offer; all these form the foundation of storytime and are key to what we share with families. Keep this in mind as you enrich your storytimes.

GARDENS

Storytime Introduction

Hello, everyone, and welcome to storytime. Let's get settled in, and we'll get started.

Opening Rhyme

Hello, Hello

Hello, ____(name)____, hello, ____(name)____ .
Hello and how are you?
I'm fine, thanks.
I'm fine, thanks.
I'm hoping you are too!

Print Motivation

Phonological Awareness

Vocabulary

Narrative Skills

Print Awareness

Letter Knowledge

Let's say some of your names again. We have Shanika, Tom, and José. Let's sing this song about names together. What happens if we give everybody's name the same first sound, using the m sound? Shanika becomes Manika, and Tom becomes Mom, and José becomes Mosé. Let's try it with everybody's name.

We're going to read a book now about how a garden grows.

Book

Planting a Rainbow

 ??

By Lois Ehlert

Read the book. Go through it again and look at the flower names. Say the name of a flower and explain that you are going to clap out the number of syllables, or parts that it has.

Look at this flower. It's a daffodil. Let's clap out the sounds in daffodil. Daff-o-dill.

Clap three times, once for each syllable.

Do this with flower names of various lengths, from rose to petunia. Instead of clapping you could stamp your feet, jump up and down, or do any other kind of motion.

Song

"Pansies and Petunias"

Traditional, as sung by Raffi on *One Light, One Sun*
(Sing to the tune of "Apples and Bananas")

This may be a challenge, but with a little practice, it will be fun.

I like to pick, pick, pick

Pansies and petunias.

I like to pake, pake, pake

Pan-says and pay-tay-nays.

I like to peek, peek, peek

Peen-sees and pee-tee-nees.

I like to pike, pike, pike

Piyn-siys and piy-tiy-nys.

I like to poke, poke, poke

Pone-soes and po-to-nos.

I like to pook, pook, pook

Poon-soos and poo-too-noos.

Repeat till most children are comfortable with the sounds.

Our next story is an alphabet book.

Book

Alison's Zinnia

By Anita Lobel

To the adults:

At home, have your child think of other words that start with the same
sound as the first sound in your child's name. Children learn best by
doing activities that have meaning to them.

Activity

*Bring in some seeds, dried beans, peas, or fruits and vegetables with
their seeds intact. Talk about the fact that the seeds are in the fruit,
that they are the future plants.*

In our next book, we see that you don't need a lot of space to have a garden.

Book

Flower Garden

By Eve Bunting

*Use this book to demonstrate dialogic reading. Remember to first label
the new words and then to ask open-ended questions related to the
children's experiences. Some questions might be*

What plants do you think grow in gardens?

What present has your mom gotten for her birthday?

What have you gotten for your birthday?

How did you feel when you got it?

Arts and Crafts

Materials needed: craft sticks, markers or crayons, paper, and glue.

Tell the children that they are going to make their own gardens like they saw in Planting a Rainbow. *After they draw their flowers, have the adults help to write the names of their plants on the art sticks, which can then be glued to the paper. It is fine if the children make up the names of their flowers and plants. Or, if you prefer, let the children cut out pictures of flowers from plant catalogs and label them.*

Closing Song

"Storytime Is at an End"

(Sing to the tune of "Twinkle, Twinkle, Little Star")

Storytime has reached its end.

Say good-bye to all your friends.

We've read some books and had some fun.

Feels like we have just begun!

Storytime is over, friends.

We have really reached the end!

Closing

Thanks for coming, everyone! Have fun playing with word sounds. Don't forget to check out some books on your way out!

Remember, when you have fun, the children and adults will too!

A VISIT TO THE KING AND QUEEN

Storytime Introduction

Hello and welcome to storytime. I am pleased to see you here with your children today. Find a spot to sit in and we'll begin.

To the adults:

Parents, an important skill that children need before beginning formal reading instruction is actually more of an attribute or even an attitude. It is called *print motivation*, or interest in and enjoyment of books. One of the ways of encouraging this is to use books as a jumping-off point into children's imaginations.

Opening Rhyme

Hello, Hello

Hello, hello.
Hello and how are you?
I'm fine, thanks.
I'm fine, thanks.
I'm hoping you are too!

Our first book is the story of a boy who became king of some wild things.

Book

Where the Wild Things Are

??

By Maurice Sendak

This book has many interesting words that can be talked about ahead of time. By talking about the words before reading the story, you decrease the disruption of the flow of the story.

Print Motivation   Phonological Awareness   Vocabulary   Narrative Skills   Print Awareness   Letter Knowledge

---

To the adults:

As I read this story, listen to the many interesting words there are, such as *gnashing*, *claws*, and *rumpus*. These words are not used in daily conversation, but are in the rich language of books. Hearing these words helps your child build vocabulary, one of the six skills that help children when they later learn to read.

??

Read the book.

Activity

Remember the wild rumpus that Max and the wild things created? Let's make our own wild time as we dance around to this music. *[Put on some good jumping/dancing around music, or even "The Monster Mash," and make your own wild rumpus. Encourage the children to say with you, "Let the wild rumpus begin!"]* When the music stops, you stop. When the music starts, you start again. Let's try it. *[Pause the music intermittently.]*

Our next kingly adventure is going to take place as we see what happens when the king is in the bathtub and won't get out.

Book

King Bidgood's in the Bathtub

??

By Don Wood and Audrey Wood

First we are going to talk a little bit about the people who help the king. They are mentioned in the story. We have a *knight*, a *squire*, a *queen*, a *page*, and a *duke*. Together they are called the *court*. They are the group of people who help to protect the king and to help him make decisions.

> *Don't forget to mention other king-specific words, like* castle *and* crown. *Read this book dialogically, asking these questions:*

Why won't the king get out of the tub?

What do you do when you don't want to get out of the bathtub?

How do you think they feel when he won't get out?

The king wouldn't get out of the tub and everyone had an idea
    on how to get him out. Listen . . .

> "Who knows what to do?
> I do, said the knight with a glub, glub, glub
> Today we fish in the tub."

Go back through parts of the story, helping the children to see the connection between the "with a _____, _____, _____" and "today we _____ in the tub." Now come up with some new pairings of activities. For example, "Who knows what to do? I do, said a motorcycle rider, with a vroom, vroom, vroom. Today we ride in the tub." Substitute some of the following, or ones you can think of:

singer / hum, sing

basketball player / throw, play

soccer player / kick, play

fiddler / strum, fiddle

baby / wha, cry

baker / mix, bake

To the adults:

When we play with the ideas that we find in a book, we are helping to make the story part of the child's life. By encouraging children to play along with the story, we are helping them incorporate the words, ideas, and energy of the story into their play. By making books and their stories fun, we are helping to motivate children to want to read more.

We're going to sing a song about a duke. Remember who a duke is? That's right, he's part of the king and queen's court, a special group of helpers.

Song

"The Noble Duke of York"

March while singing this song, going on tippy-toe and bending knees as the song indicates.

Oh, the noble Duke of York
He had ten thousand men.
He marched them up to the top of the hill
And he marched them down again.
Oh, when they're up, they're up
And when they're down, they're down.
And when they're only halfway up
They're neither up nor down!

Book

Mother Goose

(any version)

Or read a nonfiction title about kings or castles. If you choose a non-fiction title, remember to point out any new words.

Say some Mother Goose rhymes together, including the old favorites that have anything to do with a king or queen, like "Humpty Dumpty."

Activity

Materials: precut crowns, stick on jewels, dots, or whatever is on hand to decorate them, and glue, markers, or crayons.

Have the children decorate precut crowns or "dunce"-shaped hats that ladies wore. They can all call themselves King _____or Queen _____, or Lady _____.

As you talk with the adults and children, model talking with the children about what they are making. Ask open-ended questions. Give them time to think and to describe what they are doing. It is a good idea to give materials to both the adult and the child so that the adult will be more likely to allow the child to develop his own work.

Closing Song

"Storytime Is at an End"

(Sing to the tune of "Twinkle, Twinkle Little Star")

Storytime has reached its end.

Say good-bye to all your friends.

We've read some books and had some fun.

Feels like we have just begun!

Storytime is over, friends.

We have really reached the end!

Closing

Remember to make reading fun as you and your child learn about things you are interested in!

Since many adults imitate what we do, remember to keep book sharing fun.

DINOSAURS

Storytime Introduction

Hello. My name is _____. I am pleased to see you all here today at storytime. We are about to get started, so come on in and find a place to sit. Today we are going to read some books about dinosaurs.

To the adults:

Parents, one book can be used in many ways. Today we are going to look at a variety of ways that we can use books to help our children develop their early literacy skills.

Opening Rhyme

Hello, Hello

Hello, hello.
Hello and how are you?
I'm fine, thanks.
I'm fine, thanks.
I'm hoping you are too!

Did you hear what I said right before we sang our hello song? That's right, we are going to read some books about a REALLY HUGE animal that lived a long time ago. Its name starts with the letter *D* and the sound /d/. Any ideas? That's right, it's a DINOSAUR!

First, let's see how people think dinosaurs used to look.

Book

Use any nonfiction book with good pictures of dinosaurs, or use Dinosaur Bones, *by Aliki, or* Bones, Bones, Dinosaur Bones, *by Byron Barton.*

??

| Print Motivation | Phonological Awareness | Vocabulary | Narrative Skills | Print Awareness | Letter Knowledge |

Activity

Let's say the names of the dinosaurs. Clap out the syllables of the dinosaur names. For example, *T Rex* would have two claps, *Tyrannosaurus* would have five!

To the adults:

When we separate a word into its sounds, it is called *segmentation*. Playing with words this way now will help your children later in school when they have to break words into syllables as a way of decoding words.

Our next book is told by the dinosaur—a *T Rex*, in fact. It is called *T Is for Terrible*.

Book

T Is for Terrible

By Peter McCarty

This book shows parents how to see things from a different point of view, and to ask the child "How it would feel if . . ." In short, this is a dialogic reading experience! Some questions might be:

How is this dinosaur like others?

How is it different from others?

How does it feel?

How would you feel if you were this dinosaur?

To the adults:

We can use storybooks as a way of talking with our children about all kinds of things; not just "real" or factual information needs to be shared.

Who can tell me how we know about dinosaurs? What have we found left from dinosaurs? Bones, that's right. How did we find them? Someone dug them up. Let's dig! Everyone on their feet. HEH! Dig for dino. Can you hear that sound of the letter *D*?

To the adults:

You can talk about letters and letter sounds as the opportunity arises. Repetition helps, as does having fun!

Song

"Dig for Dinosaurs"

From *Sea Shanties*, by the Robert Shaw Chorale

(Sing to the tune of
"What Shall We Do with the Drunken Sailor?")

Let's dig, dig, dig for dino   *Pretend to dig with a shovel*

Dig, dig, dig for dino

Dig, dig, dig for dino

Dig for dinosaurs!

Our last book is about the kind of dinosaur that you can name! That's right, I want to call my dinosaur a *Bookasaur* because I love books. Let's read this next book and you will see what I mean.

Book

I Can Draw a Weeposaur and Other Dinosaurs

??

By Eloise Greenfield

Read this book through, making sure to finish each poem before talking about it. You might want to play with other ways of describing what each dinosaur is. For example, a speedasaurus *could also be a* fastasaurus *or a* quickasaurus. *Their opposite would be a* slowasaurus. *You get the idea.*

To the adults:

The more words kids know, the better off they will be when they learn to read. Research tells us that it is easier to read a word that you have already heard. You can use books to help expand your child's *vocabulary*. Look for words that have the same meaning, or are synonyms. You can also look at words that are opposites, or antonyms.

??

Arts and Crafts

Materials needed: photocopies of dinosaurs or bones, blown up and cut into puzzle-like pieces.

The paleontologists put the dinosaurs' bones together. They completed a puzzle. I have a puzzle here for us to do. *Hand out pictures of dinosaurs or bones. The children cut them into pieces, and then put the puzzles together.*

Closing Song

"Storytime Is at an End"

(Sing to the tune of "Twinkle, Twinkle Little Star")

Storytime has reached its end
Say good-bye to all your friends.
We've read some books and had some fun
Feels like we have just begun!
Storytime is over, friends
We have really reached the end!

Closing

To the adults:

Please, have fun using books for all kinds of learning fun! Don't forget to check some books out for this child, and for any other little ones you might have. See you next time!

Everyone responds to smiles and laughter. Make both a part of storytime.

LET'S GO SHOPPING

Storytime Introduction

Hello. My name is _____. Thanks for bringing your children to the library today. Let's get ready to begin today's adventure!

> To the adults:
>
> Today throughout storytime, I will be pointing out some activities that we are doing that support your child's early literacy development. Today we are going to be emphasizing *vocabulary*, or knowing the names of things, and *print awareness*, which is noticing print. We are also going to look at *rhyme*, another skill that helps children learn how to read.

Opening Rhyme

Hello, Hello

Hello, hello.
Hello and how are you?
I'm fine, thanks.
I'm fine, thanks.
I'm hoping you are too!

> *Asking the children some questions before the first story will help them focus on the theme.*

Today we are going to go on a shopping trip with some of our storybook friends. How many of you like to go shopping? What are some of the things you go shopping for? *[Give the children time to respond.]*

Our first book is a story about a family that is shopping for dinner. It is called *Feast for 10*, by Cathryn Falwell.

| Print Motivation | Phonological Awareness | Vocabulary | Narrative Skills | Print Awareness | Letter Knowledge |

Book

Feast for 10

By Cathryn Falwell

or

Mama and Papa Have a Store

By Amelia Carling

As you read Feast for 10, *make sure to point out the different kinds of food and products that they buy, as well as the grocery cart and other objects. You can mention the different parts of the characters' clothing, pointing out details about the mother's earrings, the children's hair decorations, and anything else you find interesting. Here are some sample questions:*

Who is going shopping?

Whom do you go shopping with?

Why do you think there are so many chairs set around the table?

Whom do you invite over when you have a feast?

For Mama and Papa Have a Store, *you can compare the kinds of products sold, the process involved in buying them, and how things are alike and different from where they live.*

To the adults:

You can help your children see the relationship between the written and spoken word by using what is called *environmental print*, or words that are part of our everyday life, like signs and labels.

Activity

Materials needed: boxes, cans, or pictures of food, enough for each child.

Talk with the children about the items they have. Have each child bring the item up to the front of the room, next to you. Using the visual clues on the food product and the initial letters, help the children guess what kind of food it is.

Song

"A Shopping We Will Go"

(Sing to the tune of "A Hunting We Will Go")

March in place, if it feels right!

A shopping we will go	A shopping we will go.
A shopping we will go	A shopping we will go.
Heigh-ho the dairy-oh	We'll check the list to see what we've missed
A shopping we will go.	A shopping we will go.

What kind of food do we have?

That's right, a _____ and an _____. *[Hold up different items.]* Let's sing the shopping song again. *[Repeat the song as many times as you wish.]*

Our next book is about a boy who can't remember what he needs to buy.

Book

Don't Forget the Bacon

By Pat Hutchinson

Read the book. There is a lot to talk about in this story. Remember to call things what they are—the fence is a picket fence, *the rope around the dog's neck is a* leash. *Choose a page to turn to and then ask some dialogic questions:*

Why do you think he kept forgetting what to buy?

What could he have done to help him remember what to get?

What do you do to help you remember what to buy when you go to the store?

Now we are going to see how some silly sheep shop. The name of this book is *Sheep in a Shop*, by Nancy Shaw.

Book

Sheep in a Shop

By Nancy Shaw

To the adults:

Notice the rhyming words in this book. Being able to rhyme helps develop *phonological awareness*, or knowing words are made up of sounds. Let's sing a rhyming song.

Song

"Rhyme Along"

(Sing to the tune of "Row, Row, Row Your Boat")

Rhyme, rhyme, rhyme along,
Rhyme along with me!
Stop and *shop* are rhyming words
So rhyme along with me!

> *Go back through the story and pick out other rhyming pairs with the children.*

Arts and Crafts

> *Materials needed: paper, pictures of food cut out from magazines and newspapers, glue, and crayons or markers.*

Let's pretend we are going shopping. We are going to make a shopping list, using pictures and words of what we are going to buy.

> *Suggest that the adults write the names of the things that they cut out, using the child's words.*

Closing Song

"Storytime Is at an End"

(Sing to the tune of "Twinkle, Twinkle Little Star")

Storytime has reached its end
Say good-bye to all your friends.
We've read some books and had some fun
Feels like we have just begun!
Storytime is over, friends
We have really reached the end!

Closing

To the adults:

Writing can be very motivating. It helps children make the connection between the spoken and the written word. Encourage your children to write. You could begin by making a shopping list together the next time you go shopping.

Are you using a favorite story? Tell everyone why you love this book!

FOOD

Storytime Introduction

Hello and welcome to storytime. Thanks for bringing the children here today. It is terrific to see so many of you coming here every week!

To the adults:

Parents, *narrative skills* is the ability to describe things and events and to tell stories. This is one of the skills that children need to have before formal reading instruction begins. One of the ways that children develop this skill is by learning that stories have a beginning, a middle, and an end. We can help encourage them to retell familiar stories as well as learn the sequences of new ones. Today, we are going to tell at least one story together.

Opening Rhyme

Hello, Hello

Hello, hello.
Hello and how are you?
I'm fine, thanks.
I'm fine, thanks.
I'm hoping you are too!

Choose a book where the sequence matters, making it easier for the children to remember the order of events. For example, in Stone Soup, *order doesn't matter, whereas in* The Little Red Hen, *it does. Remember to develop vocabulary, ask open-ended questions, and let the children help retell the story using a flannel board, puppets, or even the book itself. Use the words "what happened first," "and then," and finally, "at the end."*

Our first book tells the story of a little red hen who bakes some delicious bread.

Print Motivation	Phonological Awareness	Vocabulary	Narrative Skills	Print Awareness	Letter Knowledge

Book

The Little Red Hen

By Paul Galdone

Or read another sequential book using the basic format discussed above to highlight the beginning, the middle, and the end of the story.

Let's do a song about making bread. Follow along with what I do.

Action Song

"From Wheat to Bread"

(Sing to the tune of
"This Is the Way We Wash Our Clothes")

Suit actions to words.

This is the way we plant the wheat
Plant the wheat, plant the wheat
This is the way we plant the wheat
Said the little red hen.

Repeat with these substitutions:

. . . cut the wheat . . .   . . . bake the bread . . .

. . . grind the wheat . . .   . . . eat the bread . . .

. . . knead the dough . . .

To the adults:

As you can see, in this song the order in which things happen makes a difference. Have your child tell you the story in order. Help him or her out if needed. This helps your child develop narrative skills. The song we do with actions helps reinforce the sequence.

Activity

I have here in my bag lots of different things from my kitchen.   **?.?**

The bag should contain things like an egg timer, a whisk, measuring cups and spoons, dinner and salad fork, knife, teaspoon, butter knife, pie tins, cookie cutters, a teacup, and other things that are interesting and odd. Pull each item from your bag one by one. Say the name of it and what it is used for, allowing the children to respond as well.

You can see how talking about things we have around the house helps develop your child's vocabulary.   ??

Book for Dialogic Reading

Use any nonfiction selection about bread, like Ann Morris' Bread, Bread, Bread, or a book about cooking or food growing. Nonfiction can be an excellent source of books to use for dialogic reading. Titles that have lots of images and few words are especially good. Remember to talk about the names of things, including utensils and food names.

Let's sing a song. It is a fun song to sing because we change the sounds around to make nonsense words. It goes like this.

Song

"Apples and Bananas"

Traditional, as sung by Raffi on *One Light, One Sun*

I like to eat, eat, eat
Apples and bananas.
I like to ate, ate, ate
Ayples and banaynays.
I like to ite, ite, ite
Iples and bininis.

I like to oat, oat, oat
Oples and bononos.
I like to oot, oot, oot
Ooples and boonoonoos.

Have you ever wondered what happens to all those letters you eat with alphabet soup? What if they went to your brain and you could read? Well, in *Martha Speaks*, by Susan Meddaugh, a dog eats alphabet soup, and wait until you see what happens.

Book

Martha Speaks

By Susan Meddaugh

Because the idea of this book is so intriguing, it is fun to talk about what happened during the story. Some leading questions are

How would you feel if you had a dog who could talk?
What questions would you ask your dog if it could talk?

To the adults:

When we talk about a story after reading it with a child, we are helping him or her remember what he or she heard, and to recap it. This helps to reinforce new vocabulary words because the child has the opportunity to use the words again. It also is one of the first steps in learning how stories work, which will help children later when they begin to read. Their ability to predict stories is based on their experience with books and is an important part of being a good reader. We can help them learn how to predict what will happen next by pausing before the end of the book and asking, "If you were making your own story, what would you say would happen next?"

Activity

Materials needed: cut- or punched-out letters of the alphabet or alphabet macaroni, paper and glue.

This leads us right up to today's activity. I have some alphabet letters here. Let's make our own alphabet soup by gluing letters on to the paper. Listen to your child as he describes what he's doing or talking about the story.

You might want to have some "thought bubbles" photocopied on to paper for them to use.

Closing Song

"Storytime Is at an End"

(Sing to the tune of "Twinkle, Twinkle Little Star")

Storytime has reached its end.
Say good-bye to all your friends.
We've read some books and had some fun.

Feels like we have just begun!
Storytime is over, friends.
We have really reached the end!

Closing

To the adults:

Remember to summarize stories after you read them. You can also help children get the idea of putting activities in sequence by telling them what you are going to do. For example, first we are going to storytime, then we are going to pick out some books, and then we are going to go home.
    See you next time!

Take a moment and look around you. This is a good time to remember how much you love books and children.

MICE

Storytime Introduction

Hello and welcome to storytime. It's terrific to see you here with your children today. Find a spot to sit and we'll begin.

To the adults:

Parents, today we are going to be playing with the letter *M* and its sound, /m/. Research tells us that *letter knowledge*, or learning to name letters and to recognize them, is an important skill for children to have before they learn how to read. Along the way I will show you some ways to help your children learn some new words and practice retelling stories. These activities help develop *vocabulary*, which is knowing the names of things; and *narrative skills*, which is the ability to describe thing and events and to tell stories. Both of these skills are important to learning how to read.

Opening Rhyme

Hello, Hello

Hello, hello.
Hello and how are you?
I'm fine, thanks.
I'm fine, thanks.
I'm hoping you are too!

Today we are going to be looking at books about mice. How might a mouse sing our welcome song? Let's sing it in a squeaky mouse voice!

Repeat the Hello, Hello rhyme using a mousy voice.

Our first story is about a mouse and the huge mess she makes.

| Print Motivation | Phonological Awareness | Vocabulary | Narrative Skills | Print Awareness | Letter Knowledge |

Book

Mouse Mess

By Linnea Riley

Read the book all the way through to enjoy the rhyme and rhythm of the story. Then choose a page. Highlight some new vocabulary words, urging the children to repeat the new words. Some words you might include are needle and thread, wrist watch, postage stamps, outlet, plug, faucet, cracker, prongs of a fork, slice of cheese, *and the names of fruits and vegetables. Use some of the following questions to get the dialogue going.*

What kind of food do you think the mouse likes the best?

What food do YOU like best?

How does it taste?

What would happen if you made such a big mess?

Our next activity helps us hear the sound *M* makes, which is /m/.

To the adults:

It is important for children to know that the sounds that letters make are different from each other. This will help them later when they need to be able to decode or sound out words as they are learning to read.

Activity and Rhyme

Can you hear the first sound in the word *mouse*? It's /m/. Like mmm, mmm, good, as you rub your tummy, isn't it? Let's say the sound /m/ when we rub our tummies. That can be our sign for the /m/ sound.

Are you ready to play a listening game? I am going to say words that start with the letter *M*, which makes the sound /m/. When you hear the /m/ sound, rub your tummy! Let's stand up to begin.

I hear, with my little ear, the sound /m/.

OK, get ready to rub your tummy when you hear /m/.

tight . . . light . . . *might*

rice . . . *mice* . . . dice

my . . . sky . . . high

How about some words that end with the letter *M* and the /m/ sound!

I hear, with my little ear the sound /m/.   him . . . hit . . . hill.

rat . . . ram . . . rap   hat . . . ham . . . had

To the adults:

It is easier to hear beginning sounds than ending sounds. Don't worry if it takes them a while to catch on to any of these activities. If your child isn't quite able to do something, wait and try again next month. Keep this fun, or you will all become frustrated!

Continue this activity with nonsense and real words. They don't have to be in sets of three, either.

For our next story, we are going to see what happens when a mouse can't find his family.

Book

Whose Mouse Are You?

By Robert Kraus

This book is good for dialogic reading, and helps children talk about feelings. Some questions to ask might be

How does the mouse feel when he can't find his family?

What did he do to get his family back?

How do you think he felt when he was back with his family?

Or use any version of The Town Mouse and the Country Mouse.

Let's do a song using the letters in the word *mouse.*

Song

"M-O-U-S-E"

(Sing to the tune of "B-I-N-G-O")

Have all the children stand up. Have them make their bodies into an M, then O, then U, then S, and then E. Hold the letters up on a flannel board or use foam letters, both upper and lowercase. Then have each child decide which letter they want to be. As each letter is dropped, those children sit down and clap for their letter.

There is a creature in my house   M-O-U-S-E, M-O-U-S-E, M-O-U-S-E

And MOUSE is what it's called.   MOUSE is what it's called, oh.

Here's our last book for today about mice.

Book

Mouse Count *or* **Mouse Paint**

By Ellen Stoll Walsh

or

Mouse Look Out!

By Judy White

If you are using either of the Walsh books, you can read it multiple times, asking the children to read with you if you have a big book. It is good to model multiple readings of books. Point out that the children actually begin to memorize these short stories. Again, the emphasis is on vocabulary, naming objects, and asking questions. If you are using White's book, encourage the children to chime in on the refrain.

Arts and Crafts

Materials needed: precut letters, paper, markers or crayons, and glue.

Have some precut letter Ms available. Give them to the children to paste onto paper. Suggest that they use the Ms to make mice. Each M can be one ear, leaving them to design the mice around it. Another mouse craft is to have a mouse shape on paper, and the children draw an M for the ears. Practice in the air first.

Closing Song

"Storytime Is at an End"

(Sing to the tune of "Twinkle, Twinkle Little Star")

Storytime has reached its end.
Say good-bye to all your friends.
We've read some books and had some fun.
Feels like we have just begun!

Storytime is over, friends.
We have really reached the end!

Closing

To the adults:

Point out letters and their sounds wherever you go. The most interesting letters for most children are the ones in their names, so begin there and have fun!

Take a second and remember why you are doing this! You want everyone to love books as much as you do . . . try to convey this idea with your enthusiasm.

IN, OUT, UP, DOWN, OVER, AND UNDER

Storytime Introduction

Welcome to storytime. My name is _____ and I am happy to see you here today. If everyone is ready, we'll begin with our hello song.

To the adults:

Parents, *narrative skills,* or the ability to describe things and events and to tell stories, is one of the six skills needed by children before formal reading instruction begins. Today we are going to use some familiar stories and retell them together, while emphasizing the stories' beginning, middle, and end. We are also going to be learning about prepositions such as *in, on, under, around,* and more! *Vocabulary,* or knowing the names of things, is another important skill that children need to have.

Opening Rhyme

Hello, Hello

Hello, hello.
Hello and how are you?
I'm fine, thanks.
I'm fine, thanks.
I'm hoping you are too!

Our first story is about a family's adventures while they go on a bear hunt.

					MC AJ
Print Motivation	Phonological Awareness	Vocabulary	Narrative Skills	Print Awareness	Letter Knowledge

Book

We're Going on a Bear Hunt

By Michael Rosen

Have fun with the motions and movements of the story. Repeating the actions will help the children remember the sequence, especially of the chorus: "You can't go over it . . ."

Now that we have read it through once, let's tell the story together by looking at the pictures [*or flannel board, or whatever else you choose to use*].

To the adults:

Having actions to go with a story often helps children remember the story when they retell it. This helps with narrative skills.

Song

"London Bridge Is Falling Down"

Suit actions to words.

London Bridge is falling down
Falling down, falling down.
London Bridge is falling down
My fair lady.

Take the keys and lock her up
Lock her up, lock her up.
Take the keys and lock her up
My fair lady.

Our next story is about a family of goats that has to cross a bridge to get food.

Book

The Three Billy Goats Gruff

By Peter Asbjornsen

Have fun with the voices of the Three Billy Goats Gruff and the troll as you read the story!

OK, let's pretend we are the Billy Goats Gruff.

Pretend to stomp over a bridge, etc. Ask questions that will help them to remember the story, like "Who went first over that bridge?"

In our next book we are going to look at pictures and talk about where things are located.

Books without words are an excellent source for dialogic reading. All of Tana Hoban's and Peter Spier's books, for example, work well with this. It can be especially good to use wordless books for those who are just starting dialogic reading. However, a book need not be wordless to do dialogic reading.

Book for Dialogic Reading

All About Where

or

Over, Under and Through

By Tana Hoban

Label the new vocabulary words as you go. Ask the questions as they pertain to each image. For example, on the first page of All About Where, *mention that the girls are jumping rope. Point out the cement wall and the sneakers, tennis, or athletic shoes. For questions, ask*

Where do you think these girls are?

How can you tell?

Which season is it?

How can you tell if they are happy or sad?

You can ask similar questions of some of the pictures that follow.

Activity

Materials needed: a long, thick piece of rope, string that can be taped to the floor, or cord, or hoola-hoops for small groups, and some lively music.

Lay the rope in a really big circle on the floor. Play some lively instrumental music. Tell the children that they need to follow your directions about getting on the circle, in the circle, outside of the circle, or under the circle. You can also jump over it.

To the adults:

Words that describe spatial concepts are hard for some children. Playing a game like this develops vocabulary and an understanding of these words.

Arts and Crafts

Play Pick-up Sticks.

Materials needed: colored straws and markers.

Give each family a few colored straws. Have the children tell the adults they came with which straw they want to pick up. Before picking it up, they need to describe its position. For example: "I want to pick up the blue straw. It is on top of the red straw, and beside the yellow straw."

Closing Song

"Storytime Is at an End"

(Sing to the tune of "Twinkle, Twinkle Little Star")

Storytime has reached its end.
Say good-bye to all your friends.
We've read some books and had some fun.
Feels like we have just begun!
Storytime is over, friends.
We have really reached the end!

Closing

To the adults:

As you go about your day together, talk about what you are doing. Summarize with your child what you did this morning, or yesterday. Talk about your activities in the order that they occurred. This will help your children to become familiar with the idea that their activities, like stories, have a sequence. See you next week!

Remember, the books are the key. All of your messages to the adults should reinforce your love of books and words.

IT'S COLD OUTSIDE

Storytime Introduction

Hello and welcome to storytime. I am happy to see you here with your children today. Find a spot to sit and we'll begin.

To the adults:

Research indicates that *phonological awareness*, or the ability to hear and play with the smaller sounds in words, is an important skill for children to know before they go to school. We are going to play around with words and their sounds during storytime today as we *segment* words, or break them into their syllables. We are also going to play with some rhyming words.

Opening Rhyme

Hello, Hello

Hello, hello.
Hello and how are you?
I'm fine, thanks.
I'm fine, thanks.
I'm hoping you are too!

Our first book tells the story of a winter's day adventure.

Book

The Snowy Day

By Ezra Jack Keats

Read the book through, making sure to point out any new words. Tell the children that you are going to take some of the words from the story to do the following activity.

Print Motivation	Phonological Awareness	Vocabulary	Narrative Skills	Print Awareness	Letter Knowledge

Activity

What's a winter word you remember from the story? Let's clap the number of syllables that each word has.

Choose words with varying numbers of syllables to get things started.

To the adults:

Clapping out words into their parts or syllables with all kinds of words, wherever you might be, helps your children's *phonological awareness.*

Let's see what happens to this family of snow people.

Book

Snowballs

By Lois Ehlert

Lois Ehlert's books are excellent for dialogic reading. Remember to point out new vocabulary words such as birch tree, *the names of birds, and all of the various things they use to decorate the snowballs. Some open-ended questions might include*

Where do you think they made the snow people?

What have they put on the snow dad to make it look like a dad?

How can you tell it is a snow mom?

What else might the squirrel eat?

What would have happened if the sun hadn't been so warm?

What names could you give the snow people?

Song

"I'm a Little Snowman"

(Sing to the tune of "I'm a Little Teapot")

I'm a little snowman, round and fat.   Pebbles for my buttons, a carrot for my nose
Here is my scarf and here is my hat!   Made of snow from head to toes.

Sing the song through once and then sing it again, with emphasis on the rhyming words. Ask the children to identify which words rhyme, or sound alike.

One of the hardest parts about winter is getting ready to go out and play. Let's see what happens when one child puts all of his winter clothes on.

Activity

Everyone stand up. Let's dress for a cold snowy day.

Pretend to put on various pieces of winter clothing, talking about each as you do it.

Now let's see what happens when some animals find a mitten.

Book

The Mitten

By Jan Brett

To the adults:

The ability to *rhyme* is another part of *phonological awareness*. We have done quite a bit with rhyme, so let's see if the children are able to come up with their own rhyming words. Try rhyming with your children as you go about your daily activities. Rhyme with their names, and the things you see and do.

Who can think of some words that sound like these words from the story? Let's say words that rhyme with them.

Activity

Pick out some words from the story. Say each word and have the children repeat it.

Materials needed: paper, crayons or markers, or an assortment of craft odds and ends.

Draw a picture of how you look when you go out in the snow. Or, here are some different materials you can use to decorate your own snow people! Draw a circle on the white paper and let's see who you make.

Closing Song

"Storytime Is at an End"

(Sing to the tune of "Twinkle, Twinkle Little Star")

Storytime has reached its end.
Say good-bye to all your friends.
We've read some books and had some fun.

Feels like we have just begun!
Storytime is over, friends.
We have really reached the end!

Closing

Have fun as you rhyme your way through the day. See you next week. Don't forget to get some books to share!

Since many adults imitate what we do, remember to keep book sharing fun.

WHAT'S IN A NAME?

Storytime Introduction

Hello and welcome to storytime. I am glad to see so many of you here again today. My name is _____. Let's get started!

To the adults:

Phonological awareness, or the ability to hear and play with the smaller sounds in words, is one of the most important skills that young children need before they begin formal reading instruction. Today we are going to explore *phonemic awareness*, which is being able to recognize and work with the individual sounds in words. It is part of phonological awareness.

Opening Rhyme

Hello to You

Hello, *[substitute child's or adult's name]*.

Hello and how are you?

I'm fine, thanks.

I'm fine, thanks.

I'm hoping you are too!

There are lots of different names here, aren't there? Let's clap out the different syllables, or parts of the words. For example, *Ma-ri-a* has three claps. *Joe* has just one.

The girl in our next story has a very long name—Chrysanthemum.

 Print Motivation   Phonological Awareness   Vocabulary   Narrative Skills   Print Awareness Letter Knowledge

Book

Chrysanthemum

By Kevin Henkes

After reading this book, go back through it and clap out the syllables of the different names, as you did in the previous activity.

To the adults:

Breaking words into their parts, or syllables, is called *segmentation*. Being able to segment words will help your children later as they are learning how to read.

Now let's try a name game song that's pretty hard to do! It's called "The Name Game."

Song

"The Name Game"

By Shirley Ellis

Remember "Shirley, Shirley, Bo-Birley"? Sing the song using as many names as you can. Include some names from Chrysanthemum.

Our next book is about a girl who has one of the longest names that I have ever heard.

Book

Catalina Magdalena Hoopensteiner Wallendiner Hogan Logan Bogan Was Her Name

By Tedd Arnold

"Catalina Magdalena Hoopensteiner Wallendiner Hogan Logan Bogan" is a song, too. Sing it if you know it or can follow along with the song in the book. Otherwise, you might use "John Jacob Jingleheimer Schmidt."

Song

"John Jacob Jingleheimer Schmidt"

Traditional, as sung on *Toddler Favorites, Too!*

John Jacob Jingleheimer Schmidt
I know it's my name too.
Whenever I go out

The people always shout
JOHN JACOB JINGLEHEIMER SCHMIDT
Na, na, na, na, na, na, na, na.

There are lots of ways to try to guess someone's name. In *Rumpelstiltskin* we see what some of them are.

Book

Rumpelstiltskin

By Paul Galdone

This is a good one to read dialogically because it is so visually rich. Remember to label the words they might not know, like miller and spinning wheel. Possible questions might be

How would you feel if you were put in a room with straw and told to turn it into gold?

What do you do when you think something is too hard, or too difficult for you to do alone?

What else could she have done to find other names?

Activity

Let's play a game with name riddles. Remember in the story that the queen had to guess Rumpelstiltskin's name? Here is a guessing name game for us to play. Listen carefully.

Will the children whose names start with the sound /b/ please stand up? [Ben, Brittany]

Will the children who have the sound /t/ in their name please stand? [Tamika, Tom]

Do this for as long as needed to include all the children.

To the adults:

Phonemic awareness deals with the sounds of spoken language. In order to read phonetically, children need *phonemic awareness*, hearing the sounds, which is why it is important to work on these skills with your children.

Closing Song

"Storytime Is at an End"

(Sing to the tune of "Twinkle, Twinkle Little Star")

Storytime has reached its end.
Say good-bye to all your friends.
We've read some books and had some fun.

Feels like we have just begun!
Storytime is over, friends.
We have really reached the end!

Closing

Thanks for coming, and have fun playing name games this week!

Everyone responds to smiles and laughter. Make both a part of storytime.

FINE FEATHERED FRIENDS

Storytime Introduction

Hello, my name is _____. Welcome to storytime. I am happy to see you here with your children today. Let's all get settled in and we'll get started.

To the adults:

Letter knowledge, or knowing the names of letters, how they look, and their sounds is one of the six skills that children need to become fluent readers. Make sure that when you talk about letters, you use both the letter name and the letter sound. Today we are going to look at our feathered friends, featuring the letter *F* and the /f/ sound.

Opening Rhyme

Hello, Hello

Hello, hello.

Hello and how are you?

I'm fine, thanks.

I'm fine, thanks.

I'm hoping you are too!

Our first book is a story about a cat who tries to catch a bird for lunch, but all he gets is feathers!

Book

Feathers for Lunch

By Lois Ehlert

Talk a little about feathers before reading the book. Explain that while some animals have fur, birds have feathers to keep them warm. Repeat the word feather *a couple of times, drawing out the /f/ sound.*

Print Motivation	Phonological Awareness	Vocabulary	Narrative Skills	Print Awareness	Letter Knowledge

What is the first sound that you hear in the word *feather*? That's right, it's /f/. What is the sound that this letter *F* makes? *[Hold up a cutout of the letter F.]* What other words can you think of which start with that sound?

To the adults:

Research indicates that children benefit from learning that letters are different from each other and that they have different names and sounds at the same time.

Song

"Listen to These Words"

(Sing to the tune of "Old MacDonald Had a Farm")

What's the sound that these words share?
Listen to these words.
Fat and *feather* are these words
Tell me what you've heard (/f/, /f/, /f/).
With a /f/ /f/ here, and a /f/ /f/ there
Here a /f/, there a /f/, everywhere a /f/ /f/.
/f/ is the sound that these words share
Listen for the sound!

Here are some others words you could use: fox, fish, frog, fly, farmer.

We are going to read about a duck and an adventure it had one day.

Book

One Duck Stuck

By Phyllis Root

or

Duck in the Truck

(or any book in the series)

By Jez Alborough

We are going to read the book all the way through, and then go back through it to find the words that rhyme, or sound alike. OK, now let's find the rhyming words. That's right, *duck* and *stuck* rhyme. Let's sing them with a rhyming song.

Song

"These Words Rhyme"

(Sing to the tune of "Skip to My Lou")

Duck, stuck, these words rhyme.
Duck, stuck, these words rhyme.
Duck, stuck, these words rhyme.
We're rhyming all the time!

Look through the book and find other sets of rhyming words.

To the adults:

Rhyme is an important part of *phonological awareness* too. It helps children decode words as they learn new words and learn how to read.

Book

Goodnight My Duckling

By Nancy Tafuri

or

Farmer Duck

By Martin Waddell

Pre-identify vocabulary words. The grass near the pond is called reeds. Mention the parts of the duck's body, pointing out their beaks, their feet with flippers, that act as paddles. For Waddell's book, talk about the gloomy day, how the animals feel, what it is like to be bossed around.

？？

Next we are going to sing a song about some ducks.

Song

"Five Little Ducks"

Five little ducks went out to play
Over the hills and far away.
Mother Duck said, "Quack, quack, quack"
Four little ducks came running back.

Four little ducks went out to play
Over the hills and far away.
Mother Duck said, "Quack, quack, quack"
Three little ducks came running back.

Three little ducks went out to play
Over the hills and far away.
Mother Duck said, "Quack, quack, quack"
Two little ducks came running back.

Two little ducks went out to play
Over the hills and far away.
Mother Duck said, "Quack, quack, quack"
One little duck came running back.

One little duck went out to play
Over the hills and far away.
Mother Duck said, "Quack, quack, quack"
Five little ducks came running back.

You might ask what other numbers start with the /f/ sound. You can try float *or* flap, *using appropriate gestures.*

Our next book is about birds flying.

Book

Ducks Fly

By Lydia Dabcovich

or

Are You My Mother?

By P. D. Eastman

Or read any book you like that features birds and flight, including titles on migration.

Now for a song about flying.

Song

Fly, Fly, Fly Along

(Sing to the tune of "Row, Row, Row Your Boat")

Extend your arms out, pretending to fly.

Fly, fly, fly, along
Fly along with me.
Faster, faster, faster, faster!
I'm flying, come and see.

Show them how to draw the letter F *in the air with a certain part of their hand that starts with the letter* F. *Yes, their* fingers.

Arts and Crafts

Materials needed: feathers, paper, glue, markers or crayons.

Tell the children that they are going to make their own feathered friends, using the feathers provided. They can name their creature, or not, as they choose.

Closing Song

"Storytime Is at an End"

(Sing to the tune of "Twinkle, Twinkle Little Star")

Storytime has reached its end.

Say good-bye to all your friends.

We've read some books and had some fun.

Feels like we have just begun!

Storytime is over, friends.

We have really reached the end!

Closing

See you all next time! Enjoy playing with letters and letter sounds. Remember to play these letter games only as long as they're fun.

Bring everyone into your storytime before you begin. Remind them, and your-self, that you are about to enter the magical world of books.

ON THE FARM

Storytime Introduction

Hello and welcome to storytime. I am glad that you were able to brave the weather today! Let's get comfortable and ready to begin.

To the adults:

We have looked at a number of skills that young children need before entering school. Today we are going to be doing a combination of skill development, including *phonological awareness* and *letter knowledge.*

Remember to point to the chart or handout, or whatever it is that you use to emphasize the skills.

Opening Rhyme

Hello, Hello

Hello, hello.
Hello and how are you?
I'm fine, thanks.
I'm fine, thanks.
I'm hoping you are too!

Now, let's sing our welcome song; part of it is going to be sung with animal voices. Let's have a sheep help out first. What does a sheep say? *Baaa*, that's right! It will sound like this *[substitute all of the words with sheep talk]*:

Baaa baaaa. Baaa, baaaa.   Baaa baaaa, baa.
Baaa baa, baaa baaaaa baa baaa?   Baaa baa baaa baaaaa baa baaa!
Baaa baaaa, baa.

Now as a cow *[mooooo]*. . .
Now as a donkey *[hee-haw]*. . .

Print Motivation	Phonological Awareness	Vocabulary	Narrative Skills	Print Awareness	Letter Knowledge

Our next book is about some of the animals that live on a farm.

Book for Dialogic Reading

Big Red Barn

By Margaret Wise Brown

Or use any book you like which has pictures of farm life. (You might want to use a nonfiction title.) Pre-identify the vocabulary words that you are emphasizing. Words like silo and the different names of baby animals can be used. Point out that a baby duck is a duckling, a foal is a baby horse, and so on. Ask open-ended questions after labeling the new words. Encourage the use of the vocabulary words when you are jointly summarizing or retelling the story. For example:

What is the baby horse, or foal, doing?
What do you think the farmer keeps in this silo?
What do you think the silo looks like?

Song

"B-I-N-G-O"

This old favorite is being done with a twist to incorporate letter play. Instead of just singing the song, have the letters in "BINGO" cut out of felt. Put up all the letters and take them down as each letter is re-placed by a clap of hands. Another variation of this activity is to have the children stand up and make each letter with their bodies. Then let each child choose a letter to shape themselves into. Have them sit down as their letter is dropped.

To the adults:

Children learn best by doing. Remember that letter play should be meaningful. Show letters in the context of objects and words that they know. Use letters they can touch or play with.

Our next book shows us what happens when farm animals become sick.

Book

Barnyard Song

By Rhonda Gowler Greene

Or read any book with animal sounds.

Activity

Say It Slow, Say It Fast

Play the "Say It Slow, Say It Fast" game with two farm animals—for example, a donkey and a rooster. Use play dough or picture cards to demonstrate the game. Hold up the card with the picture of the donkey. Say this is a picture of a donkey. "Say that word with me. Now we'll say it slowly: don-key." As you say it slowly, hold up one half of the card at a time. Then say it again fast and hold up both halves of the card together.

I'll demonstrate the "Say It Slow, Say It Fast" game and you all say the words with me. First we'll try it with *donkey*, and then with *rooster*. Now let's make up some silly words. Here's the *don* from *donkey* and the *ster* from *rooster*. Put them together: *don-ster*, or *roo-key*. You can play this game at home, too.

To the adults:

Research has shown that *phonological awareness*, or the ability to hear the smaller sounds in words, can be taught and learned. Activities like the "Say It Slow, Say It Fast" game have been shown to help develop this skill. Playing with words and their parts helps children develop phonological awareness.

Now let's see how the barnyard wakes up in the morning.

Book

Rise and Shine!

By Nancy White Carlstrom

Or read any rhyming farm book.

To play with the rhyme, make up riddles based on the different kinds of animals that are in the book. You could also use some of the phrases from the book. Some riddles based on farm animals might include

I am thinking of an animal that lives on a farm . . .

It swims in a pond and rhymes with *luck*.   *duck*

Its babies are called foals and it rhymes with *course*.   *horse*

Craft Activity

Materials needed: paper, scissors, crayons or markers.

Have the children make their own cards for the "Say It Slow, Say It Fast" game. Some possible words include donkey, chicken, bunny, rabbit, chicken, rooster, puppy, *and* piglet.

Closing Song

"Storytime Is at an End"

(Sing to the tune of "Twinkle, Twinkle Little Star")

Storytime has reached its end

Say good-bye to all your friends.

We've read some books and had some fun

Feels like we have just begun!

Storytime is over, friends

We have really reached the end!

Closing

To the adults:

Take advantage of every opportunity to play with words. Make up riddles or play "I Spy" as you wait in the doctor's office, or anywhere else. Not only will your children learn, but it will also lessen the boredom and tension of waiting!

Before you begin, remember to thank everyone for being with you. Everyone appreciates being appreciated! A sincere greeting and a smile set the stage for enjoyment.

CHANGES

Storytime Introduction

Hello. My name is _____. Thanks for bringing your children to the library today. Let's get ready to begin today's adventure!

To the adults:

Narrative skills, or the ability to describe things and events and to tell stories, is one of the skills that children need to have before beginning formal reading instruction. Another skill is *vocabulary*, or knowing the names of things. By reading to children in a way that engages them, we can help them develop these skills. This way of reading to a child is called *dialogic reading*.

Opening Song

Hello, Hello

Hello, hello.
Hello and how are you?
I'm fine, thanks.
I'm fine, thanks.
I'm hoping you are too!

Our first story shows us what happens to a seed over time. It is about how it changes and turns into something else.

Print Motivation

Phonological Awareness

Vocabulary

Narrative Skills

Print Awareness

Letter Knowledge

Book for Dialogic Reading

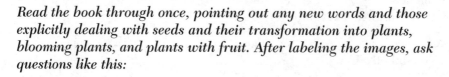

The Carrot Seed

By Ruth Kraus

or

Growing Vegetable Soup

By Lois Ehlert

Read the book through once, pointing out any new words and those explicitly dealing with seeds and their transformation into plants, blooming plants, and plants with fruit. After labeling the images, ask questions like this:

What is this called?   *Pointing to a seed*

What does a plant need to grow?

Where have you seen plants?

What kinds have you seen?

Where could you plant a seed?

Song

"From Seed to Flower"

(Sing to the tune of
"This Is the Way We Wash Our Clothes")

Suit actions to words.

This is the way we plant the seed, plant the seed, plant the seed

This is the way we plant the seed

So early in the morning.

Repeat with these substitutions:

. . . we water the seed . . .   . . . the plant comes up . . .

. . . the rain comes down . . .   . . . the flower blooms . . . on a spring day.

. . . the sun does shine . . .

You saw how the seed changed into a plant and how the plant produced flowers. What else changes? How have you changed since you were a baby? Let's see what happens in our next book.

Book

Te Amo, Bebe, Little One

By Lisa Wheeler

Or read another book about a child growing up.

Young children can easily relate to books about babies. They love talking about when they were little, and what they could or couldn't do! Take advantage of their interest, and encourage dialogue. Ask questions about what they were like when they were "little." Encouraging them to talk supports narrative skills.

How big were you when you were a baby?

What did you do when you were little?

What can you do now that you could not do when you were little?

Poem

When I Was a Baby

When I was a baby, a baby, a baby

When I was a baby, I talked like this:

BA, DA, BA.

When I was a baby, a baby, a baby

When I was a baby, I ate like this.   *Suck on your thumb as if it were a bottle*

When I was a baby, a baby, a baby

When I was a baby, I crawled like this.   *Crawl*

Now I am a big kid, a big kid, a big kid

Now I am a big kid, I talk like this:

Hi!

I eat like this   *Gesture of eating with a spoon*

And I walk like this   *Walk in place*

Because I am not a BABY!

What else changes?

Here we have a book about the seasons *[or the weather]*.

Book

Choose a book about the seasons, weather, moving, adding a family member, or anything that evokes the idea of change. Use a book such as The Cloud Book *by Tomie De Paola, or* The Seasons of Arnold's Apple Tree *by Gail Gibbons.*

Activity

Lots of things can change, including the way we do things! Are you ready? Watch. I have an invisible thing in my hand. I am going to make it into something, then you guess what it is. Then watch as I change it into something else.

Start with something easy, like shaping and bouncing a ball. Let them guess. Then make it small and it can become chewing gum. Then pull it very long and it becomes a jump rope. Let children guess as you pantomime the words.

Book

Color Dance

By Ann Jonas

or

Little Blue and Little Yellow

By Leo Lionni

Or use any other book about colors and how they change when combined.

Many children are in the process of learning colors. You can ask questions about the colors they are wearing, their favorite colors, the colors of their rooms, etc. Talk about how colors change when they are mixed *or* blended *together.*

To the adults:

Reading this way gives us lots of opportunities to help our children expand their vocabularies. It is easier for them to read words with which they are familiar. The more words they know, the better!

??

Arts and Crafts

Materials needed: paper, crayons, markers, colored chalk, or paint.

Explain that you are going to look at how colors change when they are combined. Encourage them to draw a rainbow, or to just play around with the colors.

Closing Song

"Storytime Is at an End"

(Sing to the tune of
"Twinkle, Twinkle Little Star")

Storytime has reached its end.
Say good-bye to all your friends.
We've read some books and had some fun.
Feels like we have just begun!
Storytime is over, friends.
We have really reached the end!

Closing

To the adults:

I look forward to seeing you next week. Try reading the books you borrow the way we did here today, and let me know how it went when I see you next week.

Take a second and remember why you are doing this! You want everyone to love books as much as you do . . . try to convey this idea with your enthusiasm.

BUTTERFLIES

Storytime Introduction

Hello. My name is _____. I am pleased to see you all here today at storytime. We are about to get started, so come on in and find a place to sit.

To the adults:

During the storytime today we are going to be looking at some different ways of helping your children develop their early literacy skills. Notice how I point out the words on various pages, making sure that the children see that I am reading the written words. Knowing that we read from left to right across the page in English is part of *print awareness*, one of the skills children need to have before formal reading instruction begins. We are also going to play with and talk about the letter *B* and the sound *b*. *Letter knowledge* is another skill that young children need before entering school.

Opening Rhyme

Hello, Hello

Hello, hello.
Hello and how are you?
I'm fine, thanks.
I'm fine, thanks.
I'm hoping you are too!

Today we are going to share some books about butterflies.

> *Spend a few minutes talking about the theme. Ask questions that cannot be answered with yes or no, similar to the questions you ask in dialogic reading. Some questions might be*

Where do butterflies live?
Where have you seen butterflies?

Print Motivation	Phonological Awareness	Vocabulary	Narrative Skills	Print Awareness	Letter Knowledge

Our first book about butterflies is Eric Carle's *The Very Hungry Caterpillar*. How can a book about caterpillars also be about butterflies? Let's find out!

Book with Flannel Board

The Very Hungry Caterpillar

By Eric Carle

> *Read the book. Use the flannel board and have the children help to retell the story.*

What did the caterpillar turn into? *A butterfly*, that's right. What is the first sound in the word *butterfly*? *B*, that's right. It is the sound that the letter *B* makes. It looks like this. **Hold up a cutout of the letter B and have them trace the letter in the air with their fingers.**

For out next book, we are going to read a nonfiction, or true story, about butterflies.

To the adults:

We help to motivate our children to read when we can follow their interests. It is fun, and educational, to use nonfiction books along with stories. The nonfiction books are in a different part of the library than the storybooks. I will be happy to help you find books about things you and your child are interested in at any time!

Book

> *Use any nonfiction title written for young children. Run your finger under the title and author as you say them. You can read the words as written, or if the book is too wordy, just talk about the pictures. Point out one or two new words, and encourage the children to repeat the new words that were used in the book.*

To the adults:

You might have noticed that I ran my finger under the words of the book's title and author. This simple action helps children know that it is the words we are reading, that we read from left to right, and from top to bottom. These concepts are all part of *print awareness*.

> *Make your hands into the shape of a butterfly by locking your two thumbs together and holding your other fingers together, to form a butterfly.*

Oh you see that butterfly!

Action Rhyme

Oh My! Butterfly!

Using your butterfly hands, land on parts of the body.

Oh me, oh my!
Get off of my _____
You butterfly!

??

Name the various body parts that the butterfly flies onto, such as nose, stomach, knee. Ask the children to join in with you. Continue for as long as you wish. When it is time, use the following rhyme to finish:

Oh me, oh my!

It's time to get going

You butterfly!

Get going . . . bye, bye.

As you say "bye, bye," have the butterfly "wings" turn into a wave good-bye.

Let's take another look at some butterflies.

Book

Where Butterflies Grow

By Joanne Ryder

or

Waiting for Wings

By Lois Ehlert

To the adults:

Children need to know both the letter name and the letter sound. Research indicates it is best to teach the name and the sound of the letter together. Learning about letters with crafts and activities is more fun than drilling children on the letters. Here's a craft using the letter *B*.

Arts and Crafts

Materials needed: letter Bs, paper, glue, crayons or markers.

Have you noticed how one side of the wing of a butterfly looks just like the other side? Look what happens if we take the letter *B* and put them back to back. It looks like butterfly wings! Glue the wings on to the paper and make your own beautiful butterflies!

Closing Song

"Storytime Is at an End"

(Sing to the tune of
"Twinkle, Twinkle Little Star")

Storytime has reached its end.
Say good-bye to all your friends.
We've read some books and had some fun.
Feels like we have just begun!
Storytime is over, friends.
We have really reached the end!

Closing

To the adults:

As you go through the week with your children, take advantage of signs, symbols, and all kinds of print. Talk with your youngsters about the letters they see. Print is everywhere! Have fun as you discover it together. And keep your eyes peeled for that letter *B*!

10

Build Your Own Early Literacy Storytimes

You have read about, and hopefully absorbed, the importance of empowering adults to lay the foundation for their children to become fluent readers. You have read through the sample storytimes for a variety of ages. Now you are ready to use this information to re-create your own storytimes.

Where to Start?

The best place to start is with one of your own storytimes! Choose a storytime you have done and feel comfortable with.

Get Ready to Build on It!

To build on your own storytime, if you like, use the "Storytime Planning Sheet" in appendix C. (See figure 10-1 for a completed sample.) Follow the first three steps on the planning sheet: use a storytime you enjoy; choose a skill or aspect of a skill to highlight (use the skills list on the planning sheet); decide what to say to the adults. In the planning sheet's first column, list the title of the book, song, or rhyme. In the second column, write down your early literacy messages to the adults.

FIGURE 10-1   *Sample Storytime Planning Sheet*

Storytime Planning Sheet

You may find it easier to highlight just one skill, or even just one aspect of one skill, during any one storytime (for example, only the rhyming aspect of phonological awareness).

All storytimes *must* model print motivation, the enjoyment of books and reading, whether or not you specifically articulate information about print motivation.

1. *Fill in your storytime plan* in the order you intend to do it. (You may do some modification depending on ways you highlight a skill.)

2. *Choose a skill* or an aspect of a skill to highlight. (Use list below.)

3. *Fill in what you will say* related to the skill (using "What Can I Say: From Skill to Parent/Caregiver" in appendix C as a guide, if you like) for the following:

    the opening early literacy tip

    one or two messages to adults during the storytime

    the closing

Skills

Choose one or two skills from the list below. Depending on what you want to say, you can highlight one aspect of a skill or highlight the skill in general. (You will *not* have a highlighted skill for every component.)

- ☐ Print Motivation: Enjoyment of Books
- ☐ Phonological Awareness
    - ☐ Rhyming
    - ☐ Breaking words apart and putting them together
    - ☐ Hearing beginning sounds/alliteration
- ☐ Print Awareness
    - ☐ With books
    - ☐ In the environment
- ☐ Vocabulary
    - ☐ Introducing new words
    - ☐ Explaining (not replacing) words
    - ☐ Adding new meanings to familiar words
- ☑ Narrative Skills
    - ☑ Retelling stories
    - ☐ Retelling events
    - ☐ Adding descriptions
- ☐ Letter Knowledge
    - ☐ Same and different
    - ☐ Letter shapes
    - ☐ Letter names
    - ☐ Letter sounds

FIGURE 10-1 (cont.)

STORYTIME COMPONENT	COMMENT TO ADULTS BASED ON RESEARCH
Early literacy tip	*Narrative skills, the ability to describe things and events and to tell stories, is one of the six early literacy skills that researchers say are important for laying a foundation for reading. During this storytime, I'll be highlighting some of the things you can do to support this skill while having fun together.*
Opening rhyme: Open, Shut Them	
Talk about theme— catching and being caught	*Let your child talk about the book from looking at the cover before you even start reading. This gives your child time to talk and tell you things he knows. This supports narrative skills.*
Book: *Jump, Frog, Jump,* by Robert Kalan	
Movement activity: jump like frogs	
Book: *Blue Sea*, by Robert Kalan	
Use flannel board to have children retell story	*There are many ways to encourage your child to retell a story (which develops narrative skills). It's a lot of fun. Don't worry if your child does not get every detail.*
Finger play: 1, 2, 3, 4, 5 Once I caught a fish alive	

Book: *The Gunniwolf*, by
   Wilhemina Harper,
   with puppets
	Using puppets is another way to encourage children to retell a story and make up some of their own! (Whisper: "Narrative skills")

Good-bye song: "The More We Get Together"	

Take-home craft: For *Blue Sea*—
   construction paper with
   different-size holes. Cutouts
   of different-size fish to go
   through the holes.	

Closing to adults Display/handouts	*Thank you for coming. I hope you'll enjoy listening to your child retell stories you share with them. I have displayed some books with repeated phrases and happenings that work well for retelling. Feel free to check them out. There is some early literacy information on the table which you can take as well.*

Choose the Skill
or Skills to Highlight

Now look over your storytime and think of the six early literacy skills: print motivation, phonological awareness, vocabulary, narrative skills, print awareness, and letter knowledge. Think broadly. Just because a book rhymes doesn't mean you have to highlight rhyme as a skill. You can use a rhyming book to talk about vocabulary or letter knowledge.

Use the Aids Provided Here

Figure 10-2, "General Ideas for Each Skill," will give you some ideas of what you can do with the elements you already have to highlight different skills.

Use Ideas from
the Sample Storytimes

If you found something you liked in the sample storytimes, you can add or replace something you have used with something new. Remember, *you don't need to incorporate all of the suggestions from one sample into one storytime*. They are meant to help you think differently about what you are doing, and to point the way to different kinds of activities that are fun and easy to do. After all, these are *your* storytimes! The books that we suggest are simply that—suggestions.

The icons in the right-hand column of the sample storytimes can help you identify the use of an element if you are looking for something to add to your storytime. Do not feel constricted by these aids, however. Use your imagination and your creativity. Write down your thoughts on the blank "Storytime Planning Sheet" in appendix C if you find it helpful.

What to Say to the Adults

For some of us, speaking to the adults is the most difficult part of this kind of storytime, but being prepared will give you confidence. Figure 10-3, "What Can I Say? A Sampling," may help you focus on what you can say for one or two of the components in your storytime. Also, refer to "What Can I Say? From Skill to Parent/Caregiver," in appendix C, to help you think about what to say about the skill you have chosen. Feel free to reword the messages in figure 10-3 and in appendix C to make them comfortable to you while still including the relationship to the skill. Note where in your storytime you will make a comment (a sentence or two) to the adults. To make yourself more at ease, write the phrases you are going to say on a piece of sticky paper or an index card and attach it to the back of a book until you become more comfortable with the phrases. Make sure that you know when you are going to speak directly to the adults. As time goes on this will all seem natural to you.

FIGURE 10-2   A Sampling of General Ideas for Each Early Literacy Skill

SKILL	DESCRIPTION	POSSIBLE IDEAS
Print motivation	Having a joy of and interest in reading and books	Use the storytime introduction to describe the skill. Model the fun of reading and of playing with language. Clap at the end of each book to celebrate the joy of reading it. Enjoy the book and the interaction yourself. Keep children involved. Encourage the parents to let children hold books and turn the pages. Have children and adults join in at appropriate parts. A choral reading with a big book is especially good with parents of young children. When children chime in, tell them they are doing a good job helping you read. Use nonfiction of interest to the children and that you enjoy. Have a comfortable setting where adults and children share time talking and looking at books together. As part of take-home or end-of-storytime activity, emphasize this skill. Have a selection of favorite picture books displayed in the storytime area and encourage adults to choose as many as they want to share at home.
Phonological awareness	Rhyming Breaking words apart and putting word chunks together Hearing beginning sounds	Use the storytime introduction to describe the skill. Use books that rhyme. Emphasize some rhyming words, using a song such as "These Words Rhyme" or "Rhyme Along" to do so (see sample storytimes). After reading a book, take a word from a book (whether the book itself is a rhyming book or not) and play with one of the words in the story: what rhymes with it, what words start with the same sound as your chosen word. Use books with different sounds and noises, for example, the sounds animals make. Use Mother Goose or other rhymes and poetry. Sing songs and repeat them in the same storytime and in later storytimes. Clap the syllables of the children's names and the theme word. After reading a book, choose a word or two from the story and clap out the syllables in the words. Change the initial sound of words in a song. Adapt "Apples and Bananas." Change the initial sound in a repeated phrase in the story. Play around with silly (nonsense) words; then it is not hard to rhyme or change starting sounds.

SKILL	DESCRIPTION	POSSIBLE IDEAS
		Use flannel boards or puppets to present rhymes and songs.
		Let children fill in rhyming words in stories and songs.
		Do finger plays.
		Play word games like "I Spy" using rhymes or beginning sounds.
		As part of take-home or end-of-storytime activity, emphasize this skill.
Vocabulary	Introducing new words Explaining (not replacing) unfamiliar words Introducing less-familiar meanings to familiar words; same word can have different meanings	Use the storytime introduction to describe the skill. Take time before reading the book to describe an unfamiliar word. Sometimes one word has several meanings. Even though it is used one way in the book, you can talk about its other meanings before or after reading the story. Pick out a word from the book, rhyme, or song. For an unfamiliar word, explain the word; for a familiar word, introduce a less-familiar word. Add descriptive words as you talk about pictures. Many Mother Goose rhymes have words not used in conversation; point out a few of these. Have children repeat less-familiar words. Use nonfiction as a source of materials that offer new words. Demonstrate dialogic reading. Talk about theme, adding less-familiar words and explaining them. Bring in the real items of pictures shown in the book. After reading a book, go back to an interesting picture and talk about it, adding less-familiar words. Choose books that offer children new experiences in an understandable way. Books have many words that we do not use in daily conversation. Demonstrate this with one of the books you use. As part of take-home or end-of-storytime activity, emphasize this skill.
Narrative skills	Retelling stories Retelling events Adding descriptions Telling stories or events in sequence	Use the storytime introduction to describe the skill. Take time before the book to talk about an unfamiliar word. For babies, demonstrate how we read with them, allowing time for baby to babble a reply. Have children and adults say repeated words along with you as you read a book.

(cont.)

FIGURE 10-2 (cont.)

SKILL	DESCRIPTION	POSSIBLE IDEAS
Narrative skills (cont.)		Have children do a motion as they repeat a phrase along with you as you read a book.
		Repeat a book used in a previous storytime but with different theme to bring out different aspects of the story.
		Use fewer books and expand on them more.
		Retell the story with puppets, flannel board, props, or creative dramatics.
		Allow time for children to talk about the theme. "Tell the person next to you something about (bears)." Have a way to draw the children's attention back to you.
		Demonstrate dialogic reading.
		As part of take-home or end-of-storytime activity, emphasize this skill.
Print awareness	Knowing how to handle a book	Use the storytime introduction to describe the skill.
	Knowing that we read the text, not the pictures	Write rhymes and songs on flip charts and occasionally run finger under print.
	Knowing that, in English, we read from left to right and from the top to the bottom of the page	Run finger under title or repeated phrase or both.
		Use a big book and run finger under print from time to time.
	Understanding that print is all around us	Use a big book to do a choral reading, following print with finger without interfering with story.
	Understanding that print has meaning	Talk about environmental print (signs, newspapers).
		Include books with writing as part of the story (for example, *Bunny Cakes*, by Rosemary Wells).
		Include books with signs in the pictures and varying print orientations (for example, *My Friend Rabbit*, by Eric Rohmann).
		Use name tags for both children and adults.
		Point out when illustrations show signs or print around them.
		Start with book oriented the wrong way, and play around with it.
		Point out interesting endpapers.
		Write repeated word to add to a flannel board rhyme or story.
		Allow participants to write their own names. Parents can write child's name underneath if necessary.
		As part of take-home or end-of-storytime activity, emphasize this skill.
Letter knowledge	Knowing names of letters	Use the storytime introduction to describe the skill.
	Knowing that letters are different from each other	Point out shapes.
	Knowing that the same letter can look different	Let children *feel* different shapes.
		Give opportunities to have children match and see how things are alike and different (e.g., matching games on flannel boards).

SKILL	DESCRIPTION	POSSIBLE IDEAS
Letter knowledge (cont.)	Knowing that letters make sounds	Use large foam letters during storytime. Have children make letters with their bodies. Have children make letters with their fingers. Use manual alphabet for some words in theme or book. Use an alphabet book even if you don't go through all the letters. Talk about the first letter in your theme; what does the letter look like? Give children the opportunity to write after storytime or encourage it as an at-home activity. Use variations of the "B-I-N-G-O" song, perhaps with your theme. Use name tags for both children and adults. Allow participants to write their own names. Parent can write child's name underneath if necessary. Have letters in a variety of formats and sizes available for after storytime (foam, felt, magnet, carpet squares). As part of take-home or end-of-storytime activity, emphasize this skill.

FIGURE 10-3   What Can I Say?

Sometimes when we are trying to become comfortable with new information, it helps to have a kind of script of what we want to tell others until we have internalized what we have learned, and this figure offers suggestions.

Perhaps some of these suggestions will be helpful. They are *not* meant to be limiting. They are meant as a beginning, with each of us learning new information as time goes by and sharing it with parents/caregivers. One storytime element may have more than one skill associated with it. When you do it one time, you can emphasize one skill, and when you do it at another storytime, you can emphasize a different skill.

You may be highlighting different aspects of early literacy to parents and caregivers at different programs. The following chart shows how you can use the same book or rhyme to highlight different skills at different storytimes. Be flexible.

ET = Early Talker (newborn–2 years)   **T** = Talker (2–3 years)   **PR** = Prereader (4–5 years)

STORYTIME COMPONENT	EARLY LITERACY SKILL	COMMUNICATION TO PARENT/CAREGIVER
Bounce/Song "Horsey, Horsey" song and activity, from *Lively Songs and Lullabies*, by Carol Rose Duane. **(ET)** "Five Little Ducks," from *Rise and Shine*, by Raffi, or other song that has some words with more than one syllable **(T, PR)**	Phonological awareness	Aside from being fun, singing songs with your baby or toddler helps them hear words being broken up into smaller sounds. This skill is part of phonological awareness and later helps them with reading. Singing is fun! Don't worry if you don't have perfect pitch!

(cont.)

FIGURE 10-3 (cont.)

STORYTIME COMPONENT	EARLY LITERACY SKILL	COMMUNICATION TO PARENT/CAREGIVER
Bounce / Song (cont.)		In songs, each syllable has a different note. Without really thinking about it, children are hearing words being broken down into parts. This helps them when they have to sound out words.
	Narrative skills	After you sing a song, talk with your child about what it's like to ride a horse or feed the ducks. Allow time for your child to babble or talk back. This encourages narrative skills.
Song/Body parts "Turn-a-Round," from *Getting to Know Myself*, by Hap Palmer **(T)**	Phonological awareness	Songs help children hear words broken down into syllables because there is a different note for each syllable. Children are hearing words broken down into parts. This skill is part of phonological awareness and later helps them with reading.
	Vocabulary	This song points out parts of the body, helping children learn vocabulary. When you do the song again and again, you can substitute different parts of the body so your child hears even more words. Having a large vocabulary, knowing the names of things, is one of the skills children need when they later learn to sound out words.
Song with parts of body "Little Flea," from *Wee Sing for Baby*, by Pamela Beall **(ET)**	Vocabulary	Talking with your baby or singing to him throughout the day exposes your child to a lot of language. Children who are spoken to a lot during their early years, right from birth, end up knowing many more words than when parents speak to their children very little. Even though your child cannot speak, it is important to talk with him or her. It's critical to language development.
	Phonological awareness	Even while you are diapering your baby, you can sing this song. Singing songs helps children hear that words are broken down into smaller parts, which helps them develop phonological awareness.

STORYTIME COMPONENT	EARLY LITERACY SKILL	COMMUNICATION TO PARENT/CAREGIVER
Theme talk Today we're having stories about picnics. Have any of you ever been on a picnic? What did you do? **(PR)**	Narrative skills	Let children tell you what a picnic is or what happened when they went on a picnic. This helps to develop their narrative skills, the ability to retell events.
	Letter knowledge	*You can hold up a foam letter p and say that picnic starts with p. Say, "Let's fill up a picnic basket with different things. What shall we put in? Carrots, paper plates, peanut-butter sandwiches, yum yum. Paper and plates start with p! So does peanut butter. What else shall we take on the picnic?" See how you can incorporate knowing letters into whatever you are talking about.* This is a game you can play at home, too, which develops letter knowledge.
Retell with flannel board *Blue Sea*, by Robert Kalan, then children help you retell with flannel board **(T, PR)**	Narrative skills	Once children are familiar with a story, let them tell you what happens. This improves their narrative skills, or the ability to retell events. Developing this early literacy skill helps later with reading comprehension.
	Vocabulary	This book has words that talk about the concept of size. Talk about some less-familiar words related to size and relative size. This builds your child's vocabulary, one of the six early literacy skills.
Introductory activity How many people are in storytime today? Let's count noses, all together. We have twenty-seven nice noses today! *[Hold up foam letter n]* Here's an *n* for all those noses! **(PR)**	Letter knowledge	Name the letters and their sounds based on things you do throughout the day.
	Print awareness	Using signs, like stop signs, when you are driving or walking around helps children learn letters.
Board book *Baby's Toys*, by Mark Ricklen **(ET)**	Print awareness	When you use a board book with nice clear pictures like this, you can point to the picture and show your baby the real thing. For example, point to the picture of the toy truck in the book and then show your child a toy truck. This helps your

(cont.)

FIGURE 10-3 (cont.)

STORYTIME COMPONENT	EARLY LITERACY SKILL	COMMUNICATION TO PARENT/CAREGIVER
Board book (cont.)	Print awareness (cont.)	child understand that pictures represent real things. Later your baby will learn that print represents words that represent real things. Let your baby/child turn the pages. He or she is learning how a book works.
	Print motivation	It is natural for babies to bite on books. This is how they learn about their world. You can just gently take the book from his or her mouth and open the book to show him or her the pictures. Show him or her how fun it is to share a book together, even if it is just for a couple of minutes at a time. A book is a toy at this age.
Nonfiction book True book about trains **(PR)**	Print motivation	Some children prefer true books (nonfiction) to storybooks. We have many books on subjects that young children like in our nonfiction section. Ask me for the subjects your child is interested in—trains, different animals, the planets—and I'll show you where to find them.
	Letter knowledge	*Hold up a foam capital T and lowercase t.* "This is the letter *T*, for *train*." Showing children letters based on subjects they like follows the children's interests. They are more likely to remember the letter than if you drill them. *Could do R and r for railroad.*
	Narrative skills	Let children talk about the pictures in the book. They may tell you about a time they saw a train or even went on one. Taking time to listen and to add to what they say helps them develop their narrative skills, which helps later with their ability to understand what they read.
	Vocabulary	When children tell you about a train or a certain train car, you can read more information from the book and add to their description or their information. This helps to expand their vocabulary, knowing the names of things, actions, and ideas.

STORYTIME COMPONENT	EARLY LITERACY SKILL	COMMUNICATION TO PARENT/CAREGIVER
Big book Big book edition of *Caps for Sale*, by Esphyr Slobodkina **(PR)**	Print awareness	Hold the book upside down. See if children notice that it is upside down. If not, point it out. Children need to know how to hold a book, which is the cover, and which is the back of the book. This is one fun way to find out if they know this.
	Vocabulary	A *peddler* is someone who sells things. When you come to a word that is not familiar to the child, you should use that word and explain it in a way the child would understand. This is one way to help the child learn more words. Books give us different words than those we use in conversation or that are on television. Knowing many words helps children with reading when they try to sound out words.

Book for dialogic
    reading
Cows in the Kitchen, by
    June Crebbin   **(T, PR)**
	Narrative skills, vocabulary	*Read the book together.*
		There are many ways to read a book. Reading a book through helps children understand the whole story and keeps the story line intact. Talking about the pictures and taking the child's lead increases your child's vocabulary and narrative skills. Try to ask questions that cannot be answered with yes or no.
		Choose a page and demonstrate dialogic reading.
		If you'd like more information on this way of reading with your child, I can recommend a video, or you can talk with me after the storytime.
		See appendix E for information on the Hear and Say: Reading with Toddlers video.

Add Your Introductory Remark, or "Early Literacy Tip"

Think about what you want to say for your introductory remarks, an "Early Literacy Tip." This would be where you would say the name of the skill, what it means, and why it is important. You may say, "I'll be pointing out [the skill] a couple of times during the storytime." Here are some suggestions for ways to talk about early literacy skills with the adults during storytime.

Once you have given your explanation at the beginning, you can simply whisper the name of the skill to the adults as an aside during the storytime component that highlights that skill. For example, if you decide to highlight phonological awareness, particularly the rhyming aspect, as part of your early literacy tip at the beginning, then—when you get to the part where you are doing a rhyme and singing a song that highlights the rhyming words—you can raise your eyes toward the adults and in an exaggerated whisper say, "Phonological awareness."

Another idea is to make "word bubbles" and copy them onto colored paper. You can laminate them or protect them with contact paper, and then turn them into stick puppets (see figure 10-4). Then, when you are pointing out, for example, phonological awareness, you can simply lift up your word-bubble stick puppet for a couple of seconds.

FIGURE 10-4   Word-Bubble Stick Puppet

What Will You Say
at the End, as Part of Your Closing?

As part of your closing, encourage parents and caregivers to continue these activities at home with their children. Encourage them to ask you questions. If you find it helpful, write down what you will say or whatever notes you like on the "Storytime Planning Sheet."

Look at the Whole Picture

Now think about the whole storytime experience.

Aids: Would a poster or other aid with the six skills help you as you get used to speaking with adults in your storytime?

Name tags: Are you making name tags for the adults and the children? You can talk about letters as you or they write their names.

Flip charts: Make it easier for adults to follow along with songs and rhymes by writing them on flip charts; this helps with print awareness as well.

Display: Make sure to display some early literacy information or some books that lend themselves to dialogic reading or your highlighted skill (books that rhyme, for example).

Craft: It's not *just* doing the craft; it's how the adult interacts with the child. Think about what you can say to encourage verbal interactions. Model this behavior for the parents/caregivers.

Activities: Your storytime may end with an activity time, as an added component or instead of your craft time. You can demonstrate some activities that support the highlighted skill. Have participants try things you demonstrated during storytime, or use this time to introduce and demonstrate activities that highlight a skill. For example, have the adults and children play "I Spy" with rhyming words. You could use play dough to play the "Say It Slow, Say It Fast" game. See a brief description in "Sample Storytimes for Prereaders (Four- and Five-Year-Olds)," chapter 9, "On the Farm"; for more complete information, see "Workshops for Prereaders," at http://www.pla.org/earlyliteracy.htm. You could have them play "Concentration" using pictures of things that rhyme or have the same starting sound. They make a match when the words rhyme or have the same starting sound. You can use a 6-inch-square cardboard box, and glue a picture to each of the six sides. What pictures you put on the cube depends on what skill you want to highlight. To highlight phonological awareness, have a picture of a single object (truck, dog, banana, etc.) on each side of the cube. Take turns rolling the cube. The adult says the name of the object on the top of the cube and allows the child to repeat it. Then they think of rhyming words or words that start with the same sound. To use the cube for narrative skills, choose pictures from discarded books or magazines or photos where there is something going on in the pictures. The adult and child can take turns rolling the cube and making up parts of an ongoing story.

Home connection: Share ideas that parents/caregivers can do with their children after they leave storytime that will strengthen early literacy development as they have fun together. (See appendix B.)

Keep It Fun!

The most important part of storytime is the positive feelings you can help create around books and book sharing. This can only be conveyed if you are having a good time yourself. Relax and enjoy the books, the stories, the children, and the adults. When they see that you are having fun, they will, too.

Give it a try!

PART

Keeping It Going!

11

Assessing
Your Storytimes

As we go through the process of internalizing what may now be called a "literacy enhanced" storytime and will later simply be a storytime, in a re-created form, the following tools may be useful.

The Early Literacy Storytime Planning/Observation Checklist forms (figures 11-1–11-3) are designed to serve two purposes: (1) to help assess what you are already doing or planning to do during storytime so you can think more intentionally about ways your storytime supports early literacy and (2) to help those who observe your storytimes assess them. There are three forms, one for each age-level. On each form are the six early literacy skills and some ways that you support the skill during each storytime. *All* storytimes will bring out the fun of books, reading, and language. *All* storytimes will have a couple of instances of addressing the parents regarding early literacy. The other skills will be emphasized or mentioned during various storytimes.

These checklists have been used in a variety of ways, from informal self-checks to being made part of performance evaluations with supervisors as observers. It is often hard for the presenter to be aware of all the things she or he does. It is helpful to have another library staff person observe your storytime using the checklists. Following the storytime you both can discuss what went well and what could be improved. It is a good time to share ideas. No one expects all of the skills to be emphasized equally in one storytime.

Keeping the storytimes fun and inviting is still the most important aspect. All of us, children, parents, caregivers, library staff, learn best when we are in a welcoming, friendly environment, and when we enjoy the activities.

FIGURE 11-1

Early Literacy Storytime Planning Observation Checklist

Early Talkers: Ages Newborn–2 Years

Date: _____   Time: _____

Theme (optional):_____   Emphasized Skill(s): _____

Directions: Check off items that you plan to do/observe during the storytime.
Use the back of the page to add items that support the area(s) addressed.

I. Print Motivation (*must at least be modeled, even if no parent/caregiver message*)

___ Presenter conveys the idea that reading is fun.   ___ Children seem to have fun.

___ Presenter seems to have fun.   ___ Adults in attendance seem to have fun.

II. Phonological Awareness

___ Presenter invites children/adults to chime in rhymes/fingerplays.

___ Presenter uses music/songs in storytime.

III. Vocabulary

___ Presenter calls attention to the pictures in book.

___ Presenter makes connection between pictures and real things/people (uses realia).

___ Presenter encourages the children/adults to respond through movement/music.

___ Presenter models use of language, using synonyms, adjectives.

___ Presenter models book sharing between parent/caregiver and child.

___ Presenter has rhymes/songs written out so adults can follow and children notice text.

___ Presenter *repeats* rhymes, songs, phrases in books.

IV. Narrative Skills

___ Presenter models talking with infants, leaving time for child to respond.

___ Presenter relates activity/book to experiences/situations familiar to toddlers.

___ Presenter allows toddlers time to respond.

V. Print Awareness

___ Presenter has rhymes/songs written out so adults can follow and children notice text.

___ Presenter uses board books to model how books are toys for young children to handle.

___ Presenter points to text and/or pictures intermittently when reading book.

___ Presenter uses name tags/draws attention to child's/adult's written name.

VI. Letter Knowledge

___ Presenter uses objects to note the importance of shapes and/or explains to parents.

___ Presenter talks about or demonstrates activities that emphasize alike and different.

___ Presenter demonstrates use of large foam/magnetic letters or shapes, importance of learning through senses.

___ Presenter uses name tags/draws attention to letters in child's/adult's written name.

VII. Parent/Caregiver Connection (*must be part of every storytime*)

___ Presenter explains to adults during storytime ways in which activities support early literacy.

___ Presenter encourages participation by parents/caregivers during storytime.

___ Presenter notes the important role parents/caregivers play in early literacy development.

___ Presenter makes suggestions for parents/caregivers to do at home.

___ Presenter calls attention to handouts/displays for parents/caregivers.

FIGURE 11-2

Early Literacy Storytime Planning/Observation Checklist
Early Talkers: Ages 2-3 Years

Date: _____   Time: _____

Theme (optional):_____ Emphasized Skill(s): _____

Directions: Check off items that you plan to do/observe during the storytime.
Use the back of the page to add items that support the area(s) addressed.

I. Print Motivation (*must at least be modeled, even if no parent/caregiver message*)
___ Presenter conveys the idea that reading is fun.   ___ Children seem to have fun.
___ Presenter seems to have fun.   ___ Adults in attendance seem to have fun.

II. Phonological Awareness
___ Presenter invites children to chime in rhymes/finger plays/songs and/or music in storytime.
___ Presenter uses books with alliteration or rhyming text; invites children to chime in.
___ Presenter plays rhyming game(s) with children.

III. Vocabulary
___ Presenter makes connections to concepts and vocabulary when reading.
___ Presenter explains/exposes children to vocabulary they may not be familiar with.
___ Presenter helps children become more familiar with words by using repeated phrases.
___ Presenter calls attention to the pictures in the story.
___ Presenter encourages the children to respond through movement/music.
___ Presenter gives children opportunity to respond orally by asking simple questions about the story and/or pictures.
___ Presenter demonstrates or talks about dialogic reading.

IV. Narrative Skills
___ Presenter uses puppets/props/flannel board to have children participate in retelling the story; may have children retell story.
___ Presenter talks about the events of the story.
___ Presenter helps children link the events and characters to what they know about.
___ Presenter demonstrates/models dialogic reading.

V. Print Awareness
___ Presenter calls attention to the cover of the book; points to and reads the title.
___ Presenter points to the print and occasionally runs finger along text while reading.
___ Presenter has rhymes/songs written out so adults can follow and children notice text.
___ Presenter uses nametags/draws attention to child's/adult's written name.

VI. Letter Knowledge
___ Presenter talks about shapes through use of books, flannel board, or objects.
___ Presenter talks about or does activities that emphasize alike and different.
___ Presenter demonstrates use of large foam/magnet letters or shapes, importance of learning through senses.
___ Presenter uses name tags/draws attention to letters in names.
___ Presenter uses alphabet book/activity/song.

VII. Parent/Caregiver Connection (*must be part of every storytime*)
___ Presenter explains to parents during storytime ways in which activities/techniques support early literacy.
___ Presenter notes the important role parents/caregivers play in early literacy development.
___ Presenter makes suggestions for parents/caregivers to do at home.
___ Presenter calls attention to handouts/displays for parents/caregivers.

FIGURE 11-3

Early Literacy Storytime Planning/Observation Checklist

Prereaders: Ages 4–5 Years

Date: _____   Time: _____

Theme (optional):_____   Emphasized Skill(s): _____

Directions: Check off items that you observe during the storytime.
Use the back of the page to add items that support the area(s) addressed.

I. Print Motivation (*must at least be modeled, even if no parent/caregiver message*)

___ Presenter conveys the idea that reading is fun.
___ Presenter seems to have fun.
___ Children seem to have fun.
___ Adults in attendance seem to have fun.

II. Phonological Awareness

___ Presenter invites children to chime in rhymes/finger plays/songs and/or music.
___ Presenter uses books that highlight sound awareness: rhyming text, alliteration.
___ Presenter plays games that support this skill (rhyming, beginning sounds, breaking words apart).
___ Presenter uses name tags to help children understand letter sounds.

III. Vocabulary

___ Presenter makes connections to concepts and vocabulary when reading.
___ Presenter explains/exposes children to vocabulary they may not be familiar with.
___ Presenter helps children become more familiar with words by using repeated phrases.
___ Presenter calls attention to the pictures in the story.
___ Presenter encourages the children to respond through movement/music.
___ Presenter gives children opportunity to respond orally by asking simple questions about the story and/or pictures.
___ Presenter demonstrates/models dialogic reading.

IV. Narrative Skills

___ Presenter allows children to participate in retelling of story; may use puppets/props/creative dramatics/flannel board.
___ Presenter talks about the events of the story and/or theme. Encourages children's comments.
___ Presenter reads book without much interruption so children exposed to story structure.
___ Presenter helps children link the events and characters to what they know about.
___ Presenter encourages children to make predictions before/during reading of story.
___ Presenter demonstrates/models dialogic reading.

V. Print Awareness

___ Presenter calls attention to the cover of the book; points to and reads the title.
___ Presenter points to the print and occasionally runs finger along text while reading.
___ Presenter has rhymes/songs written out so adults can follow and children notice text.
___ Presenter comments on names on name tags.
___ After storytime, there was opportunity for children to draw picture/"write" about story.

FIGURE 11-3 (cont.)

VI. Letter Knowledge

___ Presenter uses an enjoyable alphabet book/activity/song.

___ Presenter makes connections between letters in children's names and in alphabet book or book title.

___ Presenter talks about/points out letters and/or letter sounds.

___ Presenter uses name tags to help children understand letters.

___ After storytime, there was opportunity for children to play with magnetic/foam letters.

VII. Parent/Caregiver Connection (must be part of every storytime)

___ Presenter explains to parents ways in which activities/techniques support early literacy.

___ Presenter notes the important role parents/caregivers play in early literacy development.

___ Presenter makes suggestions for parents/caregivers to do at home.

___ Presenter calls attention to handouts/displays for parents/caregivers.

12

Promoting Early Literacy Activities In and Out of the Library

As they absorbed new knowledge on early literacy, library staff at the demonstration sites involved in the "Every Child Ready to Read @ your library" project were inspired to share the information in a variety of ways. Here are some of their ideas:

Reaching parents/caregivers when they are not in storytime

Doing outreach programs for parents and caregivers on early literacy

Incorporating early literacy information into reading programs

Expanding and organizing collections

Incorporating early literacy information into the one-on-one interaction (via reference and readers' advisory interviews)

Changing the library environment (to be more language rich and adult/child interactive)

Interpreting what we do for other agencies and organizations

You may want to consider implementing some of these, and you may think of ways not noted here.

Reaching Parents/Caregivers When They Are Not in Storytime

This is a challenge! When parents choose not to attend library storytime with their children or when we visit child-care centers, Head Start classes, and nursery school classes, the parents are not present when we do storytimes with their children. What are some ways to get the early literacy messages out to them?

1. Make sure that the child-care provider/teacher is aware of the importance not only of the activities but of *why* certain activities are important in supporting early literacy and will share this information with the adults.

2. Offer written tips, brief articles, or activity sheets to the caregivers to make it easier for them to share the information with their parents.

3. Encourage the parents to attend an evening or weekend early literacy workshop.

Appendix B offers some examples of handouts for parents/caregivers who are not present during the storytime. It is best if they can see and hear the library presenter so that they see the behaviors modeled. If that is not possible, however, these handouts offer some information and suggestions to the parent/caregiver. Use these handouts to develop your own. Build on what you have shared in storytime.

Doing Outreach Programs for Parents/Caregivers on Early Literacy

Incorporating early literacy information for parents/caregivers into storytimes is, in fact, an offshoot of the "Every Child Ready to Read @ your library" workshops for parents and child-care providers. These workshops were developed by researchers funded by the National Institute of Child Health and Human Development of the National Institutes of Health as a means for library staff to communicate early literacy research to parents/caregivers who are with children every day. For the workshop scripts and support materials, go to http://www.pla.org/earlyliteracy.htm or contact the Public Library Association (PLA) or the Association of Library Service to Children (ALSC) of the American Library Association (800-545-2433).

The public libraries that have implemented "Every Child Ready to Read @ your library" workshops have become more respected as providers of early literacy information because this program is based on early literacy research and because the program itself, evaluated by Sara Laughlin Associates, showed positive changes in early literacy behaviors.

Presenting workshops on early literacy to the adults who are with children on a daily basis can be a powerful introduction for them to library staff and services. The project evaluation found that the greatest gains were made when we worked with partners and did the workshops outside the walls of the public library, reaching those who are least likely to use the library. Partnerships included programs like Head Start, Early Head Start, home-visiting programs, social workers, faith communities, hospitals, public school early childhood programs and second-language departments, and teen parents.

Many of us are more comfortable doing programs for children than doing programs for adults. Try this: if you are most comfortable doing storytime programs for, say, two-year-olds, look at the script for the workshops for talkers (parents and caregivers of two- and three-year-olds). Try doing these workshops for parents and caregivers in your community, working with partners to reach those who do not already come to the library.

We can have the most positive effect on the early literacy of young children by modeling appropriate early literacy behaviors in the hope of influencing the behavior of the *adults* who care for the young children. Our programs for young children have neither the duration nor consistency of contact to have a permanent influence on their early literacy development. Our most important role is to promote early literacy, to explain it and to model behaviors for the parents and caregivers who are with the children every day.

Incorporating Early Literacy Information into Reading Programs

During the summer, many of us put our energies into summer reading programs. Some of us have reading programs during other times of the year as well. Libraries include the youngest children in a variety of ways: some have a separate read-to-me program for young children; others have one program to cover all ages. By having a program element specifically designed for children newborn to age five and their care providers, we send a strong message about the importance of reading to the youngest children. It is good to include parent-child early literacy activities, in addition to reading, that count toward the reading-game goal. Let older siblings count the time and books they read with young children for both the young children and themselves. Everybody loves to get double credit for one effort made.

Reassessing what we do in light of what we have learned, we must recognize the role of the parent/caregiver as part of the reading program. For example, most of us have coupons or other incentives for the children. How might we include incentives for the adults? Some examples include a free book for the adult; local merchants who can offer something for the adult; and small incentives that the adult would appreciate, such as a certificate or bumper sticker. We found that for many adults who do not use the library, fines are a major barrier, even if the fine occurred when they were young. Why not incorporate in the reading program that they can "read away their fines," and publicize this information?

The "Curious George Read to Me" program, a graphics CD-ROM from the American Library Association's Graphics Division (available at http:www.alastore.ala.org), offers bookmark-size activity sheets that incorporate information on each of the six skills for newborns to age five. (Appendix B offers an example of such an activity sheet.) Because the program is on disk, it allows users the flexibility to put whatever they want in the gameboard squares. Users can also print even a small number of game boards to use with partners, for example, a small group of teen parents.

Another idea is to start a reading program for parents/caregivers. Bring in speakers by partnering with another community parenting and health organization and the public schools or local college and universities. The reading program could be for a set number of weeks and could include parenting books, early literacy materials, and fiction and non-fiction with adult-child relationships as a pivotal piece in the book. Some library systems have developed early literacy calendars with an activity for each day or week.

Expanding and Organizing Collections

When we promote early literacy, we find that more parents, teachers, child-care providers, and others in the community, including political officials and policy makers, often seek out more information from us. Use the bibliography in appendix E as a starting point. Keep up with new materials by looking at catalogs or websites of Redleaf Press, Gryphon House, Brookes Publishers, National Association for the Education of Young Children, and Zero to Three, among others (see appendix E for websites). Building a strong resource collection will serve both staff and the community well. (See bibliography at http://www.pla.org/earlyliteracy.htm under "Research and Evaluation.")

As for the children's collections, you may want to build up board books, books with nursery rhymes, rhyming books, and books with rhymes from a variety of cultures and languages.

With strong collections, you can display various books while highlighting an early literacy skill or skills and make booklists that incorporate early literacy information.

Incorporating Early Literacy Information into the One-on-One Interaction

Many parents/caregivers come to choose books and other materials but cannot come to storytimes or to a library program. We can share information on early literacy in informal conversations with them. For example, a parent comes up with a five-year-old and a baby. She asks about books for her five-year-old but says nothing about the baby. In addition to finding books for the youngster, we can offer board books and talk about the importance of singing and doing rhymes with the baby. She may, of course, already have books and other materials at home for the baby, but it doesn't hurt to offer.

We may hear a parent saying to a young child, "No, not that book again. We just brought it back, and you've heard it a hundred times!" as the child offers the book to the parent as one to add to the stack. This situation offers us an opportunity to talk about dialogic reading and to offer a handout and the video *Hear and Say: Reading with Toddlers* (see appendix E) about it.

Sometimes an adult will actually approach us and express concern over a child's language development. Now that we have more information about early literacy, after listening to the concerns, we can offer specific suggestions about activities, *why* they are important, *and* the need for a positive experience as the adult and child do the activities together. We can offer handouts, books, and other materials that may be helpful to them as well. It is this personal interaction that makes a difference in how the adult may relate to the child. For instances where there may be cause for concern in development, we would always refer the adult to the appropriate developmental screening agency.

Changing the Library Environment

Using early literacy information, look for ways to make the library environment more language rich and adult and child interactive. The amount of space available, from a few sections of shelving to an entire floor, varies from library to library. Regardless of the resources, where we place our materials and how we promote them can help shape adults' and their children's early literacy experience within the library.

The goal is for the library environment to encourage interactions and communication between a child and other children and children and adults. By having things that draw the attention of both the adult and the child and staff who model verbal interactions, we can support early literacy and help parents and caregivers do some of these activities at home as well.

This approach means that there must be comfortable seating for adults in your area for young children, seating where they can be comfortable together. When you consider the youngest children, have you done everything to make a safe and welcoming place for adults and their infants? What do they see when they are crawling around?

Colorful images?

Books that face out?

How about a concave mirror on the end of a bookcase?

Do the children feel different textures? Insert a path of squares of different textures—sandpaper, vinyl, marble, short pile rug, shaggy rug, and so forth. Display text nearby that gives names to how these different textures feel.

Promote reading to babies when you are helping parents find books for their older children. A simple "May I help you find something to read with your baby?" will remind the parent that even the youngest child benefits from contact with books. When you notice a fussy baby, ask the adult if you can get a book for the baby to look at. Take advantage of every situation as it presents itself to get books into babies' hands. Take a minute and show the baby a few pages, talking all the while. Ensure that parents hear about programs for babies and that they are offered at a variety of times to accommodate working parents as well as those who stay home.

For children ages two through five, how can you make your space more adult-child interactive? Most libraries provide a simple, welcoming environment for this age group and its parents. Our challenge is to think how to encourage parent-child interaction to promote early literacy development. Consider the following:

Place photos of library events and children on bookshelf ends or on the front of the library desk.

Put a flannel board or magnet board where children and caregivers can make up stories with the pieces.

Set out puppets where children and caregivers can put on a show for each other.

Early childhood suppliers offer many kinds of hands-on materials that can easily be used in the library. Puzzles, shape sorters, and other kinds of manipulatives have a natural audience with this age group. Many of these items encourage talking about concepts like relative size, shape, colors, and special relationships. If lack of a secure space for the materials is an issue, consider investing in an AV cart, which can be rolled in and out of the children's area as needed and as supervision dictates.

We can encourage creative play and conversation among children and adults in the library. Children will play for long periods of time with a barn and farm animals, cars and trucks, and other kinds of figures. To promote using books as an impetus for creative play, we can highlight a book and then suggest to the parent the kinds of play that might take place.

Children who are two and three years old cannot write in a way that is easily decipherable; however, they need to go through the scribble stage on their way to conventional writing. When possible, set up an area where parents and children can write and draw pictures about their favorite books. Offer a writing center, where children can stamp, color, and write. Parents will be surprised to see how much their children enjoy stamping and writing their way along the road to reading.

Try early literacy stations or kiosks or bulletin boards that change regularly and are interactive. Even a metal book cart can become an early literacy spot display, highlighting a new skill each month with activities, information, and handouts. These spots can contain explicit activities for parents to do with their children. Provide simple instructions and materials for the adult to make something book related with the child. Encourage the adult to read and talk about the book with the child. Offer a poem with an activity for the parent to do with the child at home. It is important to include information about *why* the activity is important and how it supports early literacy: it is fun and it supports narrative skills (explain what narrative skills involve). This information can be in written form, or consider having a tape recorder parents can play to listen to the directions and information.

These ideas need not be limited to the children's area. It is easiest to start with the children's area, but children and their parents/caregivers use practically all the areas of the library. At the circulation desk, we can have things at child-eye level that draw their attention and use their senses. Try raised letters or shapes or colorful photos, including book covers.

In the restrooms, over the changing tables, post the words to a rhyme and change it every month.

In the adult area of the library, use the lower part of the bookshelf ends for items that appeal to young children, while the adult-eye level can contain information for parents/caregivers. For example, put a concave mirror or magnet board on a post where children can crawl up to it. Try a basket of books and a soft cushion on the floor.

An early literacy center or kiosk works best where parents accompany their youngsters to the library. In areas where this is not the case and there are young children who do not have anyone who reads to them, other options are available. Libraries have devised many innovative programs to connect young children with people who will read to them, including bookmobiles that go to family child-care homes and child-care centers. Another program is the Public Broadcasting Service's Designated Reader program, which the Chicago Public Library uses to encourage adults to read to children in libraries. Some libraries are training staff and volunteers to interact with children in a variety of settings, including health clinics and community centers.

Interpreting What We Do for Other Agencies and Organizations

Although we have long included many aspects of early literacy in our programs and services, we are now better able to articulate them for ourselves, other staff, administration, partners, and funding and governmental organizations.

Look carefully at the words used by the agencies you work with. If the wording you use as a result of implementing Every Child Ready to Read @ your library varies with that used by your state's Department of Education, you may need to adapt it or explain the connections. Montgomery County (MD) Public Libraries clearly correlated early literacy terminology with that used by the Maryland State Department of Education (see figure 12-1).

FIGURE 12-1   Montgomery County Public Library's Language Comparison Chart

Early Literacy Skills Montgomery County (MD) Public Libraries and Maryland State Department of Education	
MARYLAND STATE DEPARTMENT OF EDUCATION	**EVERY CHILD READY TO READ @ YOUR LIBRARY**
Learning about Books and Print Young children need many opportunities to learn about books and print.	**Print Awareness** Noticing print, knowing how to handle a book, and how we follow written words on a page
Learning about Letters Knowing the letters of the alphabet is an important step in learning to read.	**Letter Knowledge** Knowing that letters are different from each other, that the same letter can look different, and that letters are related to sounds
Learning about Sounds in Words Before starting school, children should be able to think about how words sound, apart from what they mean.	**Phonological Awareness** Ability to hear and play with the smaller sounds in words
Developing Comprehension Comprehension is a child's ability to understand stories and books.	[encompasses Vocabulary and Narrative Skills]
[contributes to Comprehension]	**Vocabulary** Knowing the names of things (feelings, concepts, ideas)
[contributes to Comprehension]	**Narrative Skills** Ability to describe things, to tell stories and events in sequence
Building Language Skills Language skills are a child's listening and speaking skills.	[supported through Narrative Skills]
[included in Building Language Skills]	**Print Motivation** A child's interest in and enjoyment of books

We can help others understand the value of our services by looking carefully at the services we offer (and often take for granted) in light of their value to others and by explaining these services—especially as they pertain to early literacy—in ways that allow others to see how we contribute to their goals and outcomes.

A Final Note:
Continuing the Journey

We hope that this book has given you food for thought, a solid foundation to build early literacy enhanced storytimes, and a strong start as you continue the journey, the journey to reach parents and caregivers as we all work together to improve the condition of young children and of families.

We urge you to internalize the ideas and information put forth here. We each have our own style, our own ways of planning, our own ways of presenting and sharing books and supporting language growth, and our own ways of relating to the adults who play critical parts in the children's lives.

The journey is a continuous process where we build on our previous experiences, look at the needs of our patrons and those in the community, and search for practical solutions to the problems we see.

So, continue to seek out and disseminate new research and information as it becomes available. Continue to incorporate new materials and new ideas into storytimes. Continue to experiment with new ideas as you build on familiar storytimes. Continue to find ways to connect with more parents and caregivers and to help them support their children's early literacy development.

Continue the journey! Ever onward . . .

Manual Alphabet

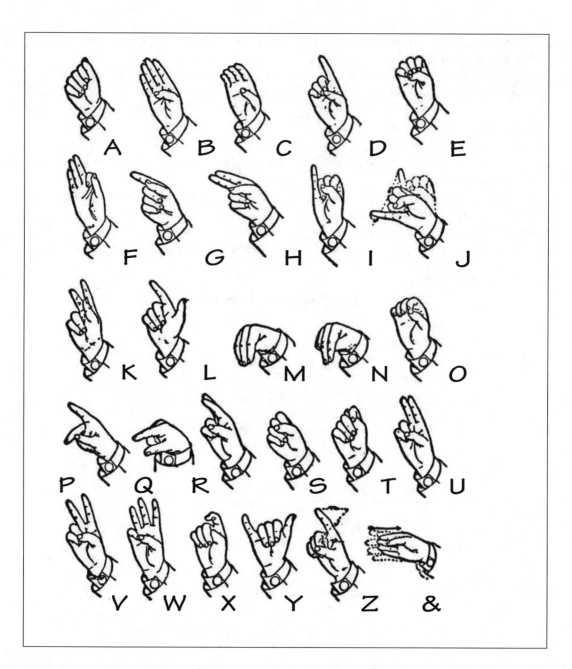

B

Encouraging Early Literacy at Home

Sample Parent Tip Take-Home Pages

We developed these sample parent pages to give you an idea of ones you can make to reflect your storytime. When you visit a child-care group or other group where the parents are not present, you can offer a "Parent Page" for the child-care provider to send home with the children. It also can serve as a talking point when the parents pick the children up.

The first "Parent Tip Take-Home" sample shows one way you can encourage parents who have attended the storytime to continue at home what you have done and modeled in your storytime. The other examples are oriented toward being handed out by a child-care provider or Head Start teacher when you have done a storytime for the children and their parents were not present. You can adapt any to your situation and, of course, make up your own! Some correspond to the sample storytimes; others do not. These samples are most appropriate for parents and caregivers of prereaders.

Parent Tip Take-Home: Narrative Skills, Vocabulary

Talking with your child about the stories we shared today will improve expressive vocabulary and strengthen narrative skills. These are two of the skills that researchers have determined lay a strong foundation for children when they are learning to read. Think about how many times a child wants to hear a favorite story. Children love repetition. Some of our stories today help a child learn to count. Others are easy to tell and retell because words or events repeat themselves in the story. Having a child tell the story back to you is important because it increases narrative skills. It may require some patience on your part. Conversation requires the use of three different parts of our brain!

- What are some of the toys Lisa put in her bed? (ball, jumping jack, dog, cat, etc.)
- Ask your child, "What do *you* do when you can't go to sleep?"
- Have your child draw some animals, one on each sheet of paper. Let your child retell the story of Ann McGovern's *Too Much Noise* using the animals she or he has drawn.

Parent Tip Take-Home: Narrative Skills

Hello! Today during storytime we read books about all kinds of things that change. Please spend some time today talking with your child about how much he or she has changed since he or she was a little baby. Here are some of the questions we asked the children:

How big were you when you were a baby?

What did you do when you were little?

What can you do now that you could not do when you were a baby?

We also read this poem together:

When I Was a Baby

When I was a baby, a baby, a baby
When I was a baby I talked like this.
Bah-bah, bah-bah
When I was a baby, a baby, a baby
When I was a baby, I ate like this.
Suck on your thumb as if it were a bottle
When I was a baby, a baby, a baby,
When I was a baby, I crawled like this.
Crawl

Now I am a big kid, a big kid, a big kid
I eat like this.
Gesture eating with a spoon
And I walk like this.
Walk in place
Now I am a big kid, I talk like this.
Hi!
Because I am not a BABY!

Please say the poem with your child and keep the conversations going!

Parent Tip Take-Home: Letter Knowledge

Hello! Today during storytime we read some books about butterflies and talked about the letter *b*, and the sound that it makes, the /b/ ("buh") sound. We sang this little song as we looked around for things that start with *b*. Please use this rhyme as you and your child keep looking for *b* things! Children need to know both the letter and the letter sound as they get ready to learn how to read.

"Rhyming Basket"

(Sing to the tune of "A Tisket, a Tasket")

A tisket, a tasket
We'll make a /b/ basket.
Help me as we look around.
Look at the *b* sounds we found!
The /b/ sound!
The /b/ sound!
Here are the words we found!

/b/ means the sound of the letter b—"buh"

When you talk about and play with the different sounds in words with your child, your child becomes more aware of the smaller sounds in words. This will make it easier for your child to sound out words when she or he learns how to read later!

Parent Tip Take-Home: Phonological Awareness

Hello! Today in storytime we read some books about farm animals. We did some rhyming riddles, like the ones below. Try to make some up with your child. It is fun to rhyme, and it will help the children later as they try to decode or sound out words once they are learning how to read.

I am thinking of an animal that lives on a farm . . .

It swims in a pond, and it rhymes with *luck*.	*duck*
Its babies are called foals, and it rhymes with *course*.	*horse*
It likes to eat bones, and it rhymes with *log*.	*dog*
It likes milk, and it rhymes with *hat*.	*cat*
Its coat is wool, and it rhymes with *beep*.	*sheep*
It quacks, and it rhymes with *moose*.	*goose*

Try making up rhyming riddles using people's names, kinds of food, or whatever else sounds like fun!

Thanks for keeping the learning going.

Parent Tip Take-Home: Print Awareness

Hello! Today in storytime we read some books about going on a shopping trip. We sang a little song to the tune of "A-Hunting We Will Go":

"A Shopping We Will Go"

A shopping we will go.	A shopping we will go.
A shopping we will go.	A shopping we will go.
Heigh-ho the dairy-oh	We'll check the list to see what we've missed
A shopping we will go.	A shopping we will go.

We talked about making a shopping list to help us remember what to buy. Please take a few minutes and make a list with your child. This activity shows your child that print has meaning and is useful. Also, while at the grocery store, point out the words on labels and signs and read them aloud. Children need to see that print is everywhere. This activity helps them develop one of the skills they need before they go to school—print awareness, or noticing that letters and print are everywhere.

Enjoy!

Parent Tip Take-Home: Letter Knowledge

Hello! Today we read some books about different kinds of noises, and we talked about the letter *n* and its sound: /n/. There are lots of different ways of helping a child learn letters. Research shows us that children learn best when they are actively involved in the process of learning. Here are some ideas of things you can do to teach letters to your child. It is best to start with these letters: *w, p, b, d, t, m, n.* Vowels, *a, e, i, o, u,* and *y,* are tricky because they change their sounds so much. Start with the letters in your child's name:

> Cut out pictures from catalogs, magazines, and newspapers that start with the letter you are learning.

> Help your child feel the letter. Draw it in the air together, with your fingers. Trace it on your child's back. Remember to do both uppercase *N* and lowercase *n,* too.

> Start every word in a sentence with the sound of your letter. Say, "Net's no," for "Let's go." You get the idea!

Remember to have fun with your child. If either of you becomes frustrated, stop the activity and try again another day. Children learn best at their own pace.

Parent Tip Take-Home: Phonological Awareness

Hello! Today we read some books about mice and learned about the letter *m* and the sound it makes. We played a game, which you can see here, that is meant to sharpen their hearing. You say three words. Only one of them can have the /m/ sound in it. Since it is easier to hear the first sound in a word, start with /m/ as the first sound. Here is a little poem that you can say to get going, along with some examples:

> I hear, with my little ear, the sound /m/.

> tight . . . light . . . *m*ight   rice . . . *m*ice . . . dice   *my* . . . sky . . . high

If your child can hear the /m/ sound at the beginning of the word, try words with the /m/ at the end of the word. This is harder than hearing the beginning sound. For example,

> tub . . . bu*m* . . . bat   sat . . . has . . . ha*m*

If this is too hard, play another time. Let your child make up the words and see if *you* can hear the sounds, too.

Once your child knows the letter and sound of *m,* move on to another letter.

Remember to point out the letter when you see it on the street and in books you share. You and your child can try drawing the letter in the air or on each other's back with your finger.

Parent Tip Take-Home: Narrative Skills

Hello! Today in storytime we read some books about food. One of the things we talked about is the order in which things happen. The ability to retell a story is part of narrative skills, when children understand what they read when they start to read on their own. It is easier for the children to remember the story and then retell it by putting the events in order.

You can help them develop this skill by talking about the things you do together in order. Summarize with your child what you did this morning or yesterday. Talk about your activities in the order that they occurred. This will help them to become familiar with the idea that their activities, like stories, have a sequence.

Here is a song that you can change to fit a variety of activities:

(Sing to the tune of "This Is the Way We Wash Our Clothes")

In the morning:
This is the way we wash our face
Wash our face, wash our face.
This is the way we wash our face
So early in the morning.
This is the way we brush our teeth . . .
This is the way we wear our clothes . . .

For shopping:
This is the way we write our list . . .
This is the way we ride the bus . . . (or drive the car)
This is the way we buy the food . . .
When we go to the store.

Have fun making up other songs as you go about your day together!

Parent Tip Take-Home: Phonological Awareness

Hello! Today in storytime we read some books about people with interesting names. This is a good time for you to tell your child the history of her name. Was your child named after someone, or does your child have a name that you just really like? Take a minute and have a conversation about your name, too.

One of the things we did with their names was to break them into parts, or segments. Each syllable, or part, gets a clap. For example, one clap for Joe, and three for De-an-dre. Which name in your family gets the most claps?

Another way to play with names is to combine the different parts of names. What would happen if you combined your name with your child's? Switch the first syllable with your child's and see what happens! For example, if your name is Rosa and your child's is Marisol, then she becomes Rorisol and you, Marsa! This ability to manipulate the smaller sounds in words is one way to develop phonological awareness. This is an important skill for children to have as they get ready to learn to read.

Have fun exploring the names of family and friends.

Parent Tip Take-Home: Phonological Awareness

Hello! Today we read some stories about ducks and the adventures they had. We are practicing rhyming because it is a skill that will help children decode words. One of the ways you can help your child improve his or her reading skills is by pointing out rhymes where you hear them. After you read a book together that has rhyming words in it, go back through the story and talk about the words that rhyme. You can sing this song together, substituting rhyming words for *duck* and *stuck*.

"These Words Rhyme"

(Sing to the tune of "Skip to My Lou")

Duck, stuck, these words rhyme.

Duck, stuck, these words rhyme.

Duck, stuck, these words rhyme,

So rhyme along with me.

Keep your ears ready to hear rhyme. You can use rhyming words from songs that you sing as well as make up your own sets of rhyming words. It is fun to play with words this way, so enjoy! You can make up words that are silly and don't make sense, just as long as they rhyme!

Parent Tip Take-Home: Phonological Awareness

Hello! Today we shared some of our favorite bedtime stories during storytime. Some of the books rhymed. We are spending quite a bit of time this year on making sure that the children can recognize words that rhyme. We are doing this because it will help them figure out new words once they are learning how to read.

Here is a little rhyming activity called "I Spy" that you can do with your child as you go about your daily lives together. You need to think of a word that is something that you and your child can see. Then think of a word that rhymes with it and use that word as your clue, as follows:

I spy with my little eye

Something that rhymes with _____.

Let's say you are in the doctor's office so you pick *clock* as the secret word. You would then say, "I spy with my little eye, something that rhymes with *sock* (clock)." You can give other clues, too, to help the child guess the secret word. Try to pick words that your child knows so that the child doesn't become frustrated.

Enjoy!

Parent Tip Take-Home: Phonological Awareness

Hello! Today we read some books about cold weather and what it is like to play outside in the snow. We sang a snowman song:

"I'm a Little Snowman"

(Sing to the tune of "I'm a Little Teapot")

I'm a little snowman, round and fat.

Here is my scarf and here is my hat!

Pebbles for my buttons, a carrot for my nose;

Made of snow from head to toes.

This next rhyming song will help reinforce the idea of rhyme. You can sing it after you pull out the rhyming words.

"Rhyme Along"

(Sing to the tune of "Row, Row, Row, Your Boat")

Rhyme, rhyme, rhyme along

Rhyme along with me!

Fat and *hat* are rhyming words

Now try along with me!

Singing this rhyming song after you and your child read a rhyming book or sing a song that has rhymes helps them understand which words rhyme. Rhyme is one part of a skill called phonological awareness, which will help your child when he or she learns how to read.

Enjoy!

Parent Tip Take-Home: Vocabulary

Hello! Today in storytime we read some stories about hands. We talked about the different parts of our hands and arms, including *wrist, knuckle,* and *finger.* It is important that we teach our children as many vocabulary words as possible. Research tells us that it is easier for a child to read a word that is familiar to him or her. Please name as many things as you can with their specific name! For some fun, dance the "Hokey Pokey," naming as many body parts as you can!

You put your right hand in
You put your hand out
You put your right hand in
And you shake it all about.
You do the hokey pokey
And you turn yourselves around.
'Cause that's what it's all about!

Remember to name left, right, and even *eyebrow* and *eyelash*! By using words for the less commonly named parts of the body, you are helping children learn lots of new words. Hearing these words over and over again helps them remember them. Later when they learn to read, it will be easier for them to sound out words they are familiar with, and also they will understand what they are reading.

You can do so much to lay a strong foundation for your child being able to learn to read!

Sample Parent Letters

When you visit a child-care center or Head Start class or do outreach where the parents are not there to observe you, you can leave a sample letter for the teachers and caregivers so that each child can take a copy home. Perhaps this will be a first step to speaking at a parent meeting.

Dear Parent,

Today _____ from the _____ public library visited our class for storytime. She talked with us about one of the six skills that children need to help them become good readers. The skill is called *print motivation*, which is a child's interest in and enjoyment of books.

Your child will acquire this skill with your help! The best way to develop print motivation in your child is to make your book-reading or book-sharing time as positive and enjoyable as you can. It is more important for this time together to be positive than it is to be long.

- You can split reading time into parts. Read one book before dinner and two before bed or part of one before dinner and finish it at bedtime.
- If your child wants you to keep reading books and there is not enough time for them all, let your child decide which to read today and which to save for tomorrow!
- Sometimes, pick the shortest books, or compromise by letting your child pick a longer book, freeing you to pick a shorter one.
- It is OK that your child wants to hear the same book over and over. Some children memorize books and actually learn to read that way!
- Try not to use book-sharing time as a reward or punishment. It should be a part of your life together, just like sharing a meal.
- If you don't have time to read a whole book, let your child choose one page and talk about the picture together.
- Keep a fresh supply of books on hand. Visit your public library.
- Build your own home library. You can find used books in good condition at library book sales, yard sales, and thrift shops.
- *Above all, have fun.* Encourage your child to love books and the stories within them. Talk about your favorite stories, repeat the rhymes, and make books a part of your lives.

Let us know how you are doing as you make book sharing an important part of your daily life.

Sincerely,

Dear Parent,

Today _____ from the _____ public library visited our class for storytime. She talked with us about one of the skills children need to help them become good readers. The skill is called *phonological awareness*, which is the ability to hear and play with the different sounds that are in the words we speak. It includes things like rhyme. We will be working on this skill off and on over the year in school.

Your child will learn this skill more quickly with your help. Please play with words and their sounds as you spend time with your child. Here are some things you can do:

- While waiting at the doctor's or in line at the grocery store, play "I Spy." Look around you and pick something out, say, for example, the wall:

    > I spy, with my little eye,
    > Something that rhymes with *ball*.

    If the child has a hard time guessing the word, give some hints that describe it. Keep it fun!

- After reading a rhyming book all the way through, go back through and talk about the words that rhyme. Sing this rhyming song to reinforce the rhymes:

    (Sing to the tune of "Skip to My Lou")

    > Rhyme, rhyme, these words rhyme.
    > Rhyme, rhyme, these words rhyme.
    > Rhyme, rhyme, these words rhyme.
    > We're rhyming all the time.

    Substitute "rhyme, rhyme," with words from the book, like "duck, muck, these words rhyme." Try this with different sets of rhyming words.

You are your children's first and most important teacher. As always we appreciate your support.

Sincerely,

Dear Parent,

Today _____ from the _____ public library visited our class for storytime. She talked with us about one of the skills that children need to help them become good readers. The skill is called *vocabulary*, or knowing the names of things. Because it is easier for children to read words that they know, it is important that they learn many, many words. The children will be learning new words at school all year long. We are hoping you will join us in teaching your child many new words.

Your child will learn this skill more quickly with your help. Here are some things that you can do to help your child learn new words:

- When you read together, label the names of the objects that you see in the book. Ask your child to repeat the names of new things after you have said them.

- Borrow *nonfiction* books, or books that tell about real people and events. They are a good way to learn new words. Try to get books about things that are interesting to your child. Ask your librarian for some ideas if you aren't sure what to borrow.

- When you are doing errands together at the grocery store and other places you go to together, point out new things and explain what they are and what they are used for. Use words like *grocery cart* and *plastic bag* as you shop.

- Conversation is important! Talk, talk, and then talk some more! Point out the clouds and the shapes they make, how the rain sounds, and how you feel. The more words children hear, the more words they will know.

- Call things what they are. If you know the name of a flower, call it by its name—rose, daffodil, or pansy. Remember not to dumb things down, but keep things on a level the child can handle.

We are excited that we will be working together to make sure that all of the kids are ready to go to school ready to read! If you have any questions or concerns, please call us.

Sincerely,

Dear Parent,

Today _____ from the _____ public library visited our class for storytime. She talked with us about one of the skills that children need to help them become good readers. It is called *narrative skills*, or the ability to describe things and events and tell stories. This skill will help them predict what is happening in stories. Predicting what will happen and remembering what did happen are both things a child needs to help him or her on the road to becoming a good reader.

We will be reading stories and asking the children to help retell the story and also to tell stories here at school. We would like to invite you to join us in this effort by doing some of the following things at home with your child:

- Read storybooks from the library or use the books you have at home. After you read a story, have your child tell you what happened. To help her get started, you can ask the following questions:

    What happened first or at the beginning?

    How did the story end, or what happened at the end of the book?

    What do you remember about the story?

- Relate the story to something in your child's experience. What did you do when . . .?

- Make a list of what you are going to do during the day. At the end of the day, you can go back through it and talk about what you did.

- Have your child draw pictures. Let your child tell you about the pictures.

- Have your child draw more pictures of something she or he does. For example, she could draw pictures of what she does to get ready to go to bed.

We have many fun projects to work on with the children. One of our goals for the year is to make sure that all of our children are ready to go to school knowing what they need to know to become good readers. We are grateful for your support and for your willingness to work with us on this important task. Please call us if you have any questions or concerns.

Sincerely,

Dear Parent,

Today _____ from the _____ public library visited our class for storytime. She talked with us about one of the skills that children need to help them become good readers. The skill is called *print awareness*, or knowing print is everywhere and understanding how to follow print on a page.

Your child will become more aware of print with your help. Here are some things you can do with your child, as the opportunity arises, to help him or her learn this skill.

To learn that print is everywhere:

■ Make a list together before you go shopping. This will also help your child learn print has meaning.

■ When you are doing errands with your child, point out signs for the different stores you visit.

■ Once you are in the store, point out the sale signs and the words on the different items.

■ If you use coupons, give some to your child so that he or she can help you by matching the coupon to the item. You can do this with the weekly sale ad papers, too.

To follow print on a page:

■ When you read a book together, point out the book's title as well as the author's name. Run your finger under both the title and the name.

■ From time to time, point out the words on the page as you read them.

■ Encourage your child to help turn the pages. This will teach him or her how to hold a book and that in English we read from left to right.

■ Pretend to read the book backward, starting from the end and flipping the pages the wrong way. Ask your child what you are doing wrong!

Have fun as you explore the world of print with your child. It is fun to watch children as they start to figure out the magic behind the written word.

As always, let us know if you have any questions or concerns.

Sincerely,

Dear Parent,

Today _____ from the _____ public library visited our class for storytime. She talked with us about one of the skills children need to help them become good readers. The skill is called *letter knowledge*, which is learning to name letters and their sounds. Research shows that it is best to teach children the name of the letter as well as the sound that the letter makes. (For example, *p* is the name of the letter. It makes the sound of "puh," which is written /p/.) Children who know their letters and letter sounds have an easier time learning to read than those who don't. We will be teaching letters and letter sounds during the year.

Your child will learn this skill more quickly with your help. Here are some things you can do:

- Teach your child the letters that are in his or her name. Concentrate on the letters that are consonants, rather than vowels (*a, e, i, o, u,* and *y*).
- Trace the letter you are working on in the air or on your child's arm and back.
- Point out letters wherever you go, from the bus stop to the restaurant and back again.
- It is fun to learn no matter where you are! Here's another version of "I Spy" that you can play. This time you are looking for letter sounds, not rhymes.

    I spy with my little eye

    Something that starts with the sound ____.

- It would be fun to play "I Spy" while grocery shopping, especially while you're waiting in line to check out.

You are your child's first and most important teacher. Remember to have fun and change activities before you or your child becomes frustrated. As always, we appreciate your support! Let us know if there is anything we can do to help you help your child as he or she gains the skills needed to be successful in school.

Sincerely,

Sample Activity Sheet

Your Curious Kid and You!

GETTING READY TO READ

Narrative Skills is the ability to describe things and events, and to tell stories. Researchers find that this skill helps children to understand what they are reading, when they start to read.

You help by:
Talking to them about what you are doing, even as you go about daily tasks
Encouraging children to speak
Listening to them carefully
Encouraging their questions
Explaining as best you can

ACTIVITIES BY AGE

BABIES

Talking to your baby is the best way to develop language. Leave time for your baby to "answer". If he turns away from you, he has had enough for now. **As you go through your day, notice when you do not talk with your baby. Look at your baby and tell her what you are doing.**

TODDLERS

Toddlers often ask questions like, "What's that?" over and over again. Add information to what they ask. If they point to a picture of a cow, tell them. "That's a cow." Say cow, and let them try to say the word. Give them lots of time to answer. Then you can add, "This cow is white with black spots." Or "Cows give us

milk." As your toddler asks you simple questions, make sure to add information to what he says.

TWO- AND THREE-YEAR OLDS

When you read a book with your child, as him, "What is happening here?" or "What do you see on this page?" Ask questions that cannot be answered with a yes or no, or by just pointing to a picture. Let him use the words he knows. If he does not know, you can tell him what you think. Then let him try to repeat.

FOUR- AND FIVE-YEAR-OLDS

Have your child draw a picture. Then let him tell you what is happening in the picture. Write down his words on his picture.

**Enjoy your time together.
If it's not a pleasant experience,
try another time.**

©2003 American Library Association. Curious George ® and © HMCo.
Activity Sheet #11-NS2

APPENDIX
C

Storytime Aids

What Can I Say?
From Skill to Parent/Caregiver

Sometimes when we are trying to become comfortable with new information, it helps to have a kind of script of what we want to tell others until we have internalized what we have learned. Feel free to reword the messages to make them more comfortable for you. However, the name of the skill should be stated.

Perhaps some of these suggestions will be helpful. They are *not* meant to be limiting. They are meant as a beginning.

ET = Early Talker (Newborn–2 Years)   **T** = Talker (2–3 Years)   **PR** = Prereader (4–5 Years)

Communication to Parent/Caregiver
Print Motivation

1. *Print motivation* is an interest in and the enjoyment of books and reading. *(ET, T, PR)*

2. Researchers have noted one of the six areas of early literacy is *print motivation*. This means having an interest in and enjoying books. Children are more likely to have print motivation when they are involved with the story. As I share the books today, you'll see different ways you can keep your children interested as you read with them.   *(T, PR)*

3. Having your child say a repeated phrase with you throughout the book keeps him or her involved.   *(T, PR)*

4. Be sure to take time every day for your child to see you read. Children who see parents reading are more likely to be readers themselves.   *(ET, T, PR)*

5. Don't worry about whether or not your child can see this big book. We'll read it together. Your child loves the sound of your voice. Use a slightly higher pitched voice and speak more clearly and slowly than when speaking with adults. This is called "parentese." Researchers find that speaking in "parentese" keeps your child's attention longer than using your regular voice. Your child will respond to your voice and to the rhythm of language. Watch your child as we read the book together.   *(ET)*

6. You may often hear the phrase "Read with your child fifteen minutes a day," or "Read with your child twenty minutes a day." No one expects young children to sit and be

read to that long at one sitting. Two or three minutes at a time is fine. It is more important for the interaction between you and your child to be a positive one than it is for it to be a long one. Researchers have found that if the interaction around books is a negative one with impatient words or negative feelings, then the child associates reading with a negative feeling. So, the more you share books and talk together, the better, but do it when it can be a positive experience for you and your child. If your child is not in the mood, look for a few minutes when your child is quietly alert. *(ET, T)*

7. When children are young, they treat books as they would any other toy. This means they put them in their mouths and explore them by pushing and pulling and sometimes tearing them. We may say, "Ohhhhh, noooo, don't put that in your mouth." But we want our children to feel comfortable with books. So, just take the book gently from your child's mouth and start showing him or her the pictures. Keep some books in their toy box. Having a positive association with books, print motivation, is one of the skills that researchers have shown is an important part of a strong foundation for reading. *(ET)*

8. When you are reading a book with your child, don't worry about whether you get to finish the book or not. Engage your child as much as you can, with your voice, by asking questions, talking about the pictures. When your child loses interest, just continue another time. By following your child's lead, you can help make book sharing a positive experience. This supports *print motivation,* a love of books. *(ET, T, PR)*

9. Parents, another important skill that children need before beginning formal reading instruction is actually more of an attribute or even attitude. It is called *print motivation*, or interest in and enjoyment of books. One way to encourage this is to use books as a jumping-off point into children's imaginations. *(PR)*

10. Have books in every room, in the car, and in the diaper bag. You can catch little times when you and your child can enjoy sharing books. *(ET)*

11. When we play with the ideas that we find in a book, we are helping to make the story part of the child's life. By encouraging them to play along with the story, we are helping them incorporate the words, ideas, and energy of the story into their play. By making books and their stories fun, we are helping to motivate them to want more. *(T, PR)*

12. Today we are going to look at some fiction and nonfiction books. *Print motivation*, or the desire to look at and use books, can be encouraged by following what children like and enjoy and by making picture book sharing fun. You can do this is by using both story and real-life books, or fiction and nonfiction books, and by picking lively, engaging stories. If you notice that your child likes a particular book, we would be happy to help you choose others like it. Just tell us what your child likes about the book, and we will try to find others that are similar. *(T, PR)*

13. Some children prefer true (nonfiction) books to storybooks. We have many books on subjects young children like in our nonfiction section. Ask me for the subjects your child is interested in—trains, particular animals, planets, anything—and I'll show you where to find books on that topic. *(T, PR)*

14. Promoting literacy does not mean creating a school-like setting in your home but rather taking advantage of the opportunities in your everyday life. *(T, PR)*

Phonological Awareness

1. One of the six early literacy skills that children need before learning to read is *phonological awareness*. This is the ability to hear and play with the smaller sounds in words, like rhyming and playing with syllables or parts of words.   *(ET, T, PR)*

   [Point to poster if you have one in the room.]

2. Do the rhymes, songs, and movements in ways that work for you and your child. There is no right or wrong way to do them. Please share different versions or ways you do them with us, if you'd like. Bring rhymes and songs you know or remember from your family. We can do them together. All this rhyming and singing is helping your child hear parts of words, one way to help develop phonological awareness. *(ET, T, PR)*

3. Today I'll be pointing out some activities that support early literacy in the area of *phonological awareness*. This is the term that researchers give to the ability to break words down into parts. Things like rhyming and hearing the beginning sounds of words are part of phonological awareness. You can see what we do here in storytime, and you may get some ideas of what you can do with your child throughout the day. *(ET, T, PR)*

4. Hearing the rhythm of language and making the animal sounds contribute to *phonological awareness*, which is hearing sounds in words, one of the skills that researchers have found helps with reading later on.   *(ET, T, PR)*

5. Nursery rhymes are fun to sing and say, and because they rhyme, they also help children develop *phonological awareness*. This is the word educators use for the ability to play with parts of words. Research shows this is an important skill for reading.   *(ET)*

6. Even though young children do not understand the meanings of the rhymes, it is important for them to hear them. By six months of age, babies are already able to recognize the sounds of the languages they hear. They also are losing those sounds they don't hear even though they were born able to learn to make them.   *(ET)*

7. Rhyming is one way that children learn to hear that words are made up of smaller parts. By doing rhymes with them you are supporting phonological awareness. This skill helps them when they later try to sound out words to read. And it's fun, too. *(ET, T, PR)*

8. As you can see, nursery rhymes expose children to words that are not used in everyday conversation. Researchers have found that children who know rhymes find it easier to learn to read.   *(ET, T, PR)*

9. Hearing and learning animal sounds help children hear different kinds of sounds. Animals make different sounds in different languages.   *(ET, T)*

10. Having your child hear and make the sounds of animals is one enjoyable way to help develop phonological awareness, to eventually be able to hear the smaller sounds in words.   *(ET, T)*

11. Reading rhyming books and sharing rhymes both help your child hear parts of words. You can play "I Spy" like this, too. "I spy with my little eye something that is white and rhymes with sock." "Clock!" You can play these games with any book or picture or even as you walk or drive around. These games are an enjoyable way to develop your child's phonological awareness.   *(T, PR)*

12. Aside from being fun, singing songs with your baby/toddler helps him or her hear words being broken up into smaller sounds. This skill is part of phonological awareness and later helps them with reading.   *(ET, T, PR)*

13. Singing is fun! Don't worry if you don't have perfect pitch! In songs, each syllable has a different note. Without really thinking about it, children are hearing words being broken down into parts. This helps them when they have to sound out words. *(ET, T, PR)*

14. Today we are going to be changing the first sounds in words and breaking words into their smaller parts. These skills are part of *phonological awareness*, the ability to hear and play with the smaller sounds in words. These are skills that will help the children once they have to try to decode words. *(PR)*

15. *Phonological awareness* involves understanding that words are made up of smaller sounds. When they have this skill, children are able to think about how words sound, separate from what they mean. *(PR)*

16. Changing initial sounds helps children see that words are made up of sounds and that those sounds can be manipulated. This will help them when they need to decode and sound out words. *(PR)*

17. At home, have your child think of other words that start with the same sound as the first sound in your child's name. Children learn best by doing activities that are meaningful to them. *(PR)*

18. When we separate a word into its sounds, it is called *segmentation*. Playing with this when children are little will help them later when they are bigger and have to break words into syllables as a way of decoding words. Clapping out the parts of words is one way to help your child hear the parts of words. *(PR)*

19. *Phonemic awareness* deals with the sounds of spoken language. To read phonetically, children need phonemic awareness, which is why it is important to work on these skills with your children. *(PR)*

20. Take advantage of every opportunity to play with rhyme and the sounds of words. Have fun this week as you rhyme around town and combine sounds, too! *(ET, T, PR)*

21. Take advantage of every opportunity to play with words. Make up riddles or play "I Spy" as you wait in the doctor's office or anywhere else. Not only will your children learn but also it will lessen the boredom and tension of waiting! *(ET, T, PR)*

22. Research has shown that children who play with sounds of words in their preschool years are better prepared to read when they get to school. *(PR)*

Vocabulary

1. *Vocabulary* is knowing the names of things and concepts, feelings, and ideas. Researchers have found that children who have heard a lot of different words and have a large vocabulary find it easier to read when that time comes. *(ET, T, PR)*

2. Today I'll be pointing out some activities we are doing that support early literacy in the areas of vocabulary and narrative skills. *[Point to poster if you have one in the room.]* I'll also be suggesting some activities you can do throughout the day. *(ET, T, PR)*

3. *[Can use when demonstrating dialogic reading.]* Today I'll be pointing out some activities we are doing that support early literacy in the areas of vocabulary and narrative skills. Researchers have found that these are two of the skills that are part of a

solid foundation for being ready to read. *Vocabulary* is knowing the names of things. *Narrative skills* is being able to describe things and events and to tell a story.   *(T, PR)*

4. *[Hand out board books.]* When you read with your child, don't just read the words. Talk about the pictures. Describe what is going on. Leave time for your child to say something back. *[Demonstrate.]* This type of interaction sets the stage for increased vocabulary and narrative skills, which research has shown will help when your child begins to read. Go ahead and do it now with the rest of the book. Keep it cozy and fun. If your child gets tired of the book, just stop and do something else.   *(ET)*

5. This is a good rhyme to do as you are bathing or diapering your child (Head and Shoulders). Use different parts of the body and words for different actions to help increase your child's vocabulary. Even though your baby does not understand everything you say, it is important for him or her to hear you speak. The wider variety of words your child hears, the larger his or her vocabulary will be, and reading will come more easily.   *(ET, T)*

6. We just went through the book from start to finish, feeling the rhythm of the text and noticing the sequence between each action. Now let's go through it again. This time we'll read it but also talk about what is happening in the pictures, the way you would with your baby or toddler. This way of sharing books helps your child develop vocabulary and narrative skills.   *(ET, T)*

7. One way you can help increase your child's vocabulary is by narrating your day, saying what you are doing while you are doing it. Or you can say what your child is doing as she or he is doing it. You might even add little stories about when you were a child. By doing this, you are exposing your child to lots of language! Leave your child time to respond, even if you cannot understand what she or he is saying.   *(ET, T, PR)*

8. When you do this rhyme at home, add on parts of the body that we may not often mention, such as elbow, wrist, and eyebrow.   *(ET, T)*

9. As you can see, nursery rhymes expose children to words that are not used in everyday conversation. Researchers have found that children who know rhymes find it easier to learn to read.   *(ET, T, PR)*

10. The language used in storybooks is different from what we use when we are speaking. Stories also have a certain structure, with a beginning, a middle, and an end. By exposing your children to storybooks, you help them become familiar with the way language is written. Reading and sharing stories with children is fun. It also will help them to know what to expect when they read stories themselves.   *(ET, T, PR)*

11. By using specific names for things, like cat and kitten, you help your child learn new words and you help them understand differences between similar things. This is one way to increase their vocabulary.   *(ET, T)*

12. You can help children understand words they may not know by offering a little explanation as you go along. If you prefer, you can explain these words before you start a book. Research notes that the more words your children know and understand, the more vocabulary they have, the easier it will be for them when they begin to read.   *(T, PR)*

13. This book (*A Place for Ben*, by Jeanne Titherington, or *On Mother's Lap*, by Ann Scott) allows you to talk about feelings. You can turn to a page and talk about what is happening in the picture. How does the child feel? You help your child talk about how he or she feels if you use the words for both what your child is feeling and what you yourself are feeling. This develops vocabulary and also helps your child talk about what he or she feels. *(T, PR)*

14. Children like to hear books over and over. We can point out different words or pictures at different times. This will help them build their vocabulary. *(T, PR)*

15. Ask us to help you find some nonfiction/ true books on things your child is interested in. We can all learn new words and new things together from these books! *(T, PR)*

16. Even in a fairly simple story like this one, there are many words that we don't use in everyday conversation. *[Give examples, such as* **Dinosaur Roar!** *by Paul Strickland, and* **The Napping House,** *by Audrey Wood.]* Even if you don't talk about the meaning of all the unfamiliar words, your child hears the words in the story and gets an idea of what they mean from hearing the story and from the pictures. *(T, PR)*

17. Jim Trelease, in his *Read-Aloud Handbook*, notes that children's books have about thirty-one rare words per thousand words; that's three times more than in conversation and 25 percent more rare words than what is on television programs. The more of these rare words the children know, the easier it will be when it comes time for school and formal learning. *(PR)*

18. The more words kids know, the better off they will be when they learn to read. Research tells us that it is easier to read a word that is known to you. You can use books to help expand your child's vocabulary. Look for words that have the same meaning, or synonyms. You can also look at words that are opposites, or antonyms. *(PR)*

Narrative Skills

1. *Narrative skills* is the ability to describe things and to talk about events and tell stories. Researchers have highlighted this skill as one of the six early literacy skills that will help your child be ready to read. *(ET, T, PR)*

2. When your baby babbles and coos, talk to him or her and add some more words. Don't worry that you can't understand what your baby is saying! *(ET)*

3. When you talk with your baby, leave time for your baby to answer with babbling or cooing. She or he is learning that conversations go two ways. This is the beginning of narrative skills. *(ET)*

4. *[Can use when demonstrating dialogic reading.]* Today I'll be pointing out some activities we are doing that support early literacy in the areas of vocabulary and narrative skills. Researchers have found that these are two of the skills that are part of a solid foundation for being ready to read. *Vocabulary* is knowing the names of things. *Narrative skills* is being able to describe things and events and to tell a story. *(T, PR)*

5. We just went through the book from start to finish, feeling the rhythm of the text and noticing the sequence between each action. Now let's go through it again. This time we'll read it but also talk about what is happening in the pictures, the way you would with your baby or toddler. This way of sharing books helps your child develop vocabulary and narrative skills. *(ET, T)*

6. The language used in storybooks is different from what we use when we are speaking. Stories also have a certain structure, with a beginning, a middle, and an end. By exposing your children to storybooks, you help them become familiar with the way language is written. Reading and sharing stories with children is fun. It helps them to know what to expect when they read stories themselves. *(ET, T, PR)*

7. *Narrative skills*, which includes the ability to retell stories, is one of the early literacy skills that researchers say children need to understand what they read. Using things you have around the house as props can help children remember a story and retell it. *(T, PR)*

8. When you ask your child questions, give him or her extra time to think and to answer you. Talking back and forth uses three different parts of the brain, so it takes him or her some time to form his or her responses. *(T, PR)*

9. Research shows that hearing a question and forming a response involve at least three different parts of the brain. You may have noticed that it takes children longer than adults to respond to questions because they have not had as much practice at it as we have. Try to wait about five seconds to give your child time to respond to what you say. *[Count off on your hand, slowly raising one finger at a time to show five seconds.]* We can even try this now as I ask you all to think of some things about our theme today. *(T, PR)*

10. Acting out stories or parts of them, having young children use their whole bodies, helps them internalize and understand what is happening in the story. They will be able to tell the story back to you, especially their favorites, which they like to hear over and over again. *(T, PR)*

11. When we talk about a story after reading it with a child, we are helping him or her remember what he or she heard and to recap it. It helps to reinforce new vocabulary words because children have the opportunity to use the words again. It also is one of the first steps in learning how stories work, which will help children when they read. The ability to predict stories is based on their experience with books and is an important part of being a good reader. *(T, PR)*

12. Remember to summarize stories after you read them. You can also help children get the idea of putting activities in sequence by telling them what you are going to do. For example, first we are going to storytime, then we are going to pick out some books, and then we are going to go home. *(T, PR)*

13. Practice telling and retelling stories. Talk about the movies and television shows that you watch together. This will help them later to talk about books. *(PR)*

14. Children enjoy talking about what they have read. It is a good way to engage them in conversation and for them to remember the story they have read. The ability to retell a story is an important skill to learn before going to school. *(PR)*

15. As you go about your day together, talk about what you are doing. Summarize with your child what you did this morning or yesterday. Talk about your activities in the order that they occurred. This will help them to become familiar with the idea that their activities, like stories, have a sequence. *(PR)*

Print Awareness

1. *Print awareness* is knowing how to handle a book, and noticing print all around us.
   (ET, T, PR)

2. Today I'll be pointing out some activities that support early literacy in the area of *print awareness. [Point to poster if you have one in the room.]* This is the term that researchers give to being aware of how books work and how we follow the words on the page. You can see what we do here in storytime, and you may get some ideas of what you can do with your child throughout the day.
   (ET, T, PR)

3. When children are young, they treat books as they would any other toy. This means they put them in their mouths and explore them by pushing and pulling and sometimes tearing them. Sometimes people keep books out of reach of young children. Of course, some books are special and will need to be kept out of reach, but allowing children to explore books is how they learn to handle them. Keep some in their toy box. If you have a bookshelf, keep some books face out, not spine out, so children can see the pictures on the covers and be drawn to them. By doing these things you help your child develop print awareness. They are learning how books work, with pages that turn. This is one of the skills that researchers have shown is an important part of a strong foundation for reading.
   (ET)

4. When you are selecting books for young children, choose ones that have pictures of things that are familiar to them. If a book has a picture of an apple, talk about the apple in the picture, for example, its color. Then get a real apple and show it to your child. Talk about how it tastes—sweet; how it feels—round and smooth; and how it feels when you bite it—crunchy. Tell children it's too hard for them to eat because they don't have teeth yet, but they eat applesauce, which is made from apples! By showing the child the real object, you help your child realize that pictures *represent* real things. Later, they will also understand that printed words represent real things.
   (ET)

5. You can run your finger under the words of the title as you say it. This helps children understand that you are reading the text, not the pictures. Do this only with the title or a repeated phrase so it doesn't get in the way of sharing the story.
   (T, PR)

6. Here is a story (*Bunny Cakes*, by Rosemary Wells) where writing is important to the story. You can have your child draw pictures and "write" lists. As you walk around or drive around, point out signs and what they say. They become aware that print is all around us.
   (T, PR)

7. Hold a book upside down or backward. See if children notice that it is upside down. If not, point it out. Children need to know how to hold a book, which part is the front, and which is the back of the book. This is one fun way to find out if they know this.
   (PR)

8. You can help your children see the relationship between the written and spoken word by using what is called *environmental print*, or words that are part of our everyday lives, like signs and labels. This is part of print awareness.
   (T, PR)

9. Writing can be very motivating. It helps children make the connection between the spoken and the written word. Encourage your children to write. You could begin by making a shopping list together the next time you go shopping.
   (T, PR)

10. The activity we just did is called *story dictation*. It helps children learn the relationship between the spoken and the written word.
    (PR)

Letter Knowledge

1. *Letter knowledge* is knowing that letters are different from each other and that the same letter can look different ways. It is also knowing that letters have sounds.   *(ET, T, PR)*

2. Researchers have noted one of the six areas of early literacy is *letter knowledge*. This means recognizing letters and knowing the names and sounds of letters. Alphabet books are one way to help children become aware of letters and how they look. It is best not to quiz your child on the letters. Just point them out as you are reading through the book. The letter your child is likely to be the most interested in is the first letter of his or her name. Make sure you point out that letter when you come to it.
   (T, PR)

3. Young children learn through their senses. Touching, smelling, and tasting are as important as hearing and seeing. Give them opportunities to feel different textures and shapes. What feels the same, and what feels different? These introductory opportunities help them later when they try to make out differences in the shapes of letters and when they try to figure out what is the same and what is different among them.   *(ET)*

4. By using specific names for things, like cat and kitten, you not only help your child learn new words, you also help him or her understand differences between similar things. This sets the stage for them seeing differences in many things, including, later, differences in the way letters look.   *(ET, T)*

5. Before children learn actual letters, they are aware of shapes. Before they have the coordination to hold a crayon and write, they can move their whole arms and bodies. Let's see you make a circle shape with your whole body!   *(T, PR)*

6. Showing children letters based on subjects they like follows the child's interest. They are more likely to remember the letter than if you drill them.   *(PR)*

7. Point out letters and their sounds wherever you go. The most interesting letters for most children are the ones in their names, so begin there and have fun!   *(PR)*

8. For most children drilling is not fun. Children can learn letters in many ways that are fun and that will keep their attention longer. For example, they can make letters using their bodies, then their fingers. They can draw letters in the water when they take a bath or with chalk on the sidewalk, or they can form letters with play dough. Keep it fun. Talk about the letters in your child's name or in a subject that the child is interested in, like trucks, volcanoes, or kittens.   *(PR)*

9. Reading alphabet books with a story is one way to expose children to letters. Some alphabet books are quite complicated. Feel free to ask me to help you find some for your child.   *(T, PR)*

10. Research indicates that children benefit most from learning both the sound and the letter name at the same time. When you teach them their letters, explain that the letter is called _____, and it makes the sound _____. Start with letters that have meaning to your child (like his or her name).   *(PR)*

11. Children learn best by doing. Remember that letter play should be meaningful. Show letters in the context of objects and words that they know and can touch or play with. *(PR)*

General Comments

1. Because *you* who are with your children throughout the day are the best ones to develop early literacy skills in your children, I will be sharing with you throughout the storytime ways that you can continue to develop ____(skill)____ with your children. *(E, T, PR)*

2. Children learn best by taking advantage of little times during the day when they are ready to learn. You know your child's routines and his moods best. During the storytime I'll be sharing some ideas and activities you can do to support some of the six early literacy skills that researchers have determined are necessary to help your child be ready to read. *(E, T, PR)*

3. In the past I have not always asked all the adults in the room to fully participate in storytime. Now, however, I have read a book/ taken training that has made me more aware of how important you—the adult who is with the child throughout the day—are to your child's early literacy development. For that reason, I am asking you to sit with your children and to participate as much as you can so that your children will follow your lead. From time to time, I will be highlighting ways you can continue to develop early literacy skills at home.

4. Children learn by repetition. Infants and young children have the most active brains. The more stimulation they receive from their environment—what they see, hear, touch, taste, and smell—the more connections are made between brain cells. After a while, there are so many connections that the ones that are not used are pruned. It is repetition that keeps connections and makes them strong. So at home or in the car, do these rhymes and songs over and again. It's fun! *(ET, T)*

5. Toddlers often have short attention spans, but they can follow shorter stories. Storybooks offer them one way to try to make sense of their world. Follow their interests, like stories that build on their own experiences—having a dog, going on a picnic. *(ET, T)*

6. Your children love to hear the sound of your voice. They also pick up on the rhythm of language, so we'll try some rhymes and songs together. As you repeat them at home, notice what your child does as she or he responds to different ones. As children get older and more familiar with them, they start to clap or do the motions to a rhyme or song they recognize. *(ET)*

7. Children of different ages need different kinds of books. An infant's vision is blurry. Infants need pictures with bright colors and stark contrast between the background and the object. As they get a little older, they focus better and enjoy looking at pictures of things that are familiar to them, especially faces. As they become toddlers, they enjoy the predictability of repeated words and actions in a book and can focus on pictures that have detail. *(ET, T)*

8. Peek-a-boo is a game young children love. It helps them learn object permanence, the concept that even if something cannot be seen, it is still there (the parent, for example). When they are under ten months old, it is good to cover your own eyes. As your baby gets older, you can cover his or her eyes. Many books play with the idea of peek-a-boo. *(ET)*

Storytime Planning Sheet

You may find it easier to highlight just one skill, or even just one aspect of one skill, during any one storytime (for example, only the rhyming aspect of phonological awareness).

All storytimes must model print motivation, the enjoyment of books and reading, whether or not you specifically articulate information about print motivation.

1. Fill in your storytime plan in the order you intend to do it. (You may do some modification depending on ways you highlight a skill.)
2. Choose a skill or an aspect of a skill to highlight. (Use list below.)
3. Fill in what you will say related to the skill (using "What Can I Say: From Skill to Parent/Caregiver" from appendix C as a guide, if you like) for the following:

>   the opening early literacy tip
>
>   one or two messages to adults during the storytime
>
>   the closing

Skills

Choose one or two skills from the list below. Depending on what you want to say, you can highlight one aspect of a skill or highlight the skill in general. (You will not have a highlighted skill for every component.)

- ☐ Print Motivation: Enjoyment of Books
- ☐ Phonological Awareness
    - ☐ Rhyming
    - ☐ Breaking words apart and putting them together
    - ☐ Hearing beginning sounds/alliteration
- ☐ Print Awareness
    - ☐ With books
    - ☐ In the environment
- ☐ Vocabulary
    - ☐ Introducing new words
    - ☐ Explaining (not replacing) words
    - ☐ Adding new meanings to familiar words
- ☐ Narrative Skills
    - ☐ Retelling stories
    - ☐ Retelling events
    - ☐ Adding descriptions
- ☐ Letter Knowledge
    - ☐ Same and different
    - ☐ Letter shapes
    - ☐ Letter names
    - ☐ Letter sounds

STORYTIME COMPONENT	COMMENT TO ADULTS BASED ON RESEARCH
Early literacy tip	
Closing to adults	
Display/handouts	

D

Early Literacy Aids

Language of Early Literacy

Phoneme

The smallest part of spoken language that makes a difference in the meaning of words
English has about forty-one phonemes. The word *if* has two phonemes (/i/ /f/). The word *check* has three phonemes (/ch/ /e/ /ck/). Sometimes one phoneme is represented by more than one letter.

Phonemic Awareness

The ability to hear, identify, and manipulate the individual sounds (phonemes) in spoken words

Phonological Awareness

The understanding that spoken language is made up of individual and separate sounds
A broad term that includes phonemic awareness in addition to work with rhymes, words, syllables, and beginning sounds.

Grapheme

The smallest part of written language that represents a phoneme in the spelling of a word
A grapheme may be just one letter, such as *b, f, p,* or *s,* or several letters, such as *ch, sh, ea,* or *igh.*

Phonics

The understanding that there is a predictable relationship between phonemes *(the sounds of the* spoken *language) and* graphemes *(the letters and spellings that represent those sounds in* written *language)*

Syllable

A word part that contains a vowel or, in spoken language, a vowel sound

---

Put Reading First: The Research Building Blocks for Teaching Children to Read, U.S. Department of Education, 2001. Available from the National Institute for Literacy, http://www.nifl.gov.

Books for Dialogic Hear and Say Reading

What kinds of books work best?
Books that
- Have clear pictures
- Have a simple story
- Are not too long
- Have pictures of things that are familiar to your child
- Show action and detail in the pictures
- Are interesting to your child

Some examples:

Benny Bakes a Cake by Eve Rice
Big Red Barn by Margaret Wise Brown
Chugga-Chugga Choo-Choo by Kevin Lewis
Cows in the Kitchen by June Crebbin
Curious George Rides a Bike by H. A. Rey
Good Night, Gorilla by Peggy Rathmann
Jesse Bear books by Nancy Carlstrom
Jump, Frog, Jump by Robert Kalan
New Road! by Gail Gibbons
Trucks by Anne Rockwell
Wind Blew by Pat Hutchins
Books by Richard Scarry

Visit your local public library.
Ask library staff for more suggestions!

Dialogic Reading Hear and Say Reading

Part I: Tips to Build Vocabulary
Ask "what" questions
    You can point, but not your child
    Questions that cannot be answered with "yes" or "no"
Follow answers with another question
Repeat what your child says
Give answer and child repeats
Help your child as needed
Praise and encourage your child
Follow your child's interests

ENJOY!

Part II: Tips to Build Sentence Skills
Ask "open-ended" questions
    What's going on here?
    Tell me what you see on this page.
Follow answers with another question:
    What else do you see?
    I wonder how . . .
    How did that happen?
    What do you think?
    How does he feel?
    When have you felt . . .?
Expand what your child says
    Add another piece of information
Help your child repeat your longer phrases

ENJOY!

Six skills your child needs to learn to read starting from birth

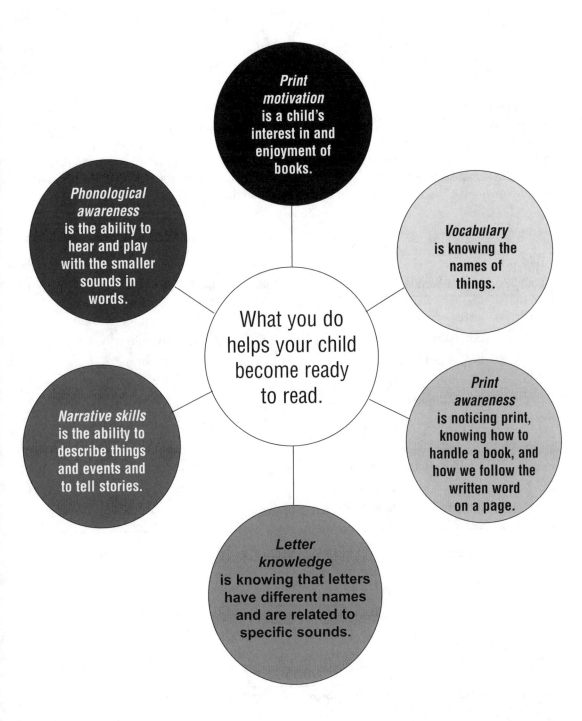

Print motivation is a child's interest in and enjoyment of books.

Vocabulary is knowing the names of things.

Phonological awareness is the ability to hear and play with the smaller sounds in words.

Print awareness is noticing print, knowing how to handle a book, and how we follow the written word on a page.

What you do helps your child become ready to read.

Narrative skills is the ability to describe things and events and to tell stories.

Letter knowledge is knowing that letters have different names and are related to specific sounds.

Letters and Letter Sounds

The following is the rough order of sounds as they develop in children's speech. You do not need to teach these sounds in this exact order. Avoid words with the initial letters q, sh, ch, and th, because the written letters do not correspond to the speech sounds (e.g., the first sound in church is not a c sound as in cat).

> Start with these letter sounds: *w, p, b, d, t, m, n, h, y.*

> Do these letter sounds next: *f, v, s, z, g, k/c.* (*k* and *c* have the same sound but are different letters. Teach them separately.)

> Do these letter sounds last: *j, l, r.*

Remember that letter-sound activities you do should be fun. Have your child listen for the *sounds* in words. Often, alphabet books choose pictures to depict a letter by the way it is *spelled*, not the way it *sounds* (e.g., *cheese* as a /c/ word; *giraffe* as a /g/ word). If you see this, do not include that word in your activity. To reduce confusion, it is important to be consistent. Choose simple words, and choose words that sound the way they are spelled. The following is a chart of letter sounds and suggested words to use in word games.

LETTER SOUND	SAMPLE WORDS	LETTER SOUND	SAMPLE WORDS
W	water, worm, wet, window	V	violin, van, vase, vacuum
P	pot, paint, pear, pool	S	sock, soap, sun, spoon
B	boy, bed, bike, ball	Z	zoo, zebra, zipper
D	door, dime, doll, dog	G	goat, gate, game, grass
T	toe, toy, truck, tree	K	kite, kangaroo, king, kiss
M	mop, mail, milk, man	C	cat, cake, cookie, car
N	net, nap, neck, nose	J	juice, jar, jacks, jelly
H	house, hill, horse, head	L	light, lion, lip, leg
Y	yogurt, yo-yo, yard, yellow	R	rake, rain, raisin, rock
F	food, fork, fox, fan		

Source: "Every Child Ready to Read @ your library" Prereader Workshop Handout, http://www.pla.org/earlyliteracy.htm.

APPENDIX

E

Resources

Books

Armbruster, Bonnie, Fran Lehr, and Jean Osborn. *Put Reading First: The Research Building Blocks for Teaching Children to Read, Kindergarten through Grade Three*. Jessup, MD: National Institute for Literacy, 2001.

Apel, Kenn, and Julie Masterson. *Beyond Baby Talk: From Sounds to Sentences—A Parent's Complete Guide to Language Development*. Roseville, CA: Prima, 2001.

Beaty, Janice L. *Early Literacy in Pre-School and Kindergarten*. Upper Saddle River, N.J.: Merrill, 2003.

Benzwie, Teresa. *Alphabet Movers*. Bethesda, MD: National Dance Education Organization, 2002.

Benzwie, Teresa, and Robert Bender. *Moving Experience: Dance for Lovers of Children and the Child Within*. Tucson, AZ: Zephyr, 1987.

Blachman, Benita A. *Road to the Code: A Phonological Awareness Program for Young Children*. Baltimore, MD: Paul H. Brookes, 2000.

Dickson, David, and Patton Tabors. *Beginning Literacy with Language*. Baltimore, MD: Paul H. Brookes, 2001.

Fox, Mem. *Reading Magic: Why Reading Aloud to Our Children Will Change Their Lives Forever*. San Diego: Harcourt, 2001.

Hall, Susan, and Louise Moats. *Straight Talk about Reading: How Parents Can Make a Difference during the Early Years*. Chicago: Contemporary Books, 1999.

Hart, Betty, and Todd Risley. *Meaningful Differences in the Everyday Experiences of Young American Children*. Baltimore, MD: Paul H. Brookes, 1995.

Jalongo, Mary. *Young Children and Picture Books*. 2nd ed. Washington, DC: National Association for the Education of Young Children, 2004.

Manolson, Ayala. *It Takes Two to Talk: A Parent's Guide to Helping Children Communicate*. Toronto, Canada: Hanen Centre, 1992.

National Reading Panel. *Teaching Children to Read: An Evidence-Based Assessment of the Scientific Research Literature on Reading and Its Implications for Reading Instruction*. Jessup, MD: National Institute for Literacy, 2000.

National Research Council. *Starting Out Right: A Guide to Promoting Children's Reading Success*. Washington, DC: National Academy, 1999.

Newman, Susan, and David K. Dickinson. *Handbook of Early Literacy Research*. New York: Guildford, 2001.

Opitz, Michael. *Rhymes and Reasons: Literature and Language Play for Phonological Awareness*. Portsmouth, NH: Heinemann, 2000.

Ramey, Craig, and Sharon Ramey. *Right from Birth: Building Your Child's Foundation for Life: Birth to 18 Months*. New York: Goddard, 1999.

Schickedanz, Judith. *Much More Than the ABCs: The Early Stages of Reading and Writing*. Washington, DC: National

Association for the Education of Young Children, 1999.

Schiller, Pamela Byrne. *Creating Readers: Over 1,000 Games, Activities, Tongue Twisters, Fingerplays, Songs, and Stories to Get Children Excited about Reading*. Beltsville, MD: Gryphon House, 2000.

Schiller, Pamela Byrne, and Pat Phipps. *Complete Daily Curriculum for Early Childhood: Over 1200 Easy Activities to Support Multiple Intelligences and Learning Styles*. Beltsville, MD: Gryphon House, 2002.

Snow, Catherine, Susan Burns, and Peg Griffin, eds. *Preventing Reading Difficulties in Young Children*. Washington, DC: National Academy, 1998.

Tabors, Patton. *One Child, Two Languages: A Guide for Preschool Educators of Children Learning English as a Second Language*. Baltimore, MD: Paul H. Brookes, 1997.

Trelease, Jim. *Read-Aloud Handbook*. 5th ed. New York: Penguin, 2001.

Weitzman, Elaine, and Janice Greenberg. *Learning Language and Loving It: A Guide to Promoting Children's Social, Language, and Literacy Development in Early Childhood Settings*. Toronto, Canada: Hanen Centre, 2002.

Video and Aids

Early literacy posters available at: http://www .pla.org/earlyliteracy.htm. (Click on "Workshops," then scroll down to "Posters and other aids.")

Huebner, Colleen. *Hear and Say: Reading with Toddlers*. Bainbridge Island, WA: Rotary Club of Bainbridge Island, 2001.

Playing Around with Words: Games and Activities to Develop Phonological Awareness in 4–5-Year-Olds. Explains and demonstrates how playing simple games throughout the day develops phonological awareness. Available from the Public Library Association: http://www.pla.org/ earlyliteracy.htm.

Playing with Words on the Go! A set of cards on a ring developed to use with children throughout the day to promote phonological awareness; available from Allen County (IN) Public Library. Proceeds go to the library's early literacy programming. Information available from Branch Youth Services Coordinator, Allen County Public Library, (260) 421-1260.

Websites

For a good selective bibliography on early literacy, go to http://www.pla.org/earlyliteracy .htm and click on "Research and Evaluation," then on the bibliography on "Background Information." Includes books, videos, and websites. The URLs lead you directly to the early literacy information on the organizations' websites.

For the "Born to Read" program and products from ALA's Association for Library Service to Children, go to http://www.ala.org/ala/alsc/ alscpubs/borntoreadprod/bornreadproducts .htm.

For the "Curious George Read to Me" program CD-ROM, go to http://www.alastore .ala.org. Search for "Curious George" under "ALA Graphics."

For storytime ideas, go to the following websites:

http://leep.lis.uiuc.edu/publish/MESTILLW/ storytime (Storytime Web Resources list, compiled by PUBYAC member)

http://www.perpetualpreschool.com/

http://kididdles.com/mouseum/alpha.html (traditional kid songs, some with music files to hear online)

The storytime plans/ideas on these websites do not include parent messages.

Books and CDs Used
in Sample Storytimes

Books

Alborough, Jez. *Duck in the Truck.*

Aliki. *Dinosaur Bones.*

Arnold, Tedd. *Catalina Magdalena Hoopensteiner Wallendiner Hogan Logan Bogan Was Her Name.*

Asbjornsen, Peter. *The Three Billy Goats Gruff* (any version).

Barton, Byron. *Bones, Bones, Dinosaur Bones.*

———. *Three Bears.*

Beckman, Kaj. *Lisa Can't Sleep.*

Brett, Jan. *The Mitten.*

Brown, Margaret Wise. *Big Red Barn.*

Bunting, Eve. *Flower Garden.*

Burningham, John. *Mr. Gumpy's Outing.*

Carle, Eric. *The Very Hungry Caterpillar.*

Carling, Amelia. *Mama and Papa Have a Store.*

Carlstrom, Nancy White. *Jesse Bear, What Will You Wear?*

———. *Rise and Shine!*

Christelow, Eileen. *Five Little Monkeys Jumping on the Bed.*

Christian, Cheryl. *Where's the Baby?*

Coats, Laura. *Ten Little Animals.*

Crebbin, June. *Cows in the Kitchen.*

Dabcovich, Lydia. *Ducks Fly.*

De Paola, Tomie. *The Cloud Book.*

Eastman, P. D. *Are You My Mother?*

Ehlert, Lois. *Feathers for Lunch.*

———. *Growing Vegetable Soup.*

———. *Planting a Rainbow.*

———. *Snowballs.*

———. *Waiting for Wings.*

Falwell, Cathryn. *Feast for 10.*

———. *Turtle Splash: Countdown at the Pond.*

Fox, Mem. *Hattie and the Fox.*

———. *Time for Bed.*

Galdone. *The Little Red Hen.*

———. *Rumpelstiltskin.*

Gibbons, Gail. *The Seasons of Arnold's Apple Tree.*

Greene, Rhonda Gowler. *Barnyard Song.*

Greenfield, Eloise. *I Can Draw a Weeposaur and Other Dinosaurs.*

Guarino, Deborah. *Is Your Mama a Llama?*

Henderson, Kathy. *Baby Knows Best.*

Henkes, Kevin. *Chrysanthemum.*

Hest, Ann. *Don't You Feel Well, Sam?*

Hill, Eric. *Spot's Birthday.*

Ho, Mingfong. *Hush! A Thai Lullaby.*

Hoban, Tana. *All about Where.*

———. *Over, Under and Through.*

Hudson, Cheryl. *Hands Can.*

Hutchins, Pat. *Happy Birthday, Sam.*

Hutchinson, Pat. *Don't Forget the Bacon.*

Jonas, Ann. *Color Dance.*

Kalan, Robert. *Blue Sea.*

Kasza, Keiko. *A Mother for Choco.*

Keats, Ezra Jack. *The Snowy Day.*

Kopper, Lisa. *I'm a Baby, You're a Baby.*

Kraus, Robert. *Whose Mouse Are You?*

Kraus, Ruth. *The Carrot Seed.*

Lionni, Leo. *Little Blue and Little Yellow.*

Lobel, Anita. *Alison's Zinnia.*

Martin, Bill, Jr. *Brown Bear, Brown Bear, What Do You See?*

———. *Polar Bear, Polar Bear, What Do You Hear?*

McCarty, Peter. *T Is for Terrible.*

McGovern, Ann. *Too Much Noise.*

Meddaugh, Susan. *Martha Speaks.*

Miller, Jane. *Farm Alphabet Book.*

Morris, Ann. *Bread, Bread, Bread.*

Most, Bernard. *Z-Z-Zoink!*

Mother Goose (any version).

Numeroff, Laura. *If You Give a Mouse a Cookie*.

O'Connell, Rebecca. *The Baby Goes Beep*.

Oxenbury, Helen. *Tom and Pippo Go for a Walk*.

Piers, Helen. *Who's in My Bed?*

Rice, Eve. *Benny Bakes a Cake*.

————. *Sam Who Never Forgets*.

Riley, Linnea. *Mouse Mess*.

Roddie Shen. *You're Too Small*.

Root, Phyllis. *One Duck Stuck*.

Rosen, Michael. *We're Going on a Bear Hunt*.

Ryder, Joanne. *Where Butterflies Grow*.

Scott, Ann. *Hi!*

Sendak, Maurice. *Where the Wild Things Are*.

Shaw, Nancy. *Sheep in a Shop*.

Tafuri, Nancy. *Goodnight My Duckling*.

Titherington, Jeanne. *Pumpkin, Pumpkin*.

The Town Mouse and the Country Mouse (any version).

Waddell, Martin. *Farmer Duck*.

Walsh, Ellen Stoll. *Mouse Count*.

————. *Mouse Paint*.

Wells, Rosemary. *Bunny Cakes*.

Wheeler, Lisa. *Te Amo, Bebe, Little One*.

The Wheels on the Bus. (any version).

White, Judy. *Mouse Look Out!*

Williams, Sue. *I Went Walking*.

Wilson, Karma. *Bear Wants More*.

Wood, Don, and Audrey Wood. *King Bidgood's in the Bathtub*.

CDs and Audiotapes

Beall, Pamela. *Wee Sing for Baby*.

Duane, Carol Rose. *Lively Songs and Lullabies* (Music for Very Little People, 14223 Masterpiece Lane, Potomac, MD 20878; 301-424-6677).

Hammett, Carol. *Toddlers on Parade*.

McGrath, Bob. *Songs and Games for Toddlers*.

Raffi. *One Light, One Sun*.

————. *Rise and Shine*.

Robert Shaw Chorale. *Sea Shanties*.

Seeger, Pete. *Birds, Beasts, Bugs and Fishes*.

Sesame Street. *Hot! Hot! Hot! Dance Songs*.

Sharon, Lois and Bram. *Mainly Mother Goose*.

Index

phonological awareness (*cont.*)
definition, 4, 255
development of, 12
ideas for storytimes, 200–201
and letter knowledge, 15
letter to parents, 236
with name tags, 21
and non-English speakers, 46
and picture books, 24–25
in rhymes and songs, 29
symbol for, 56
take-home tip sheet, 230, 231, 232, 233, 234
picture books, use of skills with, 23–29
Piers, Helen, 115, 262
planning storytimes, 51–56, 196–210
Planting a Rainbow (Ehlert), 145, 261
poems
When I Was a Baby, 189
Polar Bear, Polar Bear, What Do You Hear? (Martin, Bill), 60–61, 261
poverty and early literacy, 10–11
prereaders, 19, 54–55. *See also* Storytimes for prereaders
print awareness
comments to adults, 249–250
comments to adults at ET storytimes, 61, 80–81, 100
comments to adults at PR storytimes, 157, 160, 192, 193
comments to adults at T storytimes, 124, 125, 126, 128
definition, 4, 14
and flip charts, 52
ideas for storytimes, 202
letter to parents, 239
name tags, 20
and picture books, 27–28
in rhymes and songs, 30
symbol for, 56
take-home tip sheet, 230
and writing activities, 33
print motivation
comments to adults, 242–243
comments to adults at ET storytimes, 60, 80–81, 94
comments to adults at PR storytimes, 148, 150, 155
comments to adults at T storytimes, 109, 110, 116
definition, 4
ideas for storytimes, 200
letter to parents, 235
name tags, 20
and picture books, 24
role of parents/caregivers, 12
symbol for, 56
promotion of early literacy, 218–225
Pumpkin, Pumpkin (Titherington), 137, 262
puppets, rhymes and songs with
Furry, Furry Squirrel, 83
Hey Diddle Diddle, 85

I Had a Little Rooster, 85–86
Sippity Sup, 72
Two Little Blackbirds, 90
When Ducks Get Up in the Morning, 102–103

reading difficulties, prevention of, 9, 11
reading programs and early literacy programs, 220
reading readiness, 5. *See also* Early literacy
reading skills in school-age children, 3, 4
receptive language, 53
reference interviews with parents/caregivers, 221
repetition
and brain research, 8
comments to adults at ET storytimes, 71
in storytimes, 51–52
research on early literacy, ix, 6–15
brain research, 6–8
dialogic reading, 35
early literacy skills, 12–15
family economics, 10–11
individual risk factors, 11
shared reading, 9
television viewing, 10
rhymes. *See also* Action rhymes
Diddle, Diddle, Dumpling, 81
Five Green Apples, 116
Five Little Monkeys, 111–112
Furry, Furry Squirrel, 83
Hey Diddle Diddle, 85
Humpty Dumpty, 79, 121
Jack and Jill Went up the Hill, 78
and literacy skills, 29–31
Little Flea, 96, 204
Pizza Pickle Pumpernickel, 95
Rainbow Kittens, 111
'Round and 'Round the Garden, 96
Sippity Sup, 72
Two Little Blackbirds, 90
Rice, Eve, 125, 127, 262
Ricklen, Mark, 205, 262
Riley, Linnea, 165, 262
Rise and Shine! (Carlstrom), 185–186, 261
Roddie, Shen, 135, 262
Root, Phyllis, 179, 262
Rosen, Michael, 169, 262
"'Round and 'Round We Go" (ET), 63–69
Rumpelstiltskin (Galdone), 177, 261
Ryder, Joanne, 194, 262

Sam Who Never Forgets (Rice), 127, 262
Scott, Ann, 136, 261, 262
The Seasons of Arnold's Apple Tree (Gibbons), 190, 261

seating in library, 221–223
segmentation in phonological awareness, 30, 176
Sendak, Maurice, 148, 262
shared reading
comments to adults at ET storytimes, 68
non-English speakers, 44
research, 9
Shaw, Nancy, 158, 262
Sheep in a Shop (Shaw), 158, 262
signing for the deaf, 227
Slobodkina, Esphyr, 25, 26, 262
Snowballs (Ehlert), 173, 261
The Snowy Day (Keats), 172, 261
socialization time after storytimes, 52
songs. *See also* Action songs
Apples and Bananas, 162
B-I-N-G-O, 184
Cows in the Kitchen (Skip to My Lou), 117
Did You Ever See a Fishy? (Did You Ever See a Lassie), 87
Dig for Dinosaurs (What Shall We Do with the Drunken Sailor?), 154
Five Little Ducks, 115, 180–181
Fly, Fly, Fly Along (Row, Row, Row Your Boat), 181
I Had a Little Rooster, 85–86
I'm a Little Snowman (I'm a Little Teapot), 173
John Jacob Jingleheimer Schmidt, 176
Listen to These Words (Old Mac-Donald Had a Farm), 179
and literacy skills, 29–31
London Bridge Is Falling Down, 169
M-O-U-S-E (B-I-N-G-O), 166
The Muffin Man, 71
The Name Game, 176
The Noble Duke of York, 150
Pansies and Petunias, 146
Rhyme Along (Row, Row, Row Your Boat), 159
From Seed to Flower (This Is the Way We Wash Our Clothes), 188
A Shopping We Will Go (A Hunting We Will Go), 158
These Words Rhyme (Skip to My Lou), 180
Three Little Speckled Frogs, 89
songs with body parts, 204
sound signal, use of, 23
spatial learners, 41, 42
Spot's Birthday (Hill), 94, 261
stimulation to children and brain research, 8
storytime components, 20–33, See also *specific components*, e.g., Songs
activity time and crafts, 32–33

Saroj Nadkarni Ghoting is an Early Childhood Literacy Consultant. She conducts training and speaks at conferences nationally on early literacy. She is a consultant on the "Every Child Ready to Read @ your library" program of the Public Library Association and the Association for Library Service to Children. As Early Childhood Services Coordinator at Montgomery County (MD) Public Libraries, she helped implement the program. She has been a children's librarian since 1976. She received her BA from Oberlin College (OH) and her MLS from the Catholic University of America in Washington, DC.

Pamela Martin-Díaz is Branch Manager of the Allen County Public Library in Fort Wayne, Indiana, where she was a major writer of an early literacy grant, funded by the Lilly Foundation, that established early learning centers in branches and purchased materials for parents to use with their young children to promote letter and sound awareness. She developed a set of cards called "Playing with Words on the Go!" designed to help children with phonological awareness as well as the game "Letter Play Sets" (available through Allen County Public Library), both of which help libraries incorporate early literacy in their storytimes. Martin-Díaz has presented workshops and seminars on early literacy in several venues, including numerous training sessions locally for Head Start and other early childhood providers. She received her BA from Kenyon College (OH) and her Master of Arts in Library Science from the University of Chicago.